HENRY JAMES AND THE PAST

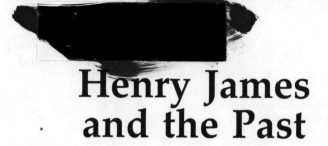

Henry James and the Past

Readings into Time

Ian F. A. Bell

Reader in American Literature
University of Keele

St. Martin's Press   New York

First published in the United States of America in 1991

Printed in Hong Kong

ISBN 0–312–06082–3

Library of Congress Cataloging-in-Publication Data
Bell, Ian F. A.
Henry James and the past: readings into time/Ian F. A. Bell.
p.   cm.
Includes index.
ISBN 0–312–06082–3
1. James, Henry, 1843–1916—Knowledge—History,   2. Historical
fiction, American—History and criticism.   3. Time in literature.
I. Title.
PS2127. H5B45   1991
813'.4—dc20
                                                    90–23880
                                                       CIP

For my mother and father,
Celia and Freddie Bell

Contents

Preface   ix

Introduction: The Jamesian Balloon   1

PART I   CONSUMING THE PAST: THE BACKWARD
          GLANCE OF *WASHINGTON SQUARE*
1   Commodity and Style   17
2   Money, History and Writing   33

PART II   CONSUMING THE PRESENT: THE PRIVATE
          SPECTACLES OF *THE BOSTONIANS*
3   Publicity and Emptiness   63
4   Language, Setting and Self   81
5   The Peculiarity of Social Life: Reform and Gender   107
6   The Personal, the Private and the Public   131

PART III ROMANCING THE PAST: *THE EUROPEANS*
          AND THE DESIGN OF DESIRE
7   Sincerity and Performance   147
8   The Self's Representations   173

Notes and References   207

Index   267

Preface

The impetus for the present book was governed by a single principle: the need to read James's early novels of the late 1870s and 1880s more historically and, concomitantly, to make a case for one of the most neglected areas in literary history, James's own historical sense. In recent years, a small body of criticism which negotiates his historical sense more attentively has begun to appear, but it continues to remain marginal within the main flow of the commentaries. My starting point is James's reworking of the Romance form at a period when the terms of the Romance form are shaped by the early period of consumer culture. The formal issues of Romance become caught up with the restructuring of questions about representation and the self by the new languages of consumption and the marketplace. Here, James engages a double project for both a critique of and a witness to the economic and commercial shifts from a system of accumulation to a system of production and reproduction as capital gives way to the expansions of finance capitalism. An introductory essay will establish the colours of the palette employed in the remainder of this analysis: the concepts and the critical positions which will organise an argument for reading James's historicism at the level of formal technique. The claim will be that the world of Jamesian fiction is a world of display, surface and performance (with all its consequences for revised notions of representation and the self which emerge during the late 1870s and 1880s), a world revealed as a system of signs and codes. James's profound ambivalence towards this world registered simultaneously a distrust of its abstractive tendencies and a deployment of fresh possibilities for imaginative liberty within a system that, as a result of its evident factitiousness, becomes available for alterability. James's ambivalence here will be a major characteristic of his historical sense.

My axis is the pairing of *Washington Square* and *The Europeans* (texts which, respectively, provide the beginning and conclusion of the argument) to graph a movement from one form of material history (economics and the transactions of commodities) to the form which becomes its most intimate expression (the strategies of consumption), from the disorder of financial speculation to its inevitable consequences in the spectacles of the shop-window. Both novels were written during those years which marked the extraordinary acceleration of industry and commerce characterising the final impetus of Reconstruction as America entered the period known as the 'Gilded Age'. From these years of dramatic and intense change, James composed the only two novels for which he chose as the setting a discernible period in America's past. The action of both novels was situated in the 1840s, the decade in which America had experienced its first series of radical transformations under the impact of newly developed industrial and commercial practices. In other words, James located both works in a period whose conditions nascently predicated the excesses and political corruptions of his contemporary situation. As such, these novels provide expressive structures from which we may begin to determine the tactics whereby James positioned himself with respect to historical and political forces.

What characterises James's positioning is his ambivalence towards a novelistic reliance upon those forms of social density by which we customarily measure a writer's alertness to contemporary conditions, and this is why that positioning suggests a more radical sense of the historical imagination; it was so closely allied to James's endless interrogations into his own practice, his analyses of the production of literary effects. The debate he conducted about technique during the 1870s and 1880s, within a nexus circumscribed broadly by his readings of the respective possibilities of Hawthorne and Balzac, engendered new models for the authorisation of history in fiction. James's sceptical negotiation of both writers instigated a wariness towards novelistic presentation (a major source of his modernity) at a moment when the world was being newly revealed as manufactured, as the product of artifice. It was his effort to deconstruct the novelistic pretensions of fiction that permitted his work its proper access to the exercises of power in history beyond the confinements of the rhetoric of realism.

While *Washington Square* and *The Europeans* (with gestures forward to *The Portrait of a Lady* and *The Tragic Muse*) remain as the poles of my discussion, the issues raised therein demanded also a consideration of *The Bostonians*. As a novel of the period that is more recognisably 'realistic' in a genre sense, *The Bostonians* would contribute to a fuller analysis of the historicism involved in James's reworking of the Romance form. James uses *The Bostonians* to investigate more richly the new realism engendered by consumption, the realism for which he finds Romance techniques to be most appropriate. Furthermore, James's use of a particular version of Emerson in *The Bostonians* registers his additional reading of the years he examines in the earlier novels. My book proposes, then, to return James to an analysable history and to essay a reading of historical writing that will eschew conventional programmes for determining social and historical density in the novelistic sense. Historical tactics here are not brought to the forefront by the substantial material of fiction but by the manufactured strategies of fiction: their reliance on absence rather than presence and their questioning of authoritative systems. By considering James's novels in this way, I hope also to suggest some re-alignments in the nature of narrative, particularly as they become expressed in the gender issues James negotiates where the male temperament is found to be inflexible and enclosing by comparison with the 'latitude' of the female.

My principal debt is to Nicola Bradbury of the University of Reading who valiantly waded through the entire manuscript with a sharp eye and considerable wisdom. Alfred Habegger of the University of Kansas brought an unparalleled knowledge to bear on my discussion of *The Bostonians*. My historian colleagues in the Department of American Studies at the University of Keele, Martin Crawford and Robert Garson, have been inexhaustible in their supply of information, and my literature colleagues, Richard Godden and Charles Swann, have presented timely suggestions and support throughout the period of composition. Over the years, the student members of my course on Henry James for the Keele MA in American Literature have constituted an excellent sounding-board for much of what follows. Friends have played a less visible role in the book's progress, but the kindness and understanding of Michael Haley and Louise Rogers have been enormously enabling. Without the patience and affection of Sue Rose, its gestation would have been even lengthier. Karen Harrison and Maureen Simkin produced the final typescript with fortitude and good humour.

I am grateful to the Departments of English in the Universities of York and Reading for invitations to test out some initial ideas, to the University of Keele for sabbatical leave and a Research Award which provided additional space for writing, and to the editors of the following learned journals for the space in which to risk a first printing of earlier drafts of various chapters: *Journal of American Studies, Connecticut Review, Notes and Queries, The Henry James Review, Modern Language Quarterly, Texas Studies in Language and Literature* and *Modern Philology*.

IAN F. A. BELL

Introduction: The Jamesian Balloon

> He has, I am convinced, one of the strongest, most abundant
> minds alive in the whole world, and he has the smallest
> penetration. Indeed, he has no penetration. He is the culmina-
> tion of the Superficial type . . . here he is, spinning about, like
> the most tremendous of water-boatmen . . . kept up by surface
> tension. As if, when once he pierced the surface, he would
> drown.

This is Wells's Reginald Boon, reading James in 1915. We would
not expect either Wells or Boon to be entirely sympathetic
towards the Jamesian enterprise, but Boon's reading turns out to
be a useful misreading which raises one of the main issues we
shall pursue: that is, his opposition of 'penetration' to 'surface'.
Boon clearly has a notion of novelistic realism lurking behind this
judgement, a realism that will prove to be entirely inappropriate
to a fiction which demonstrates above all the insufficiency of
Boon's oppositional terms within the changing history witnessed
by the final quarter of the nineteenth century. This history
records the shifts in manners and modes of social and commercial
intercourse within the development of the marketplace and the
rise of consumer culture, a history charted vividly in James's early
novels by his female characters (notably Catherine Sloper, the
Baroness Munster, Madame Merle, Verena Tarrant and Miriam
Rooth). Here, 'surface' takes on a new resonance as the reconstructed 'real' of social contact for the purposes of display and
exchange, and its major strategy of performativeness is also
picked up by Boon:

> The only living human motives left in the novels of Henry
> James are a certain avidity and an entirely superficial curiosity.

1

Even when relations are irregular or when sins are hinted at, you feel that these are merely attitudes taken up, gambits before the game of attainment and over-perception begins.[1]

Boon's notion of performativeness is generated by his marginalisation of surface. Both characteristics, in another sense, share the 'romance' features of American fiction, as Stuart Hutchinson has noted: 'Few, if any, characters in nineteenth-century American novels are confident of what they should be and do. The novels they are in are correspondingly provisional in structure. The characters feel themselves, and are represented as, the actors of uncertain roles.'[2] Boon's misunderstanding of James (or, rather, his inadvertently touching upon the main effects of James's work for the wrong reasons) may be explained in terms of the limitations in his knowledge of both American literature (Wells had read Crane and ventured amongst the realist/naturalist school, but he would not have read Melville and it is highly unlikely that he encountered Hawthorne) and of the experiential facts of America itself, the facts of advertising and the new consumerism. What I want to suggest is that James's handling of 'romance' may most usefully be read in terms of the marketplace that was America.

Surface and performance both depend upon an imagined distance – respectively, from a presumed depth and a presumed unified self – and it is precisely this distance, with its concomitant questioning of such schisms, which concerns James's fiction. Some three decades prior to Boon's reading, Robert Louis Stevenson's 'A Humble Remonstrance' of 1884 responded to 'The Art of Fiction' debate of James and Walter Besant, and Stevenson presented the opposite side of the coin. In doing so, he stressed the issue of distance through a figure James himself was to make familiar:

A proposition of geometry does not compete with life; and a proposition of geometry is a fair and luminous parallel for a work of art. Both are reasonable, both untrue to the crude fact; both inhere in nature, neither represents it. The novel which is a work of art exists, not by its resemblances to life, which are forced and material, as a shoe must still consist of leather, but by its immeasurable distance from life, which is designed and significant, and is both the method and the meaning of the work.[3]

The lesson of distance was easily available in Hawthorne, announced formally in his prefaces when he proclaimed the 'latitude' for both reader and writer that ensued from constructing a 'neutral territory' where the 'Actual and Imaginary may meet' without the hierarchical epistemology and illusory schisms of novelistic realism. James's own prefaces testify later to a similar practice, proclaiming in the preface to *The Aspern Papers* his liking for facts in the sense of 'as we say of an etcher's progressive subject, in an early "state" '. This is on the principle that 'Nine tenths of the artist's interest in them is that of what he should add to them and how he shall turn them.'[4] The preface to *The American* found him confessing that 'I have ever, in general, found it difficult to write of places under too immediate an impression – the impression that prevents standing off and allows neither space nor time for perspective.' The confession occurs in his remembering of the novel's composition where 'the tale was taken up afresh by the charming light click and clatter, that sound as of the thin, quick, quite feminine surface-breathing of Paris'.[5] As *The Ambassadors* will show abundantly, Paris for James is always 'feminine', always a world of the new surfaces which consumer culture yields. The distance James advocates in his re-working of Romance belongs to that preciosity gently (and admiringly) mocked by Boon, but understood within the terms of consumption (the distances of surface and performativeness) it is recognisable precisely as the renegotiated 'real' of social relations to which fiction bears witness.

James's summary of the Romance form in his preface to *The American* accumulates the features which he had already exploited throughout his fiction: the dissociation of the 'real' as 'the things we cannot possibly *not* know' from those that 'can reach us only through the beautiful circuit and subterfuge of our thought and desire' in the form of 'experience disengaged, disembroiled, disencumbered, exempt from the conditions that we usually know to attach to it'. It is in this manner that the forms of Romance release fiction from its illusory novelistic representation and thereby provide 'the condition of its really bearing witness at all'.[6] The Romance, then, bears witness; it does not represent in the novelistic sense. And what it bears witness to (is both caught up within and is a critique of) is the newly sanctioned world of surface and performativeness with all its implications for notions of the self which emerges in the late nineteenth century under consumption. James, whose entire canon protests against that essentially bourgeois habit of schismatic perception, does not allow final dominance to either side in his interrogations of the novel and the romance, of, say, Balzac and Hawthorne. He discriminates between formal features, certainly (between 'facts' and 'disencumbered' experience), but he always maintains that complexity of perception which refuses the comfort of taking sides. We see this complexity at work in his moments of figurative definition where he is quite clearly attempting to negotiate both sides simultaneously: in that famous, and deeply ambiguous, figure of the 'balloon of experience', for example:

> The balloon of experience is in fact of course tied to the earth, and under that necessity we swing, thanks to a rope of remarkable length, in the more or less commodious car of the imagination; but it is by the rope we know where we are, and from the moment the cable is cut we are at large and unrelated: we only swing apart from the globe . . . The art of the romancer is, 'for the fun of it', insidiously to cut the cable, to cut it without our detecting him.[7]

The figure is a calculated image for distance, and it is not under the balloon itself that we swing but under 'that necessity' of its being tied to the earth. Engagement and disengagement interfere with each other remarkably here, and that inteference dissuades us from any direct form of knowledge which James associates with mere representation. The most revealing term of James's definition is 'fun', the 'fun' of the 'hocus-pocus' that he remembers as a version of the Hawthornesque latitude in his composition of *The American*. In a particularly expressive simile, he fancifully differentiates the 'gambol' of 'frolic fancy' from the decision-making process of 'a board of trustees discussing a new outlay'.[8] The simile is powerfully reminiscent of an earlier expatriate American resistance to the completeness of representation in favour of those 'keys' and 'arrangements' which registered the true nature of art as provisory. James McNeill Whistler wrote of art's proximity to commercial enterprise in 1890, at the end of the period of those novels of James's which will most concern my present argument:

> There is a cunning condition of mind that *requires to know*. On the Stock Exchange this insures safe investment. In the painting

trade this would induce certain picture-makers to cross the river
at noon, in a boat, before negotiating a Nocturne, in order to
make sure of detail on the bank, that honestly the purchaser
might exact, and out of which he might have been tricked by
the Night![9]

Whistler's choice of image to express his resistance to the
marketplace has the same function as James's: to subvert that
form of knowledge which encourages encumbered representation. Aesthetics and commercial forms are closely entwined for
both, but while Whistler more naïvely assumes that the provisory
and disruptive functions of his 'keys' will deconstruct such
knowledge, James, on behalf of the more urgent demands of
another medium, recognises that his 'frolic fancy' itself bears a
worrying resemblance to those new shapes of social and commercial relation which they otherwise oppose. As Jean-Christophe
Agnew has noted, American literature generally in the late
nineteenth century occurs at 'a moment coextensive with the
emergence of a consumer culture among the middle class – when
the claims of romance and the claims of realism were still in the
balance', a moment where 'cultural orientation becomes one with
cultural appropriation' and in which 'We read clothes, possessions, interiors, and exteriors as representing more or less successful accommodations to a world of goods, and in so doing we
rehearse in our minds the appropriation of that social world via
the commodity. We consume by proxy. We window-shop.'[10] Our
readings become readings of the new forms of consumption in
much the same way as the famous debate between Isabel Archer
and Madame Merle reads the concomitant reconstructions of the
self precisely within these terms of surface, display and
performance.

II

My argument has been suggesting that James's formal concerns
with the construction of fiction may be productively understood
through their relations with the changes wrought by the development of a consumer culture: that aesthetic issues of representation
and character are caught up within the strategies of the marketplace. Here, the writer both exploits and is exploited by fresh

possibilities: both applauds the 'latitude' afforded by a release from illusory notions of the 'real' and of novelistic procedures, and remains caught by the precariousness of a newly discovered freedom. The precariousness of consumption has been well summarised by William Leiss who, although concerned with the post–1945 world of more evident consumerism, provides a useful perspective that is equally true of consumerism's nascent and less evident effects in America during the 1870s and 1880s:

> When the characteristics of goods change quickly and continuously . . . the categories of needing through which individuals relate to these goods are in a state of permanent fluidity. When goods become rapidly changing collections of characteristics, the individual's judgements about the suitability of particular objects for particular needs are destabilized. Characteristics are distributed and redistributed across previously distinct categories of needs, experiences and objects . . . the expression of need itself is progressively fragmented into smaller and smaller bits, which are then recombined in response to market cues into patterns that are temporary, fluid, and unstable. Previous categories of need dissolve, and the resulting fragments are subjected to regular reshufflings into new patterns. The constant revision and recombination of need-fragments renders it increasingly difficult, if not impossible, for individuals to develop a coherent set of objectives for their needs and thus to make judgements about the suitability of particular goods for them. Under these circumstances the sense of satisfaction and well-being becomes steadily more ambiguous and confused.[11]

Neither goods nor the sets of characteristics which mark the meaning of those goods for transaction possess stability. They are constantly prey to re-arrangement, and so too are the needs, the world of desire, which concomitantly mark the consumer (the self). Just as goods possess only an illusory stability, so the self which increasingly estimates itself in relation to the world of goods (Madame Merle is always the example) finds stability to be elusive. Here, to invoke the language of art, the variousness sought by the Hawthornesque latitude is expressed by the performativeness of Jamesian characters as both critique and reflection of contemporary social mores: performativeness both expresses the alterability, the recognition of otherness, which is the feature of the radical imagination that James employs against the seeming intractability of the world, *and* registers the very machinery whereby that world perpetuates itself. Certainly James would emphasise the former part of this double project; witness, for example, his 1883 assessment of Daudet in which he applauds Daudet for being 'truthful without being literal', and having 'a pair of butterfly's wings attached to the back of his observation'. He also claims that the success of a work of art may be measured by 'the degree to which it produces a certain illusion; that illusion makes it appear to us for the time that we have lived another life – that we have had a miraculous enlargement of experience'[12] – but the latter part remains an essential, and largely unacknowledged, feature in his witnessing of history.

The world of desire that is newly structured by the world of goods in the final quarter of the nineteenth century is the world in which we may recognise James's decisive refusal to dip into the storyteller's property-bag of aids to illusion and 'go behind' his characters and situations. Such a process would be to follow the novelistic reliance on that penetrative solidity of presentation which panders to the notion of an experiential unwrapping of layers in arriving at some final and absolute core. What consumption reveals above all is the *design* of things, a design which, as the quotation from Leiss demonstrates, is always changing, is always re-making the needs whereby goods become available for transaction and so, as Leo Bersani has argued, 'because experience is never without design, it's impossible to locate an original design, that is, an absolute fact or motive which could not itself be recomposed, whose nature would not be changed by changes in its relations'.[13] Bersani is one of the few critics to recognise how this release of surface from a presumed opposition to depth is James's most urgent, and indeed radical, subject[14] in its persuasion that 'our range of experience can be as great as our compositional resource', and he finds in James a 'richly superficial art' where 'hidden depths would never ironically undermine the life inspired by his own and his characters' "mere" ingenuities of design'.

Such a superficial art produces a revised notion of the self which, although Bersani does not pursue his point this far, is thoroughly in accord with those reconstructions of the self under consumption: 'By moving from causes to composition rather than from composition back to causes, James insists on the fact that fictional invention is neither evasive nor tautological; instead, it *constitutes the self*.'[15] However, Bersani's maintaining of desire's design goes a long way towards what needs to be said:

> The best talk and the best thought would be the talk and the thought which resist interpretation. Language would no longer reveal character or refer to desires 'behind' words; it would be the unfolding of an improvised and never completed psychological design. The avoidance of undeflected, unmodulated desire in both Stendhal and James is thus eminently social. It is at the highest level of civilised discourse that both novelists experiment with the disintegration of fixed definitions of being, of given structures of character.[16]

The stress on a psychological design that is 'improvised' and 'never completed' has implications beyond the presentation of character and incorporates one of the main tactics of a consumer economy where the self is shaped by manufactured desire and re-shaped incessantly (out of 'fixed definitions of being') by the changing imperatives (and the characteristics of goods) of the marketplace. Signally important here is the recognition of design which significantly recasts the Jamesian Romance. His novelistic refusals are not escapist but efforts to resist the totalising forms of the novel which he understands as being too unquestioningly reliant upon the determining forms of the 'real'; it is a resistance which aims at reconstruction, not escapism. For James, 'reality' is never a phenomenon to be dismissed or avoided: it is constructed as a pole of tension in order to enable the possibilities of design, composition and performance. Eugenia's artfulness, for example, would be meaningless without the opposing pole of New England truth and honesty through which it is tested.

Seen in this way, James's 'superficial' art registers the various-ness and mobility of desire which then becomes paramount for that versatility of the self's negotiations with its own liberties.[17] James's release of surface in its disavowal of depth, his refusal to 'go behind', has important implications for the special 'witness' his art bears, and in particular for those power struggles which provide his broadest theme. As Mark Seltzer has argued:

> The movements of power do not lie in some hidden depths, but are visible on the surfaces of the literary discourse; and the

historicity of the text is to be sought not in the grand designs and teleology of an absent History but in the microhistories and micropolitics of the body and the social body, in the minute and everyday practices and techniques that the novel registers and secures.[18]

The historicity Seltzer suggests on behalf of James is thus a matter of surface and here again we are alerted to the strategies of James's double project: performativeness, desire and surface act to disperse fixity of being and solidity of goods, but in doing so they employ those techniques of the marketplace, of advertising, which create the illusion of the fixity of goods in order to sell them, the illusion that the characteristics of goods (the means whereby they are transacted) are in fact stable. If surface as a resource of composition subverts the basic reference points for the 'real', it does so by complying with the strictures of consumption. In short, the style of the Jamesian Romance (the literary shaping for the world of desire) is the style of the advertisement. Seltzer has noted succinctly that 'the appeal of an advertising aesthetic is always implicit in James's fictional practice' and is sensitive to the way in which advertising plays a determinant role in the innovations of Jamesian representation: 'Advertising goes "beyond" a mere effect on sales because it alters the very status of the desired object. The advertising spectacle does not simply represent (or misrepresent) the object; it does not simply supplement what Strether calls the "real thing." Rather, it affirms the representation as the thing desired.'[19] When a modern analyst of the marketplace like Guy Debord claims that 'the spectacle is the *affirmation* of appearance and the affirmation of all human, namely social life, as mere appearance',[20] he echoes James's observation of 1883 that 'life is, immensely, a matter of surface'.[21]

III

James's historical sense tends to focus upon character rather than landscape and the negotiations of that sense through performativeness, surface and desire tend to express themselves within his broad concern about representation, particularly as it affects notions of the self. Here again we will encounter the extent to which James's historicism is so intimately bound up with his ideas about aesthetics. At stake will be a profound scepticism concerning the idea of the unified self[22] and an engagement with those forms of variousness which more accurately register changing understandings of the self from the latter quarter of the nineteenth century onwards.[23] The general linguistic cue is taken from Mikhail Bakhtin and his argument for dialogical forms:

> As treated by traditional stylistic thought, the word acknowledges only itself (that is, only its own context), its own object, its own direct expression and its own unitary and singular language. It acknowledges another word, one lying outside its own context, only as the neutral word of language, as the word of no one in particular, as simply the potential for speech. The direct word, as traditional stylistics understands it, encounters in its orientation toward the object only the resistance of the object itself (the impossibility of its being exhausted by a word, the impossibility of saying it all), but it does not encounter in its path toward the object the fundamental and richly varied opposition of another's word. No one hinders this word, no one argues with it.
>
> But no living word relates to its object in a *singular* way: between the word and its object, between the word and the speaking subject, there exists an elastic environment of other, alien words about the same object, the same theme.[24]

'Really, universally, relations stop nowhere' proclaimed James's preface to *Roderick Hudson*,[25] summarising a life's endeavour and a commitment to the dialogical view of language which Bakhtin maintains. In fact, Bakhtin's elaboration of his position unwittingly provides an excellent description of the characteristic Jamesian syntax:

> Indeed, any concrete discourse (utterance) finds the object at which it was directed already as it were overlain with qualifications, open to dispute, charged with value, already enveloped in an obscuring mist – or, on the contrary, by the 'light' of alien words that have already been spoken about it. It is entangled, shot through with shared thoughts, points of view, alien value judgements and accents. The word, directed toward its object, enters a dialogically agitated and tension-filled environment of alien words, value judgements and accents, weaves in and out

of complex interrelationships, merges with some, recoils from others, intersects with yet a third group: and all this may crucially shape discourse, may leave a trace in all its semantic layers, may complicate its expression and influence its entire stylistic profile.

The living utterance, having taken meaning and shape at a particular historical moment in a socially specific environment, cannot fail to brush up against thousands of living dialogic threads, woven by socio-ideological consciousness around the given object of an utterance; it cannot fail to become an active participant in social dialogue. After all, the utterance arises out of this dialogue as a continuation of it and as a rejoinder to it – it does not approach the object from the sidelines.[26]

This is exactly what happens in what is the major concern of a James novel: the conversation between characters, which is always 'dialogically agitated'. James's faith in such agitation is one of the reasons for his constant critique of schismatic perception. Here, in a positive sense, words seek their meaning through an openness to what is other, while in a negative sense (Basil Ransom is exemplary) they serve to freeze the world into manipulable categories (Ransom's schisms of male and female, public and private, for example). It is the unstable proximity of these senses which continually worries James.

Words and characters share the same operation in a James novel: both resist singularity, unity and autonomy, and both become alert to the agitation of otherness, of the alien, through the new manipulations of desire and through the strategies of the various and the performative which provide the codes of consumption. Here the self cannot be regarded as autonomous because its measurement becomes increasingly dependent upon the social forms which in turn derive their shape from these codes. However, this dependence is not to be conceived as deterministic, since James's understanding of the renewed alterability of the world, as revealed by the spectacles of the shop-window and the advertisement, enables him to recognise a radically new liberty for the self. As Ross Posnock has argued in a brilliant essay James does not cancel the subject, but rather 'clarifies its freedom, always limited and precarious, to renovate the forms it depends on', because to 'acknowledge dependence on impersonal codes of social form' involves 'recognising the otherness of non-subjective reality'.[27] In conceiving of alienation in this way, we can see performativeness as a literal incorporation of the alien within the self, liberating it from the illusion of autonomy and non-relatedness; playing for others within the rubric of social forms provides a clear instance of the need to acknowledge the self's alien elements, and provides also a re-interrogation of that comfortable dualism of self and other, subject and object which underwrites all forms of schismatic epistemology and thus plays such a large role in closing off the relational perspective that so powerfully informs James's social and aesthetic imagination. Furthermore the whole notion of the alien, the other, recognises a placing at the margin of social coding and behaviour: it is that which is excluded or resisted by the hegemony of the centre (another version of the unified, autonomous self), and is thus an exemplary testing place for the possibilities of experimentation, of openness, of alterability, of the questioning of new relations. In short, it presents a fresh critique of settled conditions and perceptions by the assertion of difference and non-identity through performativeness.

If, in so many ways, American literary history is a history of resistance to literal conceptions of the 'real' by acknowledging the world of desire, of otherness, of alterability that is so complexly caught up in its development of Romance forms, then it is entirely appropriate that the America of the late nineteenth century should witness the early development of modern consumption. As Eric Sundquist has noted, thinking generally of American realism:

> The market becomes the measure of man himself; for as the Protestant ethic divides and conquers, the gap between inherent values and their external representations widens until it dissolves altogether: inner values of the spirit are drawn outward until they appear at last to merge with the things from which one cannot be distinguished and without which one cannot constitute, build, or fabricate a self. The self becomes an *image* of the real, and the real becomes an advertisement of and for the self.

Here, as 'the distinction between aspects of the self and its implemented devices becomes increasingly obscure', performativeness becomes the prime means of social adaptation and manoeuvre:

The obsession with lying as a gesture that at once defines the environment in which one lives and expresses the necessity of masks and disguises in mastering that environment equally illuminates Wharton's and James's dramatizations of a self that is at constant risk of surrendering its powers of will and is therefore willing to perform the many roles necessary to survival in the theater of social manners.[28]

The market not only 'measures' the self, therefore; its atomising strategies (the forms of its advertisements which literally dismantle the human body and human desire), following Jean Baudrillard, actually reconstruct the 'person' into 'personality' by emphasising performative and hence marketable characteristics. Human assets become cultural commodities whose value resides in the transactions of social exchange: what are produced above all are modes of display and spectacle.[29] James recognised, however, that consumption's re-organisation of the self was not merely a matter of the deception of display, of the illusion of the image. Performativeness is conducted always in awareness of the gaze of others, and gesture is constructed with all the self-consciousness of public visibility. Such awareness makes possible a more analytical and critical attitude which can re-interrogate all those earlier seeming certainties of the self's coherence or autonomy.[30] In the marketplace, desire becomes highlighted to such an extent that both people and objects become freshly revealed as belonging to a world of manufacture, design and alterability. James's great achievement in the marketplace is to recognise the tensile relation between the prison *and* the liberation of the spectacle: his Romance recognises its own formal historicity by its witnessing and registration of consumption's practices at their early stages. James, in effect, advertises the advertisement of the history he lives through, the Romance of display, surface and performance.

Part I
Consuming the Past:
The Backward Glance of
Washington Square

Part I

1
Commodity and Style

I

It is not insignificant that *Washington Square* is the only novel for which James chose a specific locale as a title; historical time and geographical place are the issues which overtly confront the reader, to an extent (excepting *The Bostonians* and *The Princess Casamassima*) insisted upon as nowhere else in James's works. The time is, predominantly, the difficult period of the late 1830s and early 1840s,[1] and the place is that area of lower Manhattan which awkwardly defends itself against contemporary turbulence.

Dr Sloper's deliberate choices of residence are carefully located within a changing landscape,[2] and his choices match the period of Manhattan's most rapid expansion in which the Island below Canal Street was condensed by overwhelming commercial pressure.[3] This pressure was topographically initiated by the reconstruction of the Wall Street area after the fire of 1835, the year of Sloper's move to Washington Square on the outskirts of the commercial district. The two decades between the Wall Street crises of 1837 and 1857 witnessed an extraordinary economic growth,[4] and in terms of the output of goods, the decade 1844–54 (which covers most of the novel's action) was only slightly behind that of 1874–84,[5] the decade which instigated the 'Gilded Age' and in which James composed the novel. The opening-up of new markets was greatly aided by investment in the railways[6] whose advancement signalled the development of a *national* economy and the transformation from self-sufficient farming and craft production to industrial manufacture and the factory system.[7] Crucially, what Edward Pessen calls the 'speculative spirit' of the mid-1830s and 1840s provided the capital support for technology in changing the hitherto local nature of the commercial system into a national market.[8]

The speculative urge points to one of the key features of changing commercial practice: its anonymity, as symbolised by the emergence of the merchant capitalist as a necessary and dominant figure in the financing of industry,[9] by the trend towards concentrating production in larger units controlled by absentee owners[10] and by the laws of incorporation.[11] The corporate system inevitably encouraged the disengagement of the owner from the work force, particularly as, by the late 1840s, the organisation of the stock market made stock speculation (an activity wholly removed from the practice of production) an acceptable means by which to accumulate wealth. The stock market not only demonstrated further the anonymity of developing capitalism but it played a decisive role in blurring the divisions between 'old' and 'new' wealth, a process which inevitably expressed itself through the *embourgeoisement* of earlier hierarchies.[12]

Sloper's choice of location in Washington Square attempts to function both as a retreat from the city's turbulence[13] and as a resistance against it, a means (characteristic of the bourgeois mind) whereby material process may be forgotten or obliterated. The brief voice of the changing city is Arthur Townsend who, as a 'stout young stockbroker', is the voice of the distanced power structure of a market economy which provides an accurate view of living within the city's transformations: 'At the end of three or four years we'll move. That's the way to live in New York – to move every three or four years. Then you always get the last thing. It's because the city's growing so quick – you've got to keep up with it' (pp. 31–32).[14] Sloper's house, claiming the resistance of an 'ideal of quiet and genteel retirement' (p. 17), paradoxically shares this modernity,[15] but the narrative disguises its newness. With the warm glow of a backward glance,[16] James reminds the reader that he is proposing a retrospective history on behalf of his contemporary situation. He underlines his proposal by itemising the area's 'repose' through acts of domestic memory,[17] ingenuously brought to one's attention as a 'topographical parenthesis' (p. 18), which deliberately fudge the conditions of history by their naturalistic colouring and their association with the notion that the area expressed 'the look of having had something of a social history' (p. 18). Since Sloper's move to the Square occurred at its virtual nascence, it could only exhibit such a look from the retrospective of the late 1870s, the period of the novel's composition. Such dispersal of time on James's part belongs to his own tactic of removal from what he finds distasteful in the early manifestations of the 'Gilded Age', but more importantly it exposes the extent to which he is liable to be enmeshed within the practices the novel sets out to criticise. He offers the Square as being available to a kind of nostalgic recollection in order to instigate a play with his presentation, using a vocabulary of domestic memory which we know derives from his own family history. This is the only place in the novel where such vocabulary appears, and it explicitly accentuates itself as a warning against the elisions whereby nostalgic and historical recollection discolour the experience of history.

Topographically, the Square performs a clear balancing act. Any map will show how it is placed in that border area which divides the rather narrow and crooked streets in lower Manhattan from the beginnings of the broad, geometrically precise avenues to the north of the old city; the concrete names of the streets from the abstract numbers of the avenues. Its geographical equilibrium is substantiated by the solidity of Sloper's house, particularly by comparison with the only other two domiciles incorporated by the story, both of which are notable for a locational vagueness.[18] In the record of his return to New York in 1904, James is to bemoan the avenues' mathematical expression of the city's meanness as a manifestation of 'her old inconceivably bourgeois scheme of composition and distribution'.[19] The mathematical regularity of New York's grid may thus be seen as an expression of bourgeois 'consistency', straining to contain the energies of its commercial transformations in another version of balance. The idea of balance is of course central to the mathematical tenor of the bourgeois temperament, informing both the location of the Square and the scientific aptitude of Sloper himself as he lives through the birth of corporate capitalism.

II

The opening page and a half of *Washington Square* establish Sloper and his profession by an elaborate configuration which, stylistically and thematically, assumes a variety of balances. On behalf of the medical profession we are introduced to the epithet 'liberal' which is explained by a series of definitions drawn from the social realm of its operations. The first of these is a generalised judgement on the way value is ascribed: America is offered as 'a country in which, to play a social part, you must either earn your income or make believe that you earn it'. Such 'make believe' anticipates Veblen's recognition of how the 'instinct of workmanship' comes to replace the standard of 'conspicuous leisure' as a means of determining repute and value within the shifts of an expanding market economy; an instinct which relies precisely on the make believe of mere show, expressing itself 'not so much in insistence on substantial usefulness as in an abiding sense of the odiousness and aesthetic impossibility of what is obviously futile'.[20]

Within a system which confers honour by means of such a travestied purposefulness (a travesty in itself occasioned by the visibly increasing divisions between intellectual and manual labour), James's presentation of the 'healing art' claims the epithet of 'liberal' by virtue of combining 'two recognised sources of credit'. It 'belongs to the realm of the practical' (a version of manual labour) and it is 'touched by the light of science' (a version of intellectual labour). The 'healing art' is thus extended beyond medicine quite literally to 'heal', to join together the great schism of the bourgeois economy. Such healing is its social advertisement of itself, its particular 'make believe'. Hence, 'It was an element in Doctor Sloper's reputation that his learning and his skill were very evenly balanced.' This thematic balance is then mimed syntactically in the instruction 'to play a social part, you must *either* earn your income *or* make believe that you earn it' (my emphasis). The device of 'either . . . or' has been explained in its negative formulation by Roland Barthes as one of the rhetorical strategies whereby the bourgeois habitually describes the world. Again, it is a balancing device, 'a sort of intellectual equilibrium based on recognised places' whereby conflicting real-ities are anaesthetised, relieved of their specific weight and balanced out in order to immobilise choice and to freeze proper opposition.[21] This immobilisation of choice is also precisely the fate of Catherine in Sloper's hands.

The explicitness of the axioms whereby James encodes the medical profession now tends to disappear and the prose assumes a syntactical balance of expression in the succeeding sentences which implicitly summons Barthes' 'figure of the scales' into their utterance. For convenience, this is best illustrated by my emphases:

. . . he was what you might call a scholarly doctor, *and yet* there was nothing abstract in his remedies – he always ordered you

to take something. *Though* he was felt to be extremely thor-
ough, he was not uncomfortably theoretic; *and if* he sometimes
explained matters rather more minutely than might seem of use
to the patient, he never went so far . . . as to trust to
explanation alone, *but* always left behind him an inscrutable
prescription. There were some doctors that left the prescription
without offering any explanation at all; and he did not belong
to that class *either*, which was after all the most vulgar.

Sloper's 'inscrutable prescription' is a good index to the relationship of his particular temperament with the world, a relationship
characterised by the distances assumed in the precepts of mathematics and science. The inscrutability of his prescription points
the vacancy of its subject, occurring as it does at the end of a
series of propositions whose balance unites increasingly disparate
terms primarily by a syntax of negation. Both Sloper and his
profession are circumscribed by omission rather than by social
plenitude.

It matters that Sloper's profession, from a variety of possibilities, is that of a doctor, a man of science, and that he is so
conceived on behalf of a period which experienced the determinant moments of radical economic change, the beginnings of
corporate modes of production. Consistently throughout the
novel we are reminded of the 'light of science' whereby Sloper
views the world.[22] The most fruitful example occurs in a conversation with Mrs Almond which begins with a joke about geometry.
Sloper gives his conviction that Catherine will 'stick' with Morris,
and Mrs Almond asks 'shall you not relent?' The conversation
then runs:

> 'Shall a geometrical proposition relent? I am not so
> superficial.'
> 'Doesn't geometry treat of surfaces?', asked Mrs Almond . . .
> 'Yes, but it treats of them profoundly. Catherine and her
> young man are my surfaces; I have taken their measure.'
>
> (p. 152)

Sloper then goes on in a more prosaic manner to behave as a
chemist. His analogies of 'surfaces' and the 'geometrical proposition' are especially rich partly because they exhibit so clearly the
tenets of Sloper's epistemology and partly because they have such

an important role in both James's own critical theorising and his fictional practice.[23] The latter may be summarised by suggesting that 'surface' is always conceived as a social habit which is damaging when manipulated as a barrier *against* positive human intercourse, usually for the purposes of some sort of gain, and is ameliatory when employed as a device for increasing the possibilities of contact *with* the world.

Sloper clearly falls into the former category with its attendant promise of protective and exploitative distance. His assumption of the chemist's role here is one of several versions of his insistence throughout that he wishes to observe the 'mixture' of the case in question in order to see the 'third element' it produces. This is not solely a matter of dehumanised behaviour but, crucially, of economic history. Bourgeois balance fixates the world, transforms history into essential types in order to obscure, following Barthes, the 'ceaseless making of the world'. The 'motionless beam' that is bourgeois man (who, paradoxically, bases his power on science's promise of unlimited transformation) balances out potential disruptions to render nature as 'unchangeable' and 'ineffable'.[24] Mathematics provides the main vocabulary for such balance. The recent work of Alfred Sohn-Rethel has demonstrated that mathematics contributes to the abstractions of an 'ineffable' nature because it marks the only 'symbol language' that is capable of freeing itself from human activity. It thus registers not only the bourgeois disengagement from the material, changeable world, but also the divisions between intellectual and manual labour which are particularly exposed by the pressures of a developing market economy.[25]

The practices of scientific experiment and commercial enterprise are interlocked by a shared form of abstractive isolation which disguises material process. The abstraction shared by laboratory and factory is that which is characteristic of the network of exchange itself, producing a 'knowledge of nature in commodity form'.[26] The abstraction of commodities within the market is most clearly marked during their exchange when their use-value is suspended, paradoxically frozen in the material world of their real production. Sohn-Rethel summarises his point in a brilliant paragraph:

There, in the market place and in shop-windows, things stand still. They are under the spell of one activity only; to change owners. They stand there waiting to be sold. While they are there for exchange they are there not for use. A commodity marked out at a definite price, for instance, is looked upon as being frozen to absolute immutability throughout the time during which the price remains unaltered. And the spell does not only bind the doings of man. Even nature herself is supposed to abstain from any ravages in the body of this commodity and to hold her breath, as it were, for the sake of this social business of man.[27]

The commodity abstraction thus described belongs to the order of things whereby balance fixates the 'making of the world' and the 'types' of scientific positivism immobilise their objects. All three rely on a fetish of the already made, the completed object which disguises its production, its memory of manufacture. All three share the paralysis of 'homogeneity, continuity and emptiness of all natural and material content' whereby time and space (the very co-ordinates with which *Washington Square* begins) are denied their capacity for differentiation in favour of 'absolute historical timelessness and universality'.[28] All three operate as a form of equivalence which achieves its most concentrated representation in cardinal numbers and in money whose function, similarly, is to provide a uniform shape for contradictory social relations.[29] Catherine, the victim of this combination of forces, will come to display their effects as a version of a commodified object in herself.

III

Sloper's linguistic style shares these features of abstraction and paralysis through its predilection for aphorism and maxim, again a means of resisting the process of making by bearing upon objects already prepared.[30] It is a style that is rarely prepared to investigate process, to register possibilities for intervention. In the very first conversation of the novel, Sloper offers a maxim of his own, 'you are good for nothing unless you are clever', as a prelude to a play with a standard maxim in order to display the superiority of his own form: 'She [Catherine] is "as good as good bread", as the French say; but six years hence I don't want to compare her to good bread-and-butter' (p. 9).[31] When he avoids the explicit form of the maxim, his conversations frequently tend to display their enclosed nature by manipulating their circularity. He picks up on the single words of others to appropriate their reference for his own lexicon, sometimes in a cold humour (as with Mrs Penniman)[32] or, more cruelly, he elaborates on the fixed counters of Catherine's more limited range of broken statements.[33] Catherine's words, in her hesitant way, are designed as an invitation to a more engaged and expressive discourse, but the invitation is always refused: the plenitude of dialogue is not available to Sloper. It is replaced, on occasion, by a persuasive sinuosity, particularly when he feels threatened by opposition,[34] and it is a sinuosity which merely polishes the glazed surface of his ideas to render any real context impossible for the staccato utterances of others.

Sloper's rhetoric can come close to syllogism,[35] and its balance is a careful strategy in his deployment of the library scene with Catherine: 'Have you no faith in my wisdom, in my tenderness, in my solicitude for your future?' is followed by 'Don't you suppose that I know something of men – their vices, their follies, their falsities?' These statements are united by a variation on their rhythm which gives the opposition of their contents an equality of weight to mask the sharpness implied on behalf of Townsend in the latter. When the tactic fails to work on Catherine, Sloper shifts his tone from reasonable debate to absolutist assertion: as Catherine refuses to 'believe' Sloper's judgement on Townsend, he counters with 'I don't ask you to believe it, but to take it on trust.' As the text instructs us, this is an 'ingenious sophism' indeed (p. 132): when style's balance fails, the only resort is to disengage debate and substitute dogma for collaborative dialogue. At the very centre of the library scene, Sloper then plays his trump card: 'Of course, you can wait till I die, if you like. . . . Your engagement will have one delightful effect upon you; it will make you extremely impatient for that event.' This has the force of a 'logical axiom' as Catherine perceives it and here, such is the pressure upon Sloper's style, he removes even this 'scientific truth' from the field of debate: 'it is beyond a question that by engaging yourself to Morris Townsend you simply wait for my death' (p. 134). Sloper's sophistic strategy of removal prepares the ground for the falsity of the choice he offers Catherine at the end of the scene, to 'choose' between himself and Morris. It is false because, in keeping with the bourgeois temperament, it is immobilising. Sloper's rhetoric has disengaged any real possibility for choice, and its immobility is reflected in the word Sloper confiningly repeats to predict the result of his experiment: 'I believe she will stick – I believe she will stick!' (p. 137). This is to be the defining term for his expectations of Catherine from this point onwards. It reminds us vividly of the closed world inscribed by Sloper; the condition of a frozen, non-dialogical utterance and its office of removal which finds its most concentrated form in the lexicon of mathematics whose referential field is privately and internally authorised.[36] Mathematics refuses the potency of words in positions between speakers because meaning is enclosed within its own system which disavows the awkwardness of any form of otherness that might threaten its stability. It is, therefore, especially appropriate that irony constitutes the characteristic tenor of Sloper's voice. Irony, as L. C. Knights has argued, is a form of distancing designed to prevent communication. It lacks the flexibility of genuine responsiveness and is invariably intended to dominate.[37]

We may amplify Knights's observation by noting that irony's form of distancing is also a means of complex disguise. Early in the novel we are told of Sloper: 'it is a literal fact that he almost never addressed his daughter save in the ironical form'. The conjunction of 'fact' and 'form' displays the extent to which the 'ironical' is so ingrained as to become 'literal' for Sloper, the real thing. The occasion is the very first conversation between Sloper and Catherine, and it is economic: Catherine is 'this magnificent person' who is 'sumptuous, opulent, expensive', a 'regal creature' whose elaborate crimson gown renders her a package for consumption worth 'eighty thousand a year' (p. 27). The 'literal fact' that characterises the first appearance of the 'ironical form' is immediately given solidity not only by a large amount of money but by a view of Catherine as someone who is available for exchange: the evasiveness of a tone of voice has sought specific concreteness. This interplay of fact and value emerges again during Sloper's second conversation with Townsend in Chapter 12, when Townsend formally requests Sloper's approval for his engagement. He voices his assumption that Catherine 'seems to be quite her own mistress' and Sloper's reply registers his characteristic interference with the interstitial worlds of fact and value: 'Literally, she is. But she has not emancipated herself morally quite so far, I trust, as to choose a husband without consulting me' (p. 58). Here is another of Sloper's syntactical balancing acts, and its effect is not simply to confuse the worlds of fact and value for the purposes of rhetorical disguise, but to allow fact to be wholly demolished by value in order to maintain his own authority.

IV

Catherine herself is the object of play for the competing styles of Sloper, Townsend and Mrs Penniman. Her bright, expensive dresses have all the consumer-orientated opulence to attract a potential purchaser, and it is not fanciful to see the *front* parlour (which of all the rooms in the house is her 'particular province' (p. 189)), as the show-case for her display. The handsomeness of the house's frontage is stressed (p. 17) and James insists at the same time that the house 'exactly resembled' many of its neighbours: a gesture towards the uniformity of industrial production and the purchase of its commodities. The *back* parlour is ceremonially divided off from its 'more formal neighbour' by 'the great mahogany sliding doors, with silver knobs and hinges' (p. 170). All three major characters employ the vocabulary of commercial acquisition with respect to Catherine,[38] and Sloper explicitly commodifies her within a particularly nasty metaphor at the end of the European excursion: 'We have fattened the sheep for him [Townsend] before he kills it' (p. 180).

In a sense, the economic display of Catherine invokes a familiar theme of nineteenth-century English fiction since at least the time of Jane Austen: the portrayal of daughters who are regarded as trade-worthy and constituted for sale. If such invocation informs *Washington Square*, then we would need to stress that its function is to establish a point about changes in history. Sloper may be conservative, but he is not old-fashioned and it would be difficult to imagine his profession in *Pride and Prejudice*, for example. The trading of the female in, say, an Austen novel is a practice of (predominantly) social imperialism, occasioned, admittedly, by pecuniary considerations; but the point is that the female is there to be *used*. In 1813, exchange and use are *allied* but, as the market begins to change with alterations in the modes of production, this alliance is disengaged. The emerging network of commodity relations depends precisely on the *gap* between exchange and use.

Catherine is not offered for use but for exchange only, and the ghost of Austen demonstrates this very shift in the notion of trade as the experience of commodity begins its ascendancy. Sloper does not *need*, economically or socially, to 'sell' Catherine, to use her: she is there for display, on behalf of revised meanings of social selling. It is a feature of his paradoxical form of resistance to the new commerce that he refuses it by attempting to exploit its own disguising of its productivity: hence, for example, he refuses the parent's traditionally central office of organising, or causing to be organised, a series of suitors for Catherine. Revealingly, the action of the novel begins in chapter 4 with an engagement, and there is no evidence that this is an affair similar to the barter we would find in Austen. Indeed, none of the marriages in the novel, slightly presented though they are, is felt to concern the issue of trading in its older sense. Sloper's own marriage, described in Chapter 1, is 'for love', and the 'solid dowry' accompanying his bride is virtually tangential.

The distance of *Washington Square* from the world of Jane Austen may be detected further in James's portrayal of Catherine's style of speech which, by comparison with the volubility of Mrs Penniman, the loquaciousness of Townsend and the sinuosity of Sloper, is virtually a negation of style. Her narrow range of expression, her silences, are mimed materially: she chooses a meeting with her father at eleven o'clock at night when 'the house was wrapped in silence' (p. 129) and her handwriting, the most extensive use of her voice, is beautiful because of her fondness for 'copying' (p. 108), a fondness which reminds us of the reproducibility upon which market practice depends. Even her tears flow silently at the moments of her greatest distress (pp. 140–1, 254). Catherine's efforts to find her place between the competing claims of Sloper and Townsend lead at one point to a sensation which portrays exactly the divisions and paralysis of commodity abstraction, a feeling of suspension characterising the breach between exchange and use: 'She had an entirely new feeling, which may be described as a state of expectant suspense about her own actions. She watched herself as she would have watched another person, and wondered what she would do' (p. 107). And as John Lucas has noted, 'one notices how often the word "rigid" is used of her in the last pages, as though she has become arrested at a certain point forever'.[39]

In the best commentary we have on the novel, Millicent Bell has written illuminatingly of Catherine's quietude and her plain words. Opposing the linguistic worlds of those who seek to appropriate her, Catherine's muteness is to be seen as a surrender of 'style' itself, a laudable innocence of social or literary convention which bespeaks a 'new language of authenticity'.[40] While James has an obvious sympathy for that order of Romanticism which valorises quietude as a gesture towards a lost world of organic totality – and while Catherine might well share such a disavowal of the material world – her silence, as the product of the economic transformations of that world, cannot be seen so restrictively. Her limited speech may more expressively be considered as a version of the non-dialogical linguistic paralysis described by Volosinov whereby words are disengaged from a communicative position between speakers.[41] Such disengagement again suggests the frozen condition of commodities. Instead of comparing Catherine's rare-spokenness with the models of Cordelia or Billy Budd, we might remember more fruitfully the example of Bartleby, another 'copyist', in a 'Tale of Wall Street' where Melville questions his writing practice through the context of disabled liberal economics, the paper arena of 'rich men's bonds, and mortgages, and title deeds' which is wholly separated from the world of production. Thus compared, Catherine's silence can gesture only obliquely to the positivity claimed by Millicent Bell's reading; can be seen at best only as a painful reminiscence of an earlier form of linguistic sincerity that can no longer be authorised.

It is in this sense that Lucas's phrase for Catherine's final condition, a 'terrible stagnation',[42] is revealingly inappropriate: it partakes too strongly of the organic world that she rebuts and is rebutted by for the sake of her sale value. Her condition at the end of the novel is explicitly not part of nature's process: Townsend, himself now fat and balding, notes 'You have not changed', and that the years 'have left no marks' (p. 260). Catherine, like any commodity within the abstract sphere of exchange separated from the material sphere of use, is removed from alterability.[43]

Mathematics, the calculability which sanctions Sloper's placing of Townsend's 'category', and his estimate of Catherine's 'value', provides the basis simultaneously for the types of science and the prices of the marketplace.[44] The uniformity imposed by both depends upon laws governing the repeatable, and the imperishable, figuring absolutes of time and space so that 'time becomes unhistorical time and space ungeographical space'.[45] It is here that we might usefully shift our ground to approach James's composition of *Washington Square* from the stand-point of the late 1870s, because it is a feature of the novel that it progressively dissolves both time and space, those two essential properties of realistic fiction's aids to illusion.

The Square itself, by means of its topographical density and the unusual care James takes with temporal specification in the opening chapters, is categorically offered as a retreat from the bedlam of commerce. But the curious thing is that with the development of the story, the rest of the city becomes more and more evasive as an explicit context for the narrative. This may be shown by the increasing pattern of anonymity which characterises the locations chosen by Mrs Penniman for her private meetings with Townsend outside the definiteness of the Square, a pattern which moves from 'an oyster saloon in the Seventh Avenue' (p. 111), through the doorstep of a church that is a 'less elegant resort' than her usual place of worship (p. 154), to a 'street corner, in a region of empty lots and undeveloped pavements' (p. 201). As a locale, the Square is felt gradually to lose its relational contact with the city, and it is in this sense that its space becomes ungeographical (matching, perhaps, the self-sealing tenets of Sloper's perspective).

When we examine the novel's time-scheme, we find that its chronology is conflicting.[46] There are, for example, three competing sets of dates established in the opening three chapters for the commencement of the story's action: 1843, 1846, and 1838 or 1839. Equally there are three competing dates for its termination in the final meeting of Catherine and Townsend: 1851 or 1852, 1856 and 1859. Furthermore, this computation ignores the fact that the only point in the novel where a character's age is given a date tells us that Sloper married at the age of twenty-seven in 1820: thus when he dies in Chapter 33 'touching his seventieth year', the date must be 1862 or 1863, which gives a terminal date for the action as 1863 or 1864. On a more local level, we may note the discrepancy over the ages of Sloper's sisters: Mrs Almond is first given as 'younger' (p. 6) but later as the 'elder' (p. 43).[47] The conclusion we need to draw is clear: not only are we faced with sets of dates which compete amongst themselves, but that very competition is inconsistent in itself. The narrative's offering of dates and ages only at the beginning and the end, framing an untimed middle where the bulk of the action occurs, points towards James's willingness to diffuse determinant chronology. His blurring of the specific dates themselves renders that willingness a purposive tactic of historical removal.

Such removal exploits those features of the bourgeois temperament we have already noted: the obscuring of process in order to maintain uniformity and universality, which are the characteristics of commodity abstraction within the network of exchange. What needs stressing is the approximation, not the matching, of James's tactics to these features.

James is writing, of course, at the beginning of the second great phase of commercial expansion in America, the phase which expressed vividly and in large outline those forms of corporate capitalism which had begun to structure New York in the period of the novel's setting. The America James left behind in 1875 lay in the middle of the depression that followed the gold panic of 1869. During the years immediately prior to composing *Washington Square*, he had all around him the development of a disengaged, abstractive system of commercial and financial behaviour which displayed on a large canvas the outcome of its birth in the 1830s and 1840s.[48] It was a period in which the truth of his father's Emersonian lesson in 'Socialism and Civilisation' became contemporaneously accurate: 'We degrade by owning and just in the degree of our owning. . . . We degrade and disesteem every person we own absolutely, every person bound to us by any other tenure than his own spontaneous affection.'[49] From Europe James regrets, in a letter of December 1877, the declining political prestige of England and expresses the patrician hope that the country will show itself to be more than 'one vast, money-getting Birmingham'.[50] And around the time of composition itself, he writes tellingly in January 1879 of a trip to the north:

> Yorkshire smoke-country is very ugly and depressing, both as regards the smirched and blackened landscape and the dense and dusky population, who form a not very attractive element in that grand total of labour and poverty on whose enormous base all the luxury and leisure of English country-houses are built up.[51]

When we note the approximation between James's dissolving of time and space in *Washington Square* and the features of the marketplace, we note also the extent of his own site within it. Catherine undeniably focuses much of our sympathy, and if her silence and her paralysed speech are an espousal of the frozen abstraction that is her fate as a commodity, it is also, following the clue of Millicent Bell's reading, advertised as a gesture of innocence and sincerity against a shabby and loquacious materialism. We can read the novel as James's own act of resistance to the marketplace, removing himself from the excesses of the 'Gilded Age' by setting his work back in time to the point where the 'Gilded Age' was only just beginning, but we cannot read it unproblematically as an attempt to salvage possibilities for fuller, communal, more organic living in order to overcome the divisive life imposed by commodity production. The double function of Catherine's silence dissuades us from the latter because it articulates both the object of James's disquiet (by its paralysed, non-dialogical incapacity) and the flawed alternative to it (an increasingly impossible gesture towards authenticity and a freedom from lexical and institutional impositions). The flaw may be determined by the extent to which such authenticity is obliged to assume the very terms of its opposition. As Terry Eagleton notes on behalf of England (with Carlyle, Arnold and Ruskin in mind): 'As Victorian capitalism assumes increasingly corporate forms, it turns to the social and aesthetic organicism of the Romantic humanist tradition, discovering in art models of totality and affectivity relevant to its ideological requirements.'[52] And in America, the flowering of Romanticism occurs at the very moment marked by the rupture between private and corporate systems of production. The great treatises of Emerson's early work all appear shortly after Sloper's move to Washington Square. Many of the Transcendentalist positions advertised themselves as removed from the world of public affairs, but they certainly shared crucial aspects of Jacksonian reformism,[53] particularly with regard to current changes in economic life where they saw the new forms of capital and commerce as expressly threatening for traditional notions of individual liberty. It was not coincidental that one of the major documents of Transcendentalist thought, George Ripley's invitation to Emerson which sought his support for the Brook Farm experiment, adopted as its premise the division between intellectual and manual labour which focused on the most immediate consequence of corporate industry.

It is tempting to see James's wider project as an unproblematical salvaging of fine consciousness from the ravages of vulgar materialism, and to read him (with Eagleton, for example) as thereby removed from concrete history on the grounds that he displaces those material conflicts for the wealth which renders such consciousness possible.[54] Eagleton has an expressive term, '"positive" negation', for the question of consciousness in James's later work[55] that usefully may be applied to the double figuration of Catherine's quietude as paralysis and authenticity. Positivity reveals her resistance to commerce while negativity belongs to the danger of a transcendentalism which has no historical place. But the point is that these terms are not self-cancelling; they constitute a tensile nexus of epistemology in which James is to be caught up throughout the remainder of his writing. The importance of *Washington Square* lies in its exposure of this nexus. James's attempt to 'know' the offensiveness of the 'Gilded Age' locates its origins historically in order to exploit the extent to which his own discourse belongs to the ideological equipment of that which it opposes. The historical relativism exhibited in his play with an American past may then be seen to have a crucial role within his contemporaneous concerns, particularly in *Hawthorne*, his study of his most immediate literary ancestor, about the nature of fiction and the production of writing.

2
Money, History and Writing

I

James's project in *Washington Square* marks an interest in certain
forms of abstraction and human paralysis detectable in the onset
of corporate industry in America during the 1830s and 1840s. His
concern takes shape in the very structure of the novel, its
extraordinary specificity concerning time and place in the opening
three chapters becoming progressively dissolved as the action of
the story unfolds from Chapter 4 onwards. The Square itself,
conceived as an 'ideal of quiet and genteel retirement'[1] against the
commercial turbulence of lower Manhattan, loses its relational
context within the city and inhabits a kind of timelessness. Both
of these are defining features of the industrial production of
commodities. They are equally features of the bourgeois temperament that James is concerned to diagnose in the balanced, rational
discourse of Dr Sloper and the vacuous jangle of Mrs Penniman's
impoverished imagination.[2] It is these styles, in company with the
problematically 'natural' style of the socially indefinable Townsend, which compete for the commodified Catherine, worth
'eighty thousand a year' (pp. 27 and 29) within the frozen world
of market practice. Their competition, at a specific moment in
American economic history, enables us to see an intimate relationship between forms of writing, forms of history and forms of
financial behaviour, a relationship which may be focused through
one of the main questions presented by the novel: what informs
James's choice of this earlier period in American history as the
location for a work written during the late 1870s?

Millicent Bell has written well of the problem of a 'model' for
James during the time of *Washington Square*, particularly the
minutely itemised realism offered by the Balzacian novel. The
period 1878–9 seems, she rightly notes, 'to have been pivotal in

33

James's career, a time when Balzac's and all other models both teased and repelled'. She illuminatingly suggests that it was, in part, a recognition of Balzac's inappropriateness which forged the perimeters of James's own procedures, 'the use of central consciousness whose confinement of scope was its interest'.[3] More immediately, of course, there was the question of the Romance and Hawthorne, whose roles as resource were equally testing and ambivalent.[4] To schematise broadly, we might suggest that the interference of novelistic and Romantic worlds, codified by Balzac and Hawthorne respectively, may prove useful in considering the relationship between writing and the social forms of commerce which constitute the strategy of *Washington Square*.

One of the main complications of the novel is Catherine's quietude. Her rare-spokenness and broken syntax articulate both the object of James's disquiet (by its paralysed, non-dialogical incapacity) and the putative alternative to it (as an increasingly impossible gesture towards authenticity and a freedom from lexical and institutional impositions). It is thus simultaneously frozen in the material world that we experience (as a reminder of the unchangeability of commodities and a denial of their own production) and resistant to such materiality (as a Romantic refusal of discourse to taint itself by a world already given). James's sympathy is powerfully invested in both the inhumanity of the former and the possibilities of the latter, and the simultaneity of their occasion marks a point at which he may exploit the extent to which his own discourse belongs to the ideological equipment of its opposition.

In other words, the situation of Catherine may be read as an index to James's negotiation of Balzac and Hawthorne, and his interest in the urge, encouraged by novelistic convention, to locate the alternative worlds of fiction within the world we ordinarily experience.[5] His elisions of time and space (the two indispensable properties of that convention) are, again, features of the bourgeois temperament he analyses. For such a temperament, as Alfred Sohn-Rethel notes, 'time becomes unhistorical time and space ungeographical space' in order to assume a 'character of absolute historical timelessness and universality'.[6] Time, indeed, is not only elided in *Washington Square* but operates as a distinct temporal confusion whereby, despite its overwhelming 'realistic' specificity, its chronology competes within itself for historical place and emerges as an explicitly unstable resource for finding one's bearings. It is not insignificant that James also disrupts a third novelistic property at the very end of the first chapter; this is the voice which authorises our reception of the narrative, and it is disrupted in a way which confuses and disguises authorial utterance to finish with a recognisably Hawthornesque mysteriousness about its entire enterprise:

> [Catherine] grew up a very robust and healthy child, and her father, as he looked at her, often *said to himself* that, such as she was, he at least need have no fear of losing her. *I say* 'such as she was', because, to tell the truth – But this is a truth of which I will defer the telling. (my emphasis, p. 5)

Here we may invoke James's famous insistence on technique as shown by a series of geometrical metaphors, which marks a clear resistance to the material world by its advocation of surface and relationship at the expense of novelistic furniture.[7] This is not to say, of course, that we are presented with a reductive model whereby we read competing fictions of the real and the imagined, but to register James's willingness to confront the risk of alienating the novel form as a social force, a willingness that may be inferred from his interest in the complex of the novel/Romance, the material/immaterial, presented by Balzac/Hawthorne.[8] An excellent essay by Leo Bersani has attended to Jamesian geometry in order to read its distances and abstractness as more realistic than the conventional psychology of novelistic fiction:

> It's as if he came to feel that a kind of autonomous geometric pattern, in which the parts appeal for their value to nothing but their contributive place in the essentially abstract pattern, *is* the artist's more successful representation of life. . . . The only faithful picture of life in art is not in the choice of a significant subject (James always argued against that pseudorealistic prejudice), but rather in the illustration of sense – of design-making processes. James proves the novel's connection with life by deprecating its derivation from life; and it's when he is most abstractly articulating the growth of a structure that James is also most successfully defending the mimetic function of art (and of criticism).[9]

There is much valuable suggestion in this statement. It recognises that the pervasive Jamesian subject, freedom, is to be understood 'in the sense of inventions so coercive that they resist any attempt to enrich – or reduce – them with meaning'.[10] It suggests the principle of re-composition not only on behalf of James's own practice but also on behalf of the liberty of both his characters and his readers. James's analyses of his craft, his geometry of fiction and human behaviour, may thus be seen as a means of exhibiting his own production, enabling his fictions to display their own process, to escape the realms of mystification and to make themselves available for interventions (or for re-composition) by others. By maintaining this possibility for re-composition, for imagining alternative worlds (perhaps the single most important lesson he learned from Hawthorne), James refuses to appropriate the freedom of his readers. He resists the potential of his fiction to compete with a world that is solidly and confiningly familiar to us. James's predilection for the geometry of what he called 'that magnificent and masterly indirectness' enables us to see, as Todorov puts it, 'only the vision of someone and never the object of that vision directly'.[11] Liberty in style and in behaviour are thus equally guaranteed by obliquity of angle. Again we recognise here the tensile area that is the major theme of *Washington Square* through the risk James takes in the approximation between his own practice and the bourgeois temperament it seeks to denote. The abstractness of Jamesian design finds its uncomfortable correlative (albeit in a reductive form) in the paralysing categories of Dr Sloper's scientism and in the sphere of exchange breached from the sphere of use to which Sloper's equalising, non-dialogical discourse belongs.

II

Jamesian notions of freedom, then, are intimately bound up with styles of writing, with the imagining of alternatives. This intimacy was Hawthorne's great lesson, particularly in his Preface to *The House of the Seven Gables* where, having established his 'moral' (itself a cry against the impositions of one generation upon another), he wishes not 'relentlessly to impale the story with its moral as an iron rod – or, rather, as by sticking a pin through a butterfly – thus at once depriving it of life, and causing it to stiffen in an ungainly and unnatural attitude'. The 'latitude' he claims for himself in the Romance rather than the novel form is extended to the reader in warning against that 'inflexible and exceedingly dangerous species of criticism' which attempts to bring 'his fancy pictures almost into positive contact with the realities of the moment'. The desired effect is that of 'laying out a street that infringes upon nobody's private rights'.[12]

James appreciates the aesthetics of Hawthorne's position when he writes on behalf of this novel that 'Hawthorne was not a realist. He had a high sense of reality.' Despite the superabundance of the items which constitute 'realism' in the *Notebooks*, Hawthorne 'never attempted to render exactly or closely the actual facts of the society that surrounded him'.[13] The result, for James, is a sense of how 'reality' might be offered without the rhetoric of 'realism':

> I have said – I began by saying – that his pages were full of its spirit, and of a certain reflected light that springs from it; but I was careful to add that the reader must look for his local and national quality between the lines of his writing and in the *indirect* testimony of his tone, his accent, his temper, of his very omissions and suppressions.[14]

A little later, in considering the 'finest thing' in *The Blithedale Romance* (the character of Zenobia, 'the nearest approach that Hawthorne has made to the complete creation of a person'), James remembered Hawthorne's warning against too close an association between characters of fiction and those of experienced life (in this instance, Margaret Fuller):

> There is no strictness in the representation by novelists of persons who have struck them in life, and there can in the nature of things be none. From the moment the imagination takes a hand in the game, the inevitable tendency is to divergence, to following what may be called new scents.[15]

The complexity of James's understanding here (which inhibits any mechanistic valorisation of either of the complex's defining terms over the other) may be noted by comparing the above passage with his simultaneous admiration for the presentation of the narrator in this novel, a character whose standpoint has 'the advantage of being a concrete one' and who is 'no longer, as in the preceding tales, a disembodied spirit, imprisoned in the haunted chamber of his own contemplations' but 'a particular man, with a certain human grossness'.[16] Significantly, James's final judgement on *The Blithedale Romance* employs the rhetoric of realism itself to regret that the story fails, to his sense, to avail itself of 'so excellent an opportunity for describing unhackneyed specimens of human nature' so that we 'get too much out of reality, and cease to feel beneath our feet the firm ground of an appeal to our own vision of the world, our observation'. The 'brethren of Brook Farm' may well have regretted, James suggests, that Hawthorne 'should have treated their institution mainly as a perch for starting upon an imaginative flight'.[17]

The two quotations given above are, of course, taken from the study of Hawthorne published by James immediately prior to his composition of *Washington Square* and in which he describes the America of the 1840s, the period of most of the story's action, as 'given up to a great material prosperity, a homely *bourgeois* activity' where, among the 'cultivated classes', was found 'much relish for the utterances of a writer who would help one to take a picturesque view of one's internal possibilities, and to find in the landscape of the soul all sorts of fine sunrise and moonlight effects'.[18] It is difficult to detect the extent of James's irony here, expressed as it is with a sort of warmth or, at least, understanding; but this is exactly the exercise of Mrs Penniman's theatrical response to the bourgeois world which comfortably encloses her, with her 'natural disposition to embellish any subject that she touched' and her all-pervasive 'sense of the picturesque' (pp. 219 and 222). Hers is a drama which drastically fails the great Jamesian test of discrimination, a stage on which 'the idea of last partings occupied a place inferior in dignity only to that of first meetings' (p. 207). Mrs Penniman's refusal of difference matches the refusal of history and materiality within the commodity relation itself as her style, like that of Sloper, reifies the world into the immutability of exchange cut off from use. We are not, of course, proposing Mrs Penniman as a reader of Hawthorne, but noting the entanglement of James's study with his novel's temporal location and its bourgeois characteristics. As Edel notes, it was while James was working on *Washington Square* during the winter of 1879–80 that *Hawthorne* 'created its storm in the American press'.[19] And, certainly, not only James's complex of fictional strategies explored in the study but that 'storm' itself create an arena across which the novel may be read. His sense of the limits and the extent of both the Romance and the novel marks the interstitial field of the text and the insubstantiality that it risks.

One of the few concrete remarks James makes about *Washington Square* is in his famous reply to Howells's review of *Hawthorne* where he describes it as 'a tale purely American, the writing of which made me feel acutely the want of the "paraphernalia" '.[20] Here we may begin to see why James chooses to give his story an American setting rather than the English setting its 'germ' more easily suggests. The 'paraphernalia' is Howells's term for the 'items of high civilisation', such as Ascot, Eton, and so on, which James lists as absent from American life in *Hawthorne*.[21] James's reply recodes these items within their more general categories which constitute a novelist's material, 'manners, customs, usages, habits, forms', and maintains their 'realist' provenance: 'I shall feel refuted only when we have produced . . . a gentleman who strikes me as a novelist – as belonging to the company of Balzac and Thackeray.'[22] However, in *Hawthorne* itself, James's items belong to a rather more complicated sense of composition whereby the realistic and the Romantic are not to be so conveniently separated. On the page preceding his list, James quotes from the Preface to *The Marble Faun*, the only novel that Hawthorne set outside America:

> No author, without a trial, can conceive of the difficulty of writing a romance about a country where there is no shadow, no antiquity, no mystery, no picturesque and gloomy wrong, nor anything but a commonplace prosperity, in broad and simple daylight, as is happily the case with my dear native land.[23]

The items James provides are thus, in the first instance, designed to enumerate those resources available to Hawthorne, which James, thinking of Hawthorne's *American Notebooks* (understood as 'a practical commentary upon this somewhat ominous text' and characterised by 'an extraordinary blankness' despite their author's 'large and healthy appetite for detail') refers to as 'the lightness of the diet to which his observation was condemned'.[24] But James's quotation erases the awkwardness of Hawthorne's statement, leaving it as an apparently uncomplicated disposition of a 'broad and simple daylight' against the absence of 'shadow', 'antiquity', and so forth. His erasure is effected by deleting the sentences surrounding the quotation, sentences which set 'a sort of poetic or fairy precinct, where actualities would not be so terribly insisted upon as they are, and must needs be, in America' against the proposition that 'Romance and poetry, like ivy, lichens and wallflowers, need Ruin to make them grow.'[25]

Hawthorne's position in this Preface is by no means straightforward, and it is part of the function of James's erasure to render it more reductive than it is for the sake of his wider argument which will restore its complications in James's own terms. While he is not sure that Hawthorne 'had ever heard of Realism', he finds himself 'not fanciful' in suggesting that Hawthorne 'testifies to the sentiments of the society in which he flourished almost as pertinently (proportions observed) as Balzac and some of his descendants – MM. Flaubert and Zola – testify to the manners and morals of the French people'.[26] James's placing of Hawthorne in this company occurs within a page of a famous passage which suggests that his later catalogue of items is precisely a catalogue of rhetorical resources (what Howells's review termed 'those novelistic "properties"'[27]) rather than cultural condemnation. The passage emphasises the 'valuable moral' James derives from Hawthorne, a 'moral' which suggests the invidiousness of 'contrasting his proportions with those of a great civilisation': 'This moral is that the flower of art blooms only where the soil is deep, that it takes a great deal of history to produce a little literature, that it needs a complex social machinery to set a writer in motion.' This is of course only half of the 'moral' (the half which is so often attended to in isolation) and, too conveniently, it matches the later complaint about the absence of resources for the American writer. The gritty practicality of the second half drastically modifies any urge to make such a match: 'American civilisation has hitherto had other things to do than to produce flowers, and before giving birth to writers it has wisely occupied itself with providing something for them to write about.'[28] The sturdiness of James's recognition here, wonderfully undermining the metaphor of the first half of the passage, suggests how he is able to see Hawthorne, 'in spite of the absence of the realistic quality', as 'intensely and vividly local';[29] and furthermore appropriating such localism for his own purposes by reconstituting the conventions of realism.

James's appropriation of Hawthorne, particularly in his thoughts about *The House of the Seven Gables*, extends beyond a willingness to disorient the comfort of conventional categories of writing and even beyond his insistence on possibilities for the reader's flexibility. The liberty proclaimed by Hawthorne's Preface in the 'moral' he offers for the story, and in the latitude he wishes his form to maintain, enables James to describe Hawthorne as 'an American of Americans' which he defines by noting that, despite a sense of Hawthorne's conservatism, 'it is singular how often one encounters in his writings some expression of mistrust of old houses, old institutions, long lines of descent'.[30] Hawthorne's 'moral' ('the folly of tumbling down an avalanche of ill-gotten gold, or real estate, on the heads of an unfortunate posterity, thereby to maim and crush them'[31]) thus matches the latitude he claims formally for himself and his reader. The debate about the ownership of property which constitutes the story itself elaborates this intersection of imaginative and material liberty. Brook Thomas has offered a sound argument, premised on the American political system's founding on eighteenth-century models of impersonal authority freed from subjective interests and justified by invoking natural law, in which he claims:

> The status given a deed of property confirms the idea that an owner's authority to possess land is embodied in a text. A deed allows a person whose name is affixed to it to claim ownership of a piece of land. In a sense the document and the piece of property merge. The owner of the deed is the owner of the land. The owner's name coincides with the land. . . . But Hawthorne is acutely aware that sign and signifier do not coincide. Texts – including legal documents – have human authors and therefore derive their authority from human actions, not natural law. Furthermore, a document may as easily come from the irrational area of imagination as from the rational.

Thus, for Thomas, Hawthorne's story 'questions the impersonal, rational authority of a democracy's most sacred texts – its legal documents'.[32] Hawthorne's questioning of texts is, then, simultaneously a questioning of a material ideology, and it is within the intersection of the two that his concern with his own expression in the Preface needs to be read. It is also within this intersection of materiality and textuality that we need to read James's analysis in *Hawthorne* at the time of *Washington Square*'s alertness to the impositions of a bourgeois economy. Possession of property is the most material form of appropriation and of confining the freedom of others, particularly within a political system largely defined from the start by Lockean epistemology. The evanescence of portrayal, justified by Hawthorne and the object of both admiration and disquiet by James, itself has a function to resist the materiality that is the clearest product of such impersonal rationality. Impersonal rationality shares the guarantee of concealed authorship, fiction's sense of its own production; both are advertised as free from the excesses of the individual subjective imagination. Hence both most appropriately rely upon the rhetoric of realism, the nomenclature not only of politics and law but also of science (the major sanction for realistic fiction's self-advertisement) which seeks its authority from the same rationality. While Judge Pyncheon is an appropriator of property, Dr Sloper is an appropriator of linguistic capital.

III

James's interest in an author who concerned himself with, as it were, the hidden histories of the real through his restructuring of the relationship between imagination and felt experience, texts and contexts, words and deeds, suggests that we need to think of the moment of *Washington Square* across the key issue which dominated both those periods of accelerated commercial expansion occasioning its action and its composition. This was the issue of money: specifically the debates about 'soft' and 'hard' money, paper and coin, which caused such intense public interest at the end of the Jacksonian era and during Reconstruction. By maintaining the tensile relationship between competing modes of style in *Hawthorne* and *Washington Square*, the connections and disconnections between the rhetoric of imagination and that of realism, James is involved in an aesthetic arena that is especially appropriate to the field where debates about coinage and paper money were conducted. Both raise the question of symbolism in general, the relations of words or signs to their objects, and the immaterial to the material. James's displacements of style and the dematerialised centre of the novel's action mark a flexibility that is, in one sense, the more positive aspect of the instability in the hurly-burly of the commercial world whose main expression, money, is notoriously uncertain of its own status.

James's principal indictment of the bourgeois economy that figures the story's setting in the 1830s and 1840s and the period of its composition in the late 1870s is clearly in his characterisation of Sloper, almost an archetype (if James thought in such terms) of the bourgeois temperament.[33] He offers Sloper as a man of science rather than as a man of business because the latter would be too reductive an invitation to enjoin 'fictional' and 'realist' comparisons. It would also elide the nexus of relationships that makes possible the history of corporate market practice: relationships between abstract thought, numbers, science, technology and industry. Furthermore, the etymological relation between the 'species' and 'specimens' of scientific enquiry and the 'specie' of the money debates enables James obliquely to suggest the linguistic and ideological worlds in which he is willing to operate. Their shared Latin root means 'appearance', so that both belong to an epistemology which relies on the 'form', or the 'look', of its objects at the risk of an unstable or distorting distance from the 'reality' of those objects. Paradoxically, in common usage both sets of terms acquire a strong empirical solidity or specificity.

The questions concerning representation raised by James's structuring of the Hawthorne/Balzac complex and by the money debates during the Jacksonian period and Reconstruction thus circumscribe an area in which our faith about the truth of our means of expression and exchange is to be tested through an interplay between the offices of aesthetics and those of money. Both, crucially, incorporate questions about freedom. Part of our cue may be taken from an argument by Marc Shell, who is thinking about Poe's 'The Gold Bug' (a story of the early 1840s):

> Credit or belief involves the very ground of aesthetic experience, and the same medium that seems to confer it in fiduciary money (banknotes) and in scriptural money (created by the process of bookkeeping) also seems to confer it in literature. That medium is writing. The apparently 'diabolical' 'interplay of money and mere writing to a point where the two be[come] confused, involves a general ideological development: the tendency of paper money to distort our 'natural' understanding of the relationship between symbols and things.[34]

The possibility of dis-credit, the gap between sign and substance, is thus a danger for both aesthetics and financial speculation.

James is interested in that gap both as a characteristic of the abstractions within the system of exchange and as a resource for writing which requires the real without the rhetoric of realism, which insists on imaginative free play. Again we recognise here, in the simultaneous positivity and negativity of the exercise, the risk James is taking.

As Shell acknowledges, 'America was the historical birthplace of widespread paper money in the Western World, and a debate about coined and paper money dominated American political discourse from 1825 to 1845.'[35] It was a debate which expressed itself most clearly in the political sphere through the argument about the banks and their appropriation of power. One of the best commentators on the issue, James Roger Sharp, has emphasised its politicisation, claiming that 'To Jackson and his hard-money followers, banks occupied privileged positions in society and exercised tremendous and virtually unchecked power', and that 'In an age dominated by an egalitarian spirit, the banks sym- bolized aristocratic privilege on the one hand, and the rapid and uncomfortable transition the country was undergoing from an agrarian to a commercial society on the other hand.'[36] Sharp also argues (and this is crucial for the historical positioning of *Wash- ington Square*) that the bank debate reflected a wider argument about money which characterised the whole century,[37] so that by the time of the 'Gilded Age' itself the money issue focused the political rhetoric of the Populists just as acutely as it had that of the Jacksonians.[38] The mania for land speculation during the 1830s was made possible to a great extent by the absence of a national paper currency; the circulating medium consisted of specie and the paper money issued by hundreds of local banks. The Jacso- nians, in attempting to control the inevitable instability which accompanied (and, indeed, in large part enabled) such specula- tion, viewed the banks as a threat to an avowedly free and democratic society and maintained a faith in specie as 'a kind of perpetual and infallible balance wheel, regulating the workings of the banking system'. Specie, they felt, had 'an intrinsic and independent value of its own and could not depreciate as could paper money'.[39] Predictably then, the uncertain symbolism of paper money was countered by an argument for the seemingly more solid symbolism of gold and silver; we have the clear paradox of one form of abstraction competing with another on the contradictory grounds of its supposedly 'natural' materiality.

William Leggett, in a well-known essay on 'Equality' for the New York *Evening Post* of 6 December 1834, categorically places the issue in terms of class struggle and the dominance which inhibits the freedom of others: 'The scrip nobility of this Republic have adopted towards the free people of this Republic the same language which the feudal barons and the despot who contested with them the power of oppressing the people used towards their serfs and villains, as they were opprobriously called.' Throughout, Leggett opposes what he variously terms 'would-be lordlings of the Paper Dynasty' and 'phantoms of the paper system' to the 'class which labours with its own hands'. Here is a clear application of the abstractions and distances based on a differentiation of intellectual and manual labour, a differentiation whose consequences become vividly apparent under the conditions of commodity production, of the shift from agrarian to industrial practice. The former group is constituted by those whose 'soul is wrapped up in a certificate of scrip or a bank note', and the only enemy facing the 'labouring classes' is the 'monopoly and a great paper system that grinds them to the dust'.[40] Jackson himself utilises the same opposition in his Farewell Address of 1837: 'The agricultural, the mechanical, and the labouring classes have little or no share in the direction of the great moneyed corporations.'[41] Jackson's speeches in the 1830s exhibit succinctly the rhetoric of opposition to the questions of banks in general and paper money in particular, elaborating an immovable equation between banks, paper money and the abuse of democratic rights, along with manifest opportunity for fraud.[42] The instability of money characterises the 1830s by means of its consequences: inflation and speculation. To control both, the administration issued the 'Specie Circular' in 1836 which provided that only gold and silver could be accepted by government agents in payment for public lands, the object of the most intense speculation by the middle of the decade. Against such appropriation of public property by means of uncertain currency, the Circular concluded:

> The principal objects of the President in adopting this measure being to repress alleged frauds, and to withhold any countenance or facilities in the power of the Government from the monopoly of the public lands in the hands of speculators and capitalists, to the injury of the actual settlers in the new States,

and of emigrants in search of new homes, as well as to
discourage the ruinous extension of bank issues, and bank
credits, by which those results are generally supposed to be
promoted.[43]

Such was Jackson's distrust of the possibilities for making
something out of nothing that he chose to devote virtually the
whole of his Farewell Address in 1837 to the question of currency.
Arguably it is the single most sustained attack on the 'evil' of
paper money and the most rigorous justification of the 'constitutional currency' of gold and silver of any public document. It
begins by stressing the instability of contemporary conditions
engendered by the untrustworthy symbolism of the paper
medium:

> The paper system being founded on public confidence and
> having of itself no intrinsic value, it is liable to great and
> sudden fluctuations, thereby rendering property insecure and
> the wages of labor unsteady and uncertain. The corporations
> which create the paper money can not be relied upon to keep
> the circulating medium uniform in amount. In times of pros-
> perity, when confidence is high, they are tempted by the
> prospect of gain or by the influence of those who hope to profit
> by it to extend their issues of paper beyond the bounds of
> discrétion and the reasonable demands of business; and when
> these issues have been pushed on from day to day, until public
> confidence is at length shaken, then a reaction takes place, and
> they immediately withdraw the credits they have given, sud-
> denly curtail their issues, and produce an unexpected and
> ruinous contraction of the circulating medium, which is felt by
> the whole community.[44]

The 'ebbs and flows' of the currency 'naturally' engender a 'wild
spirit of speculation' which is morally harmful because it diverts
attention from 'the sober pursuits of honest industry' and fosters
an 'eager desire to amass wealth without labour'. The temptation
to create something out of nothing 'inevitably' leads to an
undermining of 'free institutions' and a corruption of authority by
locating power in the hands of a privileged few. Jackson's sense
of currency's impoverished symbolism, made particularly expressive in the obvious dangers of counterfeit notes, encourages him

to articulate his argument in terms of dominance and class,[45] and to see such counterfeits as encroaching upon human freedom by the 'natural associations' of the paper money system: 'monopoly and exclusive privileges'.[46]

The debates about money during the 1830s, the period in which Dr Sloper architecturally appropriates a portion of New York land as an act of resistance against the city's commercial practices, thus marks the coalition of a series of social and aesthetic questions concerning the nature of symbolism, its material referents and its consequent role in redefined understandings about the nature of power and liberty. Political interest in the symbolism of money becomes revived during the years of Reconstruction and particularly during the 1870s, the decade which James ends by composing his study of *Hawthorne* and *Washington Square*.

The Coinage Act of February 1873 (nominated by latterday Jacksonians as the 'crime of '73') put an end to the standard silver dollar. This demonetisation of silver in effect redefined 'coin' as gold and added considerably to the size of taxes. The Specie Resumption Act of early 1875 deflated the currency until it was at a par with gold. These acts were seen by the populists as conferring a privileged monopoly on the banks 'which drew interest in gold on the government bonds the banks bought, and interest a second time on the notes the banks were then empowered to create and lend',[47] and the money question itself became paramount during the remainder of the decade which experienced one of the country's worst depressions.[48] A single statement in support of silver against gold by the Democrat, Richard Bland, to Congress in August 1876 reveals the extent to which the Reconstruction debate on 'soft' versus 'hard' money continued the rhetoric of the 1830s. Bland was speaking on behalf of a Bill to remonetise silver which he saw as 'a measure in the interest of the honest yeomanry of this country'. He saw the Public Credit Act of 1869 and the Coinage Act of 1873 (which promised payment of government bonds in coin rather than the paper money with which they were originally purchased, and then redefined 'coin' to be gold alone at the expense of silver) as being wholly in the interests of 'stock-jobbers and speculators'. To argue that the taxpayer must pay only in gold was 'robbery, nothing more, nothing less', since creditors would benefit enormously to the detriment of debtors:

Because a measure is for once reported to this Congress that has within it a provision for the welfare of the people of the country against the corrupt legislation that has gone on here for the last sixteen years in the interest of the moneyed lords, it is here denounced as full of rascalities, and all this by the party that had perpetuated these injustices and brought corruption, fraud, infamy, and dishonour upon the country . . . Mr. Speaker, the common people of the country cannot come to this Capitol. They are not here in your lobby. They are at home following the plow, cultivating the soil, or working in their workshops. It is the silvern and golden slippers of the money kings, the bankers and financiers, whose step is heard in these lobbies and who rule the finances of the country.[49]

Bland's statement relied for its effect on the full complex of ideas we associate with the Jacksonian position: the symbolism of money, the concentration of power and the consequent limiting of free voice and free action, and the division (admittedly nostalgic in expression) between intellectual labour (the paper world of the speculators) and manual labour (the concrete productivity of soil and workshop). The opposition of notes and specie during the earlier period has become recomposed into an opposition of silver and gold, but we should not assume that the apparent materiality of silver coin presents a more satisfactory symbolism than the more obviously immaterial bank note. Coinage is also seen as an abstract form of representation, as Sohn-Rethel has urged:

A coin has stamped upon its body that it is to serve as a means of exchange and not as an object of use . . . Its physical matter has visibly become a mere carrier of its social function. A coin, therefore, is a thing which conforms to the postulates of the exchange abstraction and is supposed, among other things, to consist of an immutable substance, a substance over which time has no power, and which stands in antithetic contrast to any matter found in nature.[50]

We might remind ourselves that Sohn-Rethel establishes a discernible historical connection between the evolution of coined money and abstractive thought in the establishment of a monetary economy in the early Greek states which created conditions for 'the capacity of conceptual reasoning in terms of abstract universals, a capacity which established full intellectual independence from manual labour'.[51] This connection exposes vividly the valorised oppositions on which capitalist economics and business practices rely and which in turn place the figuration of Sloper's bourgeois temperament most accurately: the abstract vocabulary of science, geometry and cardinal numbers (in the form of monetised value) by which Catherine becomes available as a commodity.[52]

It is not so much the details of the debate about 'soft' and 'hard' money which concern us, but rather the fact that it has to do with modes of material expression, with questions interrogating the forms of solidity and meaning that may be attached to a crucial order of symbolism. And that symbolism may be seen to have a determinant place within the structures from which James wrote. The debate about money during the two periods in American history which witnessed such notable accelerations of industry and its allied commercial practices may be seen to share many of the features of an aesthetic concern to compose, across James's readings of Hawthorne and Balzac, readings which probe the materiality of writing itself. The debate about money suggests, above all, the indeterminancy of currency's symbolism and of its rhetoric, and the inadequacy of an empiricist or mimetic base for evaluation and expression. These features become exacerbated by their visibility during a period of social instability, the re-alignment of class and interest groups and economic depression immediately prior to the excesses of the Gilded Age. Treatises such as George M. Beard's *American Nervousness: Its Causes and Consequences* (New York, 1881) provided physiological evidence for the damaging impact of advanced industrial practices upon mind and body, offering, as it were, a material metaphor for those wider areas of instability which the present argument has attempted to locate.[53] And such work reminds us that the abstractions which so concern James in *Washington Square* are not to be confined to the further abstractive realm of ideas, but are material events which infect the very structures of feeling and behaviour.

IV

It would be a mistake to view the instability of a world rapidly being revealed as a marketplace for commodities solely in terms of the more apparent changes in the means of production. The development of the machines for industry should not be allowed to conceal the effects of concomitant changes in perceptions of money itself. Gerald T. Dunne has written well on this aspect of the transformations during the early nineteenth century of America's shift from an agrarian to an industrial economy:

> The rise of banking cut the fabric of tradition with an especial sharpness. Though the significance of the change was barely grasped and rarely articulated, the growing importance of banking amounted to a revolution in the traditional system of credit, which forced profound changes in outlook and values. Sharply challenged were the old agrarian views under which gold and silver, like fields and flocks, were the true essence of wealth. Rather, wealth was changing in form to the intangible – to paper bank notes, deposit entries on bank ledgers, shares in banks, in turnpikes, in canals, and in insurance companies. More important, perhaps, debt was no longer necessarily the badge of improvidence and misfortune. And from the creditor's point of view debt, in the form of bank notes or bank deposits became an instrument of power.[54]

Brook Thomas, in commenting on Dunne's description, has recognised the fuller abstraction and instability of what Dunne leaves as the 'intangible' form of wealth:

> In the new economy, the old theory that value was determined by the inherent properties of an object gave way to a subjective theory of value, in which the value of an object was determined by laws of supply and demand. In capital-poor but land-rich America, the land itself becomes just another commodity, fluctuating in value according to market conditions, the enterprise of developers, and the confidence games of speculators.[55]

Nowhere may the tissue of uncertainty be seen so clearly as within this paradox of a structure where economic power is measured by notes and documents, and where the 'real' is constituted by the fabric of paper with all its inadequate and dangerous symbolism.[56] In the America of the 1840s, as Marc Shell tells us, 'comparisons were made between the way a mere shadow or piece of paper becomes credited as substantial money and the way that an artistic appearance is taken for the real thing by a willing suspension of disbelief.'[57] The paper that Dr Sloper leaves behind as part of his 'explanation' to his patients is thus an 'inscrutable prescription' (p. 2), his only form of writing. We see here a clear contradiction of Sloper's office which mimes exactly the artistry of his science; it is a joke about the material appearance of writing that is to be taken seriously and literally. At both the fictional and material levels, 'inscrutable' writing requires further acts of re-composition to demystify its content, to make it publicly readable. The activity of forcing the signs of Sloper's writing to yield their substance and meaning is analogous both to the contemporary interrogation of the substance of money and its expression, and to the general habit of Sloper's profession, 'dividing people into classes, into types' (p. 101). Both these latter activities involve a willingness to believe in the accuracy of their modes of representation, and both specie and specimen rely on the 'look' of their expressions, sanctioned by a shared valorisation of mathematics. In the case of money, particularly paper notes, we witness a dissociation of writing and its content which quite literally mimics the breach of intellectual and manual labour within the world conceived as an industrial marketplace. The final conjunction which this equation enables is aesthetic; it is articulated in James's reading of both Hawthorne and Balzac at the time of *Washington Square*, as has been suggested, but it achieves its most famous expression in 1836, the year following the building of Sloper's house, in a statement from the chapter on 'Language' in Emerson's *Nature* (a text powerfully encoded by the transcendentalist response to America's first industrial revolution), where we find the question of literary and philosophical symbolism explicitly maintained through the figure of pecuniary fraud:

A man's power to connect his thought with its proper symbol, and so to utter it, depends on the simplicity of his character, that is, upon his love of truth and his desire to communicate it without loss. The corruption of man is followed by the corruption of language. When simplicity of character and the sovereignty of ideas is broken up by the prevalence of secondary desires, the desire of riches, of pleasure, of power, and of praise – and duplicity and falsehood take place of simplicity and truth, the power over nature as an interpreter of the will is in a degree lost; new imagery ceases to be created, and old words are perverted to stand for things which are not; a paper currency is employed, when there is no bullion in the vaults. In due time the fraud is manifest, and words lose all power to stimulate the understanding or the affections.[58]

This statement occurs, of course, in that section of Emerson's essay which pervasively attempts to express the analogies of Swedenborgian 'Correspondence' in aesthetic terms: the ways in which the imagination frames and operates within the relationship between symbols and their referents. As a counter to the 'rotten diction' of a corrupted language, Emerson posits the urge to 'fasten words again to visible things' in order to create a 'picturesque language', a phrase where 'picturesque' is intended literally as a means to effect a 'commanding certificate' of truth. Hence he argues for the materiality of the images employed in true discourse, their 'emblematic' office within a system whereby 'the whole of nature is a metaphor of the human mind', exhibiting how the 'laws of moral nature answer to those of matter as face to face in a glass' or the 'axioms of physics translate the laws of ethics'.[59] Emerson's willingness to employ metaphors from science marks an arena shared by Sloper (and, indeed, by James himself in his disquisitions on the writing of fiction), but while Sloper's science characterises an urge to privatisation and dominance, that of Emerson functions as a metaphor to permit fluidity and interconnectedness. It is instructive that Emerson's essay on Swedenborg in 1850 was capable of using technology (from, admittedly, the pre-industrial era) to maintain the sturdiness of Swedenborg's metaphysics. James felt incapable of Emerson's confidence in an 'exact relation' of symbol to its substance, but he well remembered with affection in his essay of 1887 Emerson's reading of the 'Boston Hymn' which clearly suggested the exploitative economic base of the concern with symbols in *Nature*. The occasion was the meeting in the Boston Music Hall in 1863 to celebrate Lincoln's signing of the proclamation which freed the Southern slaves. James recalls the 'immense effect' with which Emerson's 'beautiful voice' pronounced the lines:

> Pay ransom to the owner
> And fill the bag to the brim.
> Who is the owner? The slave is owner,
> And ever was. Pay *him*![60]

Whereas what Emerson elsewhere termed 'nature's geometry' provides a decided consolation for the transcendentalist temperament, James's more acute geometry emphasises crisis and instability on behalf of the allied areas of science, commerce, aesthetics and human relationships. It is in this sense that the silence which so awkwardly expresses the commodification of Catherine has its double function: to register a resistance to the commercial world and to betoken the paralysis of genuine intercourse. It is also in this sense that we are invited to notice a curious image on behalf of James's own activity of composition.

The image occurs at the beginning of Chapter 10 when Townsend, reluctantly, visits Catherine at home following his unspoken argument with her father. He is received on Catherine's own choice of ground, a 'New York drawing room', which is given a temporal description as 'furnished in the fashion of fifty years ago'. In other words, its furnishing belongs to a pre-industrial era, but by this stage in the novel we have lost our sense of the insistent specificity of time which marks its opening; such temporal detail is non-existent in the main action of the story which underlines its occurrence here as indicative of the nostalgia that Catherine never utters. We are then presented with a more definite description (the only one of its kind in the whole novel) of a particular item: as Townsend begins his assertions, he glances at

> the long narrow mirror which adorned the space between the two windows, and which had at its base a little gilded bracket covered by a thin slab of white marble, supporting in its turn a backgammon board folded together in the shape of two volumes, two shining folios inscribed in letters of greenish gilt, *History of England*   (p. 70).

Opened up here is a play between the loosely novelistic gesture of 'fifty years ago' (matching that of the story's own opening, 'During a portion of the first half of the present century, and more particularly during the latter part of it' which in itself signals a cavalier play with the specificity of time), denoting, presumably, an American past, and the embellished masquerade of a different past, that of England which, within a more domestic history, provided the germ of the story.[61] It is a play which receives attention in the correspondence with Howells about the 'items of high civilisation' in *Hawthorne* from which James proposes *Washington Square* as a determinedly 'truly American' tale.

The mirror would inevitably reflect not only Townsend's self-conscious 'glance' (the 'gilt' in its turn rather crudely punning the guilt of his occasion), but also the surface of the *History* itself, a precious object whose only reality, concealed by its surface, is a game whose chance and hazard are further concealed by the geometry of its rules. The description distances itself from the rhetoric of novelistic expression (measured in part, for example, by James's description of Mrs Montgomery's house at the beginning of Chapter 14) and has no local function to expand our sense of character or place. It merely lies there in the text as an abstracted item which contributes nothing to the narrative; it is sheer decoration. Neither is it an item of more fanciful or mysterious allegory such as we might find in Hawthorne. The mirror's surface (one of the most important of Jamesian value-terms) is literally mimetic, positioned so that it reflects not the vista of the outside world beyond the two windows which frame it (a framing of an internal view by the possibilities for an external view which thereby cancels a traditional figure for mimesis), but only an imitation text. James's self-regarding irony here suggests the catalogue of propositions about writing through which *Washington Square* negotiates its exploratory course. It permits only one form of material solidity, the 'gilt' letters inscribing the *History* (sustained, in both senses, by the slab of marble on its 'gilded' bracket) that provide a reminder of the economic conditions enabling the building of houses in Washington Square and the writing of novels about them.

V

By way of conclusion let us briefly consider the situation of Morris Townsend, partly because he has received such a uniformly bad press of the kind which elides his significance in the novel,[62] and partly to realign that unsympathetic treatment in order to locate him more concretely within the social historicism of *Washington Square*. Townsend needs, quite simply, to be understood as having a definite role to play in James's explicit critique of New York's bourgeois economy, regarding its origins in the accelerated commercial practices of the 1830s and 1840s from the point of view of its more expressive characteristics in the late 1870s. To this end, it is a mistake merely to dismiss Townsend through the stereotypes of a heartless lover or an interloper, since such categorisation inevitably seals him off from the material history that is probed by the novel's general project. It is to the presentation of a material history that the following remarks propose to return Townsend: to the social and economic forces through which the novel realises itself.

We may begin by noting the proximity of Townsend's features to those of Dr Sloper, who is himself offered as exemplary of the bourgeois temperament which sustains a view of the world as a marketplace for commodities by a balanced, rational discourse authorised by the types of science and the precepts of mathematics. Like Sloper, Townsend, when under the pressure of choosing his appropriate strategy, is capable of viewing Catherine, and indeed himself, as economic quantities,[63] and of figuring their situation in mathematical terms.[64] Sloper's tone is particularly apparent in the patronising irony of Townsend's voice during his second secret meeting with Mrs Penniman (pp. 154–7), and she is later, predictably, to acclaim the 'charm' of what she recognises as his 'formula' for giving up Catherine (p. 205). Townsend's final letter to Catherine, explaining this decision, invokes a view of themselves thoroughly within a notion of scientific computation as 'innocent but philosophic victims of a great social law' (p. 232). Earlier, having wished that Catherine would 'hold fast' to her relationship with himself (p. 116), he rapidly appropriates Sloper's own determinant hope that she will 'stick' (pp. 150, 155), a term which, foremost in Sloper's lexicon of his daughter, accentuates exactly the paralysed world maintained by both science and business practice.[65]

Townsend's approximation to the abstractive sensibility of Sloper comprises, however, only part of his force in the novel. He is given the first item of direct speech as the action of the narrative begins in Chapter 4: 'What a delightful party! What a charming house! What an interesting family! What a pretty girl your cousin is!' (p. 22). Here, rushed together, are the discrete units for the more expanded discourse of polite conversation. The speech approximates the non-dialogical tenor of Sloper's linguistic manner but is clearly less dominating; the difference is that Townsend's condensed utterance (with its implicit reluctance for discursive leeway) marks his distance from, and perhaps his awkwardness within, the social occasion. The observations he makes are, we are told, 'of no great profundity', but from Catherine's stance he goes on 'to say many other things in the same comfortable and natural manner' (p. 22). Her own social awkwardness leads her to see his loquaciousness as oddly paradoxical:

> Catherine had never heard anyone – especially any young man – talk just like that. It was the way a young man might talk in a novel; or, better still, in a play, on a stage, close before the footlights, looking at the audience, and with everyone looking at him . . . And yet Mr Townsend was not like an actor; he seemed so sincere, so natural.   (pp. 24–5)

This paradoxical mixture of the theatrical and the natural is picked up by Townsend himself a little later during the first conversation he has alone with Catherine in Washington Square. Revealingly, it is offered in the context of one of the most important Jamesian tenets, the liberty of individual perception:

> He had been to places that people had written books about, and they were not a bit like the descriptions. To see for yourself – that was the great thing; he always tried to see for himself. He had seen all the principal actors – he had been to all the best theatres in London and Paris. But the actors were always like the authors – they always exaggerated. He liked everything to be natural.   (p. 41)

Nevertheless, we know his naturalness to be the main feature of his social artifice. Sloper himself is shortly to make a joke about the same topic; when Mrs Almond argues that 'the thing is for Catherine to see it', he replies: 'I will present her with a pair of spectacles!' (p. 53). The abstractions of the novel are such that naturalness itself becomes enlisted on behalf of a determinant artifice; John Lucas, in disagreeing with Richard Poirier's reading of *Washington Square* as a play with 'a melodramatic fairy-tale', points us in the right direction when he notes: 'if the characters *do* become like stock types in stage melodrama and fairy tale . . . it is because they see themselves called on to play parts created by their self-conscious awareness of what their society requires of them.'[66] Lucas's argument suggests the linguistic disablement of social conditions, the conditions of accelerated industrial and commercial enterprise which impose the abstract structure of commodity exchange, breached from use, upon human relationships. Catherine is unable to see Townsend's conversation in any but theatrical terms because it is so unfamiliar to her and she has no other available resource; she acknowledges an artifice so unreal (by comparison, let us say, with that of Mrs Penniman)[67] that it seems a form of the natural. Sloper displays his control of the idea when he informs Townsend that 'I am not a father in an old-fashioned novel' (p. 90).

If any single word dominates *Washington Square*, it is 'natural' or its variants. And, substantially, by far the largest number of its occasions refers to Townsend. It provides the theme of his first open tribute to Catherine: ' "That's what I like you for; you are so natural. Excuse me," he added, "you see I am natural myself" ' (p. 41). His sense of his 'fine natural parts' (p. 159) combined with a confidence of manner form the basis of his physical attractiveness to which not only Catherine but even Sloper responds. Despite the fact that such naturalness constitutes a large part of his social artifice, there is a curious way in which it may be read in its own terms. To dismiss Townsend as a social climber or a fortune-hunter serves only to fix him too unproblematically. What is insisted upon is his sense of being out of place; he feels 'a great stranger in New York. It was his native place; but he had not been there for many years' (p. 24), and Catherine's early impression, coupled with her theatrical metaphors, is that 'He's more like a foreigner' (p. 33). His main feature is mobility, having travelled extensively abroad prior to the commencement of the story; travels to which he returns after his failure with Catherine. We know little of his family history, save that he has a sister in reduced circumstances, that he has been 'wild' in his youth (a notoriously indeterminate term), and that his branch of the Townsends is not 'of the reigning line' (p. 44). The interstitial social area in which James locates Townsend is, of course, characteristic of a period of intense development and change whereby existing class-lines become blurred and the great effort is to move beyond them, to articulate some proper social shape. The problem for the artist, as Forster is to encounter with Leonard Bast, Lawrence with Paul Morel, and, to a lesser extent, Dreiser with Clyde Griffiths during a later period of accelerated transformations, is to render this mobility of social place; how is such newness to be described in the world, this new style which is invariably at odds with existing social styles?

When she is told that Townsend has no 'business', Catherine expresses the surprise of one who had never heard of a young man 'in this situation' (p. 34). At the top of Sloper's list of enquiries about Townsend is the question 'What is his profession?' (p. 45). In the work of a writer where we rarely find anyone having to suffer the iniquities of a 'profession' in its full material sense, we are especially alert to this insistence in *Washington Square*. It is, after all, a novel which begins with an extraordinarily complex diagnosis of 'profession', that of Sloper which provides the entire social and economic base on which its history rests. James's monograph on Hawthorne makes a famous statement on the subject:

> It is not too much to say that even to the present day it is a considerable discomfort in the United States not to be 'in business'. The young man who attempts to launch himself in a career that does not belong to the so-called practical order; the young man who has not, in a word, an office in the business-quarter of the town, with his name painted on the door, has but a limited place in the social system, finds no particular bough to perch on.[68]

The profession that concerns James principally here is, of course, that of author and its social reception, but his stress on the necessity of being 'in business' remains valuable on its own; it is the distinguishing feature of Townsend's condition that, in the social and commercial world of lower Manhattan, he 'finds no particular bough to perch on'. The absence of a profession is, then, a prime cipher of the mobility and indeterminacy which circumscribes Townsend's 'naturalness' as a tactic against the styles of Washington Square. His position is natural in the sense that there exists no available societal vocabulary whereby it may be given expression; it has no name.

The kind of job that we are told Townsend eventually acquires is particularly germane to the period in which the novel is set.[69] He gains a partnership with a 'commission merchant' (p. 183). His function thereby is to mediate between manufacturers and the selling of their products in foreign markets and, as such, the commission merchant is probably 'the most important figure in the foreign trade organisation of both the United States and Great Britain'. This is particularly true of the state of New York for which the Census of 1840 lists 1044 commission houses as contrasted with 469 commercial houses.[70] What is illuminating about this choice of profession for Townsend goes beyond its specific historical typicality; it incorporates that form of agency which is disengaged simultaneously from the systems of production and the immediate systems of selling. In other words, it exposes a most apposite figure for the forms of disengagement and abstraction which characterise a period of rapid industrial development, those very forms which in turn provide the focus for James's critique of bourgeois economy and his sense of how they infect the structures of feeling constituting the liberty of human relationships. The world of Townsend's eventual 'profession' (like that of his cousin, the 'stout young stockbroker' who is the brief spokesman for the city's transformations – pp. 31–2 – as the novel's only other businessman) is a paper world, wholly devoid of material process or any real contact with productivity, and, as paper, is reminiscent of the alarming instability of that final abstraction, money itself (an issue which dominated American political thought during both the period of the novel's action and the period of its composition). The location of Townsend's supposed office in 'a place peculiarly and unnaturally difficult to find' (p. 201) duplicates exactly the shadowy nature of the job itself and, more generally, his membership of a new, emerging, changing class.[71]

To read Townsend as a social climber is to do no more than incorporate the partiality of Sloper's own typology; he presents a threat, but its real danger is that it cannot be fully formulated, not only because of his uncertain social positioning but because of a specific feature of Sloper's bourgeois temperament. As Roland Barthes notes, it is a feature of the bourgeois mind (and, we may add, of the exchange relation which characterises the dispersal of commodities, the defining objects of the bourgeois universe) that it obscures 'the ceaseless making of the world'.[72] What Townsend's mobility and his interstitial placing threaten above all is exactly an exposure of the 'making' of the world via his putative progress through it. To resist (to paralyse) Townsend is, in effect, to erase the 'making' of Sloper's own location because the bourgeois idea of itself is, in Barthes's definition, of 'the social class which does not want to be named'.[73] The potential interruption of Townsend marks precisely the path Sloper himself has followed. Townsend thus most profoundly threatens nothing so crude as Sloper's own position, or even the financial spoliation of his daughter, but the revelation of change, of alterability, of moving beyond the confines of his classification. His fluidity, his 'naturalness', proposes to dissolve the geometry by which Sloper and the Square are maintained paradoxically against the 'mighty uproar' of 'trade' and the 'base uses of commerce' (pp. 16–17), those disturbances which themselves seek sanction from the abstractions of science and mathematics. Sloper's treatment of Townsend is a paradigm of the conservative resistance to the new, of the bourgeois disguising (or deliberate blinding) of itself. We may see, then, that Townsend becomes the novel's less obvious victim and, more clearly, the victim of the period's transformations as he struggles within its simultaneous promise of economic amelioration and its damnation of those whom its accelerations leave behind.

Part II
Consuming the Present:
The Private Spectacles of
The Bostonians

3
Publicity and Emptiness

The Bostonians is about 'publicity'; about the issues of 'personal', 'private', 'public' relationships (almost obsessively highlighted as the novel's key terms) and their re-alignments at the onset of consumer culture in America during the 1870s and 1880s;[1] that moment in economic history when, within the practices of industrial capitalism, forms of accumulation began to give way to the imperatives of reproduction.[2] It is through these re-alignments as a function of such history that we may detect the 'very national, very typical' features of a novel which aimed insistently to be 'very characteristic of our social conditions',[3] features given insufficient weight even by those rare modern Jamesian critics who are properly concerned to register his historicism.[4] The subject of the novel – and the source of its typicality – is precisely James's anxieties about the reconstitutions of these terms 'publicity', 'public', 'personal', and 'private', about the reconstitutions of ideas concerning the self and its possibilities for relationships under the impact of the new world of consumerism. Publicity, the agency whereby the world advertises and perpetuates itself, becomes James's synecdoche for the changing culture in which all his characters are caught up. The general shape of the argument pursued here is suggested by Jean-Christophe Agnew's observations on the intrusions of the market economy:

What James sees violated in almost every case is 'privacy,' a term he uses quite broadly to refer to the indispensable conditions of familiarity upon which the fragile structure of human communities is formed. What dissolves the foundation of this familiarity is almost invariably 'publicity,' a word he uses with equal expansiveness to refer to the values and instrumentalities of a market society: the traffic in commodities, the habit of display, the inclination to theatricality, the worship of novelty and quantity.[5]

Agnew, rightly, takes *The American Scene* as providing 'the single most explicit judgement on his encounters with consumer culture', but the very directness of that example displays its insufficiency for present purposes; not only because of the twenty-year period which separates the record of James's return to America from the composition of *The Bostonians*, but because the explicit critique contained in the later text somehow inhibits James from providing anything more than a statement of distaste which fails to incorporate the diagnostic complexity we find in the fiction. Here is the reason for the misplaced confidence whereby Agnew wields those crucial terms 'privacy' and 'publicity', a confidence which invests a settled meaning that the novel disavows.

II

The title of *The Bostonians* may be allowed to invoke its issue of publicity: Boston not only as the city of reform but as the city of the advertisement, as Richard Godden has proposed: 'Boston appears to have been good ground in which to grow advertising agents; Rowell and Dodd opened there in 1865 and, via the *Advertisers Gazette*, pioneered and taught the skills of purchasing newspaper space and retailing to advertisers. The "new science" was Bostonian in origin.'[6] However, in the 1880s advertising was, of course, 'national' (the characteristic which James allied to the 'typical' in his ambition for the novel[7]), an industry whose volume multiplied more than tenfold by the end of the century.[8] The vehicles for the new industry were the newspapers and the magazines which proliferated enormously during the period under consideration, receiving their chief source of revenue from advertisements themselves and instigating decisive changes in their modes of presentation as mere information about a product gave way to the persuasion of its attractiveness.[9] These changes signal a further shift which we might categorise as a move from 'public' to 'publicity', from the language of fact and reason to the language of desire, where any assumed autonomy of the self becomes radically precarious as part of the general effect of consumer culture in which an assumed solidity of all values vibrates in a state of flux.

Matthias Pardon, who belongs to the new world of the newspapers and is a principal voice for publicity in the novel, 'indispensably' constitutes a strong part of James's claim for the 'typical', a figure whom he deploys (stridently forcing one of the novel's most problematical terms) to emphasise the 'vulgarity and hideousness' of 'the impudent invasion of privacy – the extinction of all conception of privacy'.[10] The urgency of James's repetition of 'privacy' suggests the difficulty of maintaining the word's singularity under changing conditions. The presentation of Pardon is uncompromisingly straightforward, anticipating the broad picture that Agnew finds in *The American Scene*. He is devoted to 'the cultivation of the great arts of publicity', a man for whom 'all things referred themselves to print'. The novel insists above all on his modernity, the very feature which characterises his typicality as 'the ingenuous son of his age'; as:

> a thoroughly modern young man; he had no idea of not taking advantage of all the modern conveniences. He regarded the mission of mankind upon earth as a perpetual evolution of telegrams; everything to him was very much the same, he had no sense of proportion or quality; but the newest thing was what came nearest exciting in his mind the sentiment of respect.[11]

Here we find the key features of publicity: its contemporaneousness, its technological up-to-dateness and, predominantly, its fetishisation of the 'new', expressed precisely as conditioned by the uniformity (having 'no sense of proportion or quality') of mass-production. 'New', in the form of novelty, is the major item in Pardon's lexicon: he wants to see Verena's name 'in the biggest kind of bills and her portrait in the windows of the stores' because she has the attractiveness of novelty, exactly that component which is valorised by publicity: 'she would take a new line altogether. She had charm, and there was a great demand for that nowadays in connexion with new ideas' (p. 110). For Verena to address Harvard College 'would be the newest thing yet' (p. 116). We might remember that one of James's early putative titles for the novel was 'The Newness'.[12]

Pardon's primary image of modernity is, appropriately, the telegram: the material agency for gathering and disseminating the 'news' with topical speed. The immediate effect of this mechanism was to render all newspapers the same in the replication of the stories they covered. Readers, irrespective of *which* large city daily they read, shared in consuming the 'news' exactly that illusion of sharing they enjoyed in their consumption of the 'new' products of publicity; those products which belonged to the same typographical space as the stories themselves. It is commonplace that advertisements and factual items could be seen as inter-changeable, but the slippage of the 'new' into 'novelty' in both areas is one of the main effects of publicity itself. For both newspaper editor and advertising agency, novelty became the necessary instrument whereby the individual immediacy of story or product could be effected. Newspapers colluded, then, in advertising's more apparent structuring of a consumer culture; and that collusion, as Alan Trachtenberg has argued brilliantly, dramatised a central paradox of metropolitan life:

> the more knowable the world came to seem as *information*, the more remote and opaque it came to seem as *experience*. The more people needed newspapers for a sense of the world, the less did newspapers seem able to satisfy that need by yester-day's means, and the greater the need for shock and sensation, for spectacle.[13]

The device of novelty is instrumental beyond any battle for circulation. It attempts to overcome the deadened familiarity of uniformity by pandering to a different form of familiarity; that which the consumptive reader can internalise as his or her own. Paradoxically, however, that same device, particularly within the transience of a newspaper item, serves to disengage the reader from any sense of experiential compact with the item itself. The 'spectacle' provided by the newspaper in Trachtenberg's argu-ment, following Walter Benjamin, thus expresses the 'estrange-ment of a consciousness no longer capable of free intimacy with its own material life',[14] or, as Guy Debord claims, it is 'that which escapes the activity of men, that which escapes reconsideration and correction by their work. It is the opposite of dialogue.'[15] Trachtenberg provides a fine summary of the newspapers' collu-sion within the materially abstractive habits of perception encour-aged by the commodity relation in general:[16] 'The form in which it projected its readers' assumed wish to overcome distance con-cealed its own devices for confirming distance, deepening mys-tery, and presenting the world as a spectacle for consumption. Surrogate or vicarious familiarity served only to reinforce strangeness.'[17]   With experience itself, however, the sense of 'strangeness' is felt initially as excitement. This is certainly the case with Verena, herself the novel's main 'spectacle' who, in the transformative atmosphere of New York and while maintaining the 'real life' of 'Boston earnestness', cannot help but succumb to the fantasy of publicity's very promise: the 'vogue' she might enjoy in New York. She becomes caught up in the 'vastness and variety' of the city, its 'infinite possibilities' and, revealingly, invokes the image of the telegram to register its liveliness: 'Certainly, the people seemed very much alive, and there was no other place where so many cheering reports could flow in, owing to the number of electric feelers that stretched away everywhere' (p. 251). The disengagements and abstractions of publicity's fantasies are profoundly troubling for James in this novel, but he is not so solemnly cerebral or so theoretical as to forget their experiential delight in a city that is 'bright, amusing', where 'the elements seemed so numerous, the animation so immense, the shops so brilliant, the women so strikingly dressed' (p. 253). Indeed, it is precisely through such delight that publicity may intimately restructure the perception of things: novelty *is* attractive, and hence its danger.

Telegrams are contradictory affairs. They both expand and contract the world. Their usage by the business-orientated temperament of Christopher Newman in *The American*, for example, the temperament which walks in 'seven-league boots', disturbs Madame de Bellegarde by a range that threatens the sanctity of her 'select circle' but yields 'interest' for Newman himself.[18] Immediately before writing *The American*, in his 1875 review of the *Correspondence of William Ellery Channing, D.D., and Lucy Aikin*, James revealed his worries about the telegram's condensation, a condensation of not only geographical but linguistic space:

> The telegraph, now, has made even our letters telegraphic, and we imagine the multiplication of occasions for writing to have acted upon people's minds very much as it has done in their hands, and rendered them dashy and scrappy and indistinct. In fact, it may be questioned whether we any longer write letters in the real sense at all. We scribble off notes and jot down abbreviated dispatches and memoranda, and at last the postal card has come to seem to us the ideal epistolary form.[19]

The occasion of James's worries was a comparison beteen contemporaneity and 'those spacious, slow-moving days' of the *Corre-*

spondence itself, the 1830s and 1840s when 'quiet Hampstead' and 'tranquil Boston' provided 'a sort of perfume of leisure' for epistolary matters.[20] The primitive form of this comparison anticipates the more complex comparisons invoked by *The Bostonians* on the issue of reform itself. That issue belongs to a story that is too lengthy for inclusion here, but we may note how the comparison between present frenzy and past leisure prompts a diatribe against what James defines as 'the pestilent modern fashion of publicity':

> A man has certainly a right to determine, in so far as he can, what the world shall know of him and what it shall not; the world's natural curiosity to the contrary notwithstanding. A while ago we should have been tolerably lenient to noncompliance on the world's part; have been tempted to say that privacy was respectable, but that the future was for knowledge, precious knowledge, at any cost. But now that knowledge (of an unsavoury kind, especially) is pouring in upon us like a torrent, we maintain that, beyond question, the more precious law is that there should be a certain sanctity in all appeals to the generosity and forbearance of posterity, and that a man's table-drawers and pockets should not be turned inside out. This would be our feeling where even a truly important contribution to knowledge was at stake, and there is nothing in Dr. Channing's letters to overbear the rule.[21]

Clearly we are on similar ground to that of James's broad distaste for the newspapers' assault on 'privacy' in the provisional sketch for *The Bostonians* in his *Notebook*; but again the reductiveness of his view outside its fictional representation can be misleading in its suggestion that this simple intrusion defines the extent of his concern. The cramped space of the telegraphic form had consequences beyond stylistic aberrations, beyond even its material role in encouraging a uniform image of the 'news' which itself required in turn the illusory friction of novelty. These consequences belonged to the disturbing instability of the world revealed through the telegram's compression of time and geography, an instability vividly expressed by the physician George M. Beard in his treatise of 1881, *American Nervousness: Its Causes and Consequences*. Beard argued unequivocally that the telegraph was one of the main items of modern civilisation (he listed the others as steam power, the periodical press, the sciences and 'the mental activity of women') to contribute to the contemporary spread of mental and physical disorder in America:

> The telegraph is a cause of nervousness the potency of which is little understood. Before the days of Morse and his rivals, merchants were far less worried than now, and less business was transacted in a given time; prices fluctuated far less rapidly, and the fluctuations which now are transmitted instantaneously over the world were only known then by the slow communication of sailing vessels or steamships; hence we might wait for weeks or months for a cargo of tea from China, trusting for profit to prices that should follow their arrival; whereas, now, prices at each port are known at once all over the globe. This continual fluctuation of values, and the constant knowledge of those fluctuations in every port of the world, are the scourges of business men, the tyrants of trade – every cut in prices in wholesale lines in the smallest of any of the Western cities, becomes known in less than an hour all over the Union; thus competition is both diffused and intensified. Within but thirty years the telegraphs of the world have grown to half a million miles of line, and over a million miles of wire – or more than forty times the circuit of the globe. In the United States there were, in 1880, 170,103 miles of line, and in that year 33,155,991 messages were sent over them.[22]

The telegram, then, emerges not so much as an invasion of privacy through the new world of publicity (in that form, it is as easily encoded and hence dismissed as James's non-fictional prose would suggest), but it poses fresh difficulties for the stability of privacy within the new commercial order. In this sense, the 'private' and the 'personal' may be returned to the general debate about the self in relation to the accelerating industrialism of the nineteenth century, a return in which we can determine the transformation of the self as unique or original (the terms which most frequently advertise the value of Verena's talent) into the spectacle of novelty.

Rachel Bowlby has recently provided a timely reminder of the debate's basic outline:

> It is no coincidence that the 'romantic genius' of the early part of the century came trailing his clouds of glory into the world at

precisely the historical moment when the industrialization of literature could be read as a fatal compromise of his authorial freedom. Poetic genius pitted itself against the demands of an all-too-workaday commercial world.[23]

In other words, both the worker and the artist were forced into new assertions of self-hood at the onset of mass-production; and we know, too, that James himself was thoroughly caught up in the 'industrialization of literature' through his perennial concerns over readership and his negotiations over contracts and serial rights. But what needs to be added here is that the rhetoric of the battle between 'genius' and the 'commercial world' becomes increasingly fragile as that world enters the stage of consumption. It is precisely the effect of consumption to render such rhetoric inadequate in its simple bipartite opposition of what may be assumed to be 'private' (the self) and what may be assumed to be 'public' (the world). That opposition, transformed into the difficulties of what can only be schematised roughly as 'personal' and 'publicity', loses the comfort of its presumed dichotomy to become radically uncertain. James is concerned not only with the fundamental uncertainty of these terms he wields with such seeming briskness throughout *The Bostonians*, but with the schismatic perception which, simultaneously, attempts to restore them to their earlier single antithesis.

The debate which Bowlby outlines has attracted, revealingly for the purposes of the present argument, the more detailed attention of Alfred Habegger. As part of a general argument that one of the great innovations of the 'realist' genre lay in its refusal to give readers 'the sort of satisfaction the novel generally afforded', Habegger usefully relates commercial practice to that of popular literature in establishing a shared image of the self which is disrupted by realism:

> The surge of industrial activity in nineteenth-century America puffed up the ego with dreams of stunning personal success, of inevitably triumphant personal nobility. Realism was a critical response to the simultaneously inflated and privatized ego that was made hungry by contemporary society and fed by the fantasies in popular fiction. That is one of the reasons realism was often 'pessimistic' – it insisted that the self was limited and conditioned and not capable of the apotheosis promised by mass fantasy.[24]

It is mainly through such limiting of the self that 'realist' fiction (and *The Bostonians* seems to belong to that genre) disturbs the most fundamental of satisfactions: what Habegger rightly categorises as 'ego-pleasure', where the reader is encouraged to identify with one character in particular. Autonomy of character, and by implication of self, surrenders to the play of desire (that notorious confusion of need and want, of essence and image) which, in conjunction with the limiting social possibilities for character, not only denies the reader satisfaction but disestablishes the ground for integrating a presumed authenticity of the self in the first place.

Publicity thus belongs to the strategies of commercial practices and popular literature in creating an illusion of the self which bases its rhetoric on the resources of the 'unique', the 'original'; resources which, in the age of consumption, derive their impetus from a notion of the authentic conveyed through the spectacle of novelty. As Theodor Adorno has maintained, during the later phase of that age, the unique or the genuine does not emerge as an alternative to, but is produced within, the practices of mass-production and commodity culture:

> The more tightly the world is enclosed by the net of man-made things, the more stridently those who are responsible for this condition proclaim their natural primitiveness. The discovery of genuineness as a last bulwark of individualistic ethics is a reflection of industrial mass-production. Only when countless standardized commodities project, for the sake of profit, the illusion of being unique, does the idea take shape, as their antithesis yet in keeping with the same criteria, that the non-reproducible is the truly genuine . . . The ungenuineness of the genuine stems from its need to claim, in a society dominated by exchange, to be what it stands for yet is ever able to be.

At the moment when James is beginning to work against the older novelistic autonomy of character and to probe the possibilities for its relational presentation (a process that begins most forcefully with *The Europeans* and *The Portrait of a Lady*), the world of publicity simultaneously displays the alarming impossibility for the self to be 'wholly and entirely' what it 'is',[25] the disturbing fluctuations of the 'private'. *The Bostonians* makes it abundantly clear that, for James, the altering notions of the self and its relationships which organise his fictional innovations are exposed through the transformations of publicity as themselves profoundly embedded within the most disturbing aspects of consumption; his liberations of character from the autonomy that is both an illusion of freedom and a prison are at the same time a worrying testimony to those features of consumer culture which caused him the deepest unease. That unease will be tracked in the novel through the slippages of 'private', 'personal', 'public' and 'publicity'.

These slippages are explored predominantly in the complex usages of Ransom and, to a lesser extent, Olive Chancellor; but even in the broad presentation of publicity that we see in Matthias Pardon they appear in a determinant key. His 'cultivation of the great arts of publicity' has meant that 'all distinction between the person and the artist had ceased to exist' and such erasure immediately produces James's pun whereby 'the writer was personal, the person food for newsboys, and everything and every one were every one's business'. The syntactical sinuosity of the pun becomes compounded by the play of 'everything' and 'every one', so that by the time we arrive at the indictment of seemingly straightforward intrusion three lines later ('He poured contumely on their private life, on their personal appearance', p. 107), Pardon's erasures have rendered very tenuous any meaningful dissociation of 'private' and 'personal'.

Olive's response to Pardon at this moment in the novel, the tea party at Monadnoc Place, gives a prescient indication of her role within the cultivation of consumption. Echoing Ransom's patrician disdain for Miss Birdseye's *soirée* earlier, where he judged Verena an 'exhibit' for a 'multitude' (p. 84), Olive dismisses the vulgarity of Pardon's publicity, sensing that the other guests are treating Verena 'as a show, as a social resource', and she proclaims loftily: 'Your mission is not to exhibit yourself as a pastime for individuals, but to touch the heart of communities, of nations' (p. 114). Olive's invocation of an opposition between 'individuals' and 'communities' is symptomatic of her own advertising system for Verena. Her condemnation of publicity as exhibitionism does not indicate her divorce from that world; rather, the converse is true, for what she objects to fundamentally is that it is publicity on too small, too parochial a scale and, crucially, engineered by others instead of herself. In effect, she substitutes one form of publicity for another: and it is not accidental that it is here that Pardon first proposes the idea of displaying Verena at the Boston Music Hall 'at fifty cents a ticket' (p. 111), which is of course exactly Olive's ambition – while denying the profit motive (p. 125) – in the largest display of publicity imaginable at the novel's climactic conclusion.

III

Matthias Pardon offers one of two voices in the novel which expose the procedures of publicity. Selah Tarrant both confirms and extends those procedures. Again, it is the newspapers rather than advertisements or the big department stores which provide the agency for Tarrant's perception, and in a much more exaggerated and idealised form than is the case with Pardon. The hyperbole used to express his commitment is in excess of simply registering his excitement as a wide-eyed onlooker who lacks the restraint of a professional practitioner (such as Pardon), and in excess also of Dickensian satire. 'Human existence to him, indeed, was a huge publicity', and:

> The newspapers were his world, the richest expression, in his eyes, of human life; and, for him, if a diviner day was to come upon earth, it would be brought about by copious advertisement in the daily prints . . . his ideal of bliss was to be as regularly and indispensably a component part of the newspaper as the title and date, or the list of fires, or the column of Western jokes. The vision of that publicity haunted his dreams, and he would gladly have sacrificed to it the innermost sanctities of home.
>
> (p. 89)

Hyperbole cannot conceal the literalness of that sacrifice which incorporates the 'personal' in one of its changing forms:

> He looked with longing for the moment when Verena should be advertised among the 'personals', and to his mind the supremely happy people were those (and there were a good many of them) of whom there was some journalistic mention every day in the year. Nothing less than this would really have satisfied Selah Tarrant. . . . Success was not success so long as his daughter's *physique*, the rumour of her engagement, were

not included in the 'Jottings', with the certainty of being extensively copied.

(p. 89)

As 'personals' became 'Jottings', so their bastardised form enters into the reproducibility that is the imperative of consumption. Tarrant's machinations are even more perverse. His sacrifice of home, expressed through his philandering and his sale of Verena, marks a significant change in the history of nineteenth-century industrialism. The general effect of that history had been to enforce the gender-based divisions of home and work-place, leisure and labour;[26] but, with the shift from production to consumption, the home itself (hitherto the female site of domestic privacy) becomes quite literally invaded by the designs of the new publicity. Mrs Tarrant's general encouragement of Olive's visit and her specific worries about decorum during the tea-party sequence at Monadnoc Place (p. 103) are sufficient indication of the changing nature of ideals of hospitality in the home (ideals increasingly structured by the imperatives for display encouraged by the advertising agencies). The home is no longer the haven of personal domesticity; it is now exposed to the imagined views of others. As Jackson Lears has noted, thinking forward to a slightly later history, 'Guests were everywhere.'[27]

In sacrificing his home to publicity, Selah Tarrant registers the shifts of contemporaneity: the more the home came to imply, in Trachtenberg's phrasing, a 'transcendence of labour', the more it emerged as a 'pervasive image of freedom', so the more it became linked to the requirements of publicity, to the choice of goods, 'the market from which the home seemed a refuge'.[28] A more glaring example is Olive Chancellor's residence in Charles Street, seen through the explicitly masculine perception of Basil Ransom (we are told that his artistic sense is not highly cultivated and that his conception of material comfort consists in 'the vision of plenty of cigars and brandy and water and newspapers, and a cane-bottomed chair of the right inclination') which nevertheless recognises its deformed gesture of the self: 'he had never seen an interior that was so much an interior as this queer corridor-shaped drawing-room . . . he had never felt himself in the presence of so much organized privacy' (p. 15). Both the two other residences we enter in the novel are at the other extreme in being wholly open to guests and visitors and both are given a quasi-public aspect; overtly in the case of Miss Birdseye's apartment, which has the 'similitude of an enormous street-car' (p. 28), and covertly in the impression the Burrage mansion gives of a small theatre (p. 215). We are to imagine the home of Mrs Farrinder to be, in a sense, unnecessary to James's argument since, in the role of the most 'public' figure we meet, she is advertised with broad irony as someone who spans both worlds: 'She was held to have a very fine manner, and to embody the domestic virtues and the graces of the drawing-room; to be a shining proof, in short, that the forum, for ladies, is not necessarily hostile to the fireside' (p. 28).

Not only is the idea of home as refuge seen to be fraught with the paradox of consumer culture, but it marks a clear distortion of meaningful privacy: as privacy begins to assume the shape of refuge, so it loses the shape of its traditional compact with public. We are told of Mrs Tarrant's ambitions for her daughter's marriageability that 'she hoped the personage would be connected with public life – which meant, for Mrs Tarrant, that his name would be visible, in the lamplight, on a coloured poster, in the doorway of Tremont Temple' (p. 86). Here, 'public' substitutes unquestioningly for publicity, but James is sophisticated enough to recognise that the glamour of the latter is not always wholly illusory for those who fall under its spell. Mrs Tarrant is not 'eager' about this 'vision' because she is aware of the experience it conceals: 'a tired woman holding a baby over a furnace-register that emitted luke-warm air'. Nevertheless the idea of home is, as for 'most American women of her quality', an idea for which she holds 'extreme reverence', having 'preserved the spirit of this institution' through all the vicissitudes of the past twenty years', and so the prospect of the alternative to Verena's marriage (a 'really lovely friendship' with Olive Chancellor) becomes pictured for her by the attractiveness of 'having two homes'. If the home 'should exist in duplicate for Verena', then 'the girl would be favoured indeed'. Even in the act of recognising the 'sterner fate' of marriage and the home, Mrs Tarrant thus continues to maintain their ideal 'spirit'. In testing one image of publicity, she replaces it with another; but her husband's sacrifice of the home involves more damaging consequences.

The damage is to Verena, and it is articulated in nicely understated but quite implicit terms of physical ravage. Twice we are told of Dr Prance's opinion (the only opinion in the novel

which seems unquestioningly trustworthy) that Verena is 'anaemic' (pp. 40 and 51). On the first occasion the opinion is domestic, offered as a moment of textual neutrality ('Doctor Prance
would be surprised if she didn't eat too much candy'), but on the
second occasion it is singularly vibrant; the dramatic red of her
hair, the defining feature which remains to Olive's anguished
imagining of her drowned featurelessness at Marmion (p. 356),
looks as if her 'blood had gone into it' (it is appropriate that her
fan – p. 54 – is also red). The image implies vampiric possession:
her father's hands extract at the same time as they infuse; Verena
is drained as she is inspired, and this is to be her fate as a
commodified spectacle not only in the literal hands of Selah
Tarrant but in the metaphorical handling by Olive Chancellor and
Basil Ransom. All exploit what is rather worryingly naturalised by
the narrative: 'it was in her nature to be easily submissive, to like
being overborne' (p. 285). James's outline for the novel[29] includes
the 'rare confession'[30] of his specific textual source, Daudet's
L'Evangéliste, and in his 1883 essay on the French novelist, James
designates Madame Autheman, the model for Olive, as 'the
theological vampire' of Daudet's story.[31] The image of vampiric
possession is entirely apposite for the publicity of commodities
because it is precisely the office of publicity to dissolve the solidity
of its products by a stress upon their characteristics or attributes
(texture, convenience or style, for example, which pander to
images of taste, health, social respectability and so on). Under
consumption, objects are drained; or, in Marx's phrasing: 'As a
value, the commodity is an equivalent; as an equivalent, all its
natural properties are extinguished.'[32]

The novel gives literal expression to this extinguishing: again, it
is left to Dr Prance to note the slimness of Verena's physique
(p. 335). Under consumption, the status of a product as a 'real'
object is subservient to the play of desire that is manufactured for
its presentation in the market. We witness the precarious
instability of things which belongs to the general amnesia of
commodity culture: the forgetfulness in objects of their material
relations through a suppression of their productive history.[33] Thus
any solidity Verena might be assumed to possess is a problem
throughout the novel. Not only do the languages used to describe
her and the actions in which she participates permit only a limited
sense of specificity on her behalf, but Selah Tarrant is concerned
to emphasise the 'impersonal' nature of her success (pp. 49, 56).

Admittedly this is in part the rhetoric of his promotion of Verena, but the word's inversion of 'personal' and its physical relation to the idea of possession demand that we read it beyond the confines of that rhetoric. Verena herself reinforces it by reiterating 'it isn't me' (pp. 48, 49, 50, 69, 194), and the most common adjective to be applied to her performances is 'inspirational', which not only has its own historical specificity (as an instrumental term for spiritualism generally, or as a defining doctrine for the religious asceticism of the Amana Society, for example), but also suggests an infusing of ideas from without that further isolates her from place and history. It is instructive that the only moment where she is seen to move away from 'inspiration' occurs in the final, decisive third of the novel when she is rehearsing what is to be imagined as her first great public encounter: 'She wasn't going to trust to inspiration this time; she didn't want to meet a big Boston audience without knowing where she was. Inspiration, moreover, seemed rather to have faded away' (p. 339). And the point is, of course, that this is an encounter which is to be evaded.

On the smaller scale of her first performance at Miss Birdseye's *soirée*, we witness precisely the draining of 'anaemic' Verena's solidity through attention to her attributes. Our guide is Basil Ransom; appropriately at this point in the novel, the unprepared consumer of the new product on which his gaze settles for the first time and under whose gaze Verena dissolves into a plethora of melodramatic images. She is 'attractive but ambiguous'. Although we are to acknowledge this judgement of ambiguity as a symptom of Ransom's provincialism which the novel maintains throughout, the provincialism of one who is disturbed initially by the 'surprises' of Boston, who 'liked to understand' (p. 7), and whose conception of vice was 'purely as a series of special cases, of explicable accidents' (p. 18), it is a judgement sufficiently shared by Olive (see, for example, p. 70) to allow us to take it as intrinsically accurate. Ransom is caught by the attributes of colour and brightness which he then dissolves further through the language of theatre:

He had never seen such an odd mixture of elements; she had the sweetest, most unworldly face, and yet, with it, an air of being on exhibition, of belonging to a troupe, of living in the gaslight, which pervaded even the details of her dress, fashioned evidently with an attempt at the histrionic. If she had produced a pair of castanets or a tambourine, he felt that such accessories would have been quite in keeping.

(p. 51)

Within this language, Verena's smile becomes fixed into art ('like the glisten of a gem') and romantic fiction (she 'looked like an Oriental' and 'resembled Esmeralda'), and even these gestures towards a recognisable solidity are then decomposed back into the primary impression of colour: her dress is disingenuously ordinary ('light brown') but its shape is 'fantastic', her petticoat is 'yellow', her sash 'crimson' and her beads 'amber'.

The narrative itself colludes here in noting her 'melodramatic appearance' (p. 52), a collusion already initiated in its first substantial presentation of Verena where her contradictory effects become summarised in a paradoxical theatricality:

> She had expressed herself, from the first word she uttered, with a promptness and assurance which gave almost the impression of a lesson rehearsed in advance. And yet there was a strange spontaneity in her manner, and an air of artless enthusiasm, of personal purity. If she was theatrical, she was naturally theatrical.

(p. 46)

What conspires with the dispersive effect of theatricality here is the positioning of 'personal'. Adjectivally, it picks up the values of the brief list which prepares for it, 'strange' and 'artless', and then anticipates 'naturally' where the latter's oxymoronic play with 'theatrical' disarranges its ground completely. This disarrangement is further qualified by the immediate context of the passage: the eager publicity of Matthias Pardon who perceives 'the material of a paragraph' in 'a new style, quite original', and the frozen 'eminently public manner' of Mrs Farrinder, aware of herself solely as the object of the 'collective heart' of 'many ovations'. Mrs Farrinder reiterates the paradox in a predictably rigid form whereby 'public' discourse produces nothing more than a reductive schism of familiar domesticity, wondering 'whether Miss Tarrant were a remarkable young woman or only a forward minx' (p. 47). Between the fashionableness of publicity and the cautionary reservation of public judgement, the 'personal' occupies a fragile perch amongst the threats of competing codes.

Ransom's theatrical vocabulary is a characteristic rhetoric in his appropriation of Verena. He wonders a little later, for example, whether her smile is part of the 'training' of a 'perfect little actress' (p. 60), and he is aware of the financial possibilities in a 'big career' that is comparable to that of a 'distinguished actress or singer' (p. 277). Prior to her performance at the Burrage mansion, again he extracts her from the reality of the moment; she is 'like an actress before the footlights, or a singer spinning vocal sounds to a silver thread', and her voice, universally agreed to be her salient talent, is emptied of utterance at the expense of indeterminant musicality. She is then further removed as a consequence of being portrayed as 'the *improvisatrice* of Italy', in which she becomes 'a chastened, modern, American version of the type, a New England Corinna, with a mission instead of a lyre', and such is his anxiety about the potential failure of her performance that he resorts to an image from the burlesque, the circus: 'Ransom became aware that he was watching her in much the same excited way as if she had been performing, high above his head, on the trapeze' (p. 228).[34] This language is shared by Olive's sense of Verena as 'strange' and 'different'; Verena 'seemed to belong to some queer gypsy-land or transcendental Bohemia. With her bright, vulgar clothes, her salient appearance, she might have been a rope-dancer or a fortune teller.' It is then enmeshed within Olive's perception of her own social mission: 'this had the immense merit, for Olive, that it appeared to make her belong to the "people", threw her into the social dusk of that mysterious democracy' (p. 70). Olive's 'romance of the people' (p. 31) desubstantiates Verena even further. She sees Verena's past as having the 'merit' of initiating her into 'the miseries and mysteries of the People', an initiation which, in Olive's reading, depends upon breaking apart the Greenstreet and Tarrant genealogies of Verena's family history:

> It was her theory that Verena (in spite of the blood of the Greenstreets, and, after all, who were they?) was a flower of the great Democracy, and that it was impossible to have had an origin less distinguished than Tarrant himself. His birth, in some unheard-of place in Pennsylvania, was quite inexpressibly low, and Olive would have been much disappointed if it had been wanting in this defect.

Not only does Olive's 'romance' deconstruct Verena's lineage, but it leaves its 'merit' only as instigatory; her own patronage will render it obsolete altogether: 'what she would have liked to impose on the girl was an effectual rupture with her past' (p. 96). That rupture empties Verena of her history absolutely, and is of course finally achieved by her purchase of the girl.

In part, the effect of the theatrical language is to suggest the historical newness, as opposed to novelty, of Verena. It proposes the discourse of social non-comprehension towards the alterability of historical process itself (comparable, perhaps, to the language of superstition and approximation whereby Pearl in Hawthorne's *The Scarlet Letter*, a character similarly seen as emerging at a point of historical change, is melodramatically figured as 'elf' or 'sprite'); the discourse which seeks extravagant terms in order to approach a collective meaning, a more accurate lexicon for what has indeterminate outline, is only dimly seen and understood. It would be misguided to ignore this effect, particularly since the novel so explicitly establishes itself at the beginnings of one of the most radical shifts in American history;[35] but equally we need to recognise its major role within that history which is to propose the draining of objects and persons under consumption. Ransom's theatrical language, characteristically deployed in his imagining of Verena, operates beyond the registration of social uncertainty, of the newness that has difficulties of accommodation. It emerges as a definite programme of propaganda, a re-creation of Verena for self-concerned purposes. Most shockingly, and fully congruent with the novel's interest in the power relations of speech itself, Ransom's ambition immediately prior to their excursion in Central Park is precisely to 'strike her dumb' (p. 278): to empty her of her major attribute.

4
Language, Setting and Self

The discourses deployed by Basil Ransom in his appropriation of Verena are drawn from the vocabulary of the theatre and, especially, the vocabulary of the arcadian and the pastoral. By draining Verena of any substantive content, they maintain her as a creature of his own imagining, a 'private' figure to be shored against the intrusions of publicity. Paradoxically, such a draining is precisely the tactic of publicity itself in its promotion of the spectacular: instead of 'saving' Verena in any way, Ransom's manipulative language succeeds in substituting one form of publicity, although admittedly on a minor scale, for another; his designs, in short, share all the features of the system they aim to subvert. Let us begin by tracking the main line of Ransom's arcadian language and its support for the schismatic perception whereby he attempts to rigidify the world that is, again, a feature of publicity's vision. Then let us see how the disposition of this language belongs to the wider concern of James's interest in the realist setting within the architecture of consumption and, finally, to the inflation of self which he regards as one of consumption's most insidious infections.

I

Ransom first uses the language of the theatre at his first sight of Verena, but when her performance on that occasion begins, he slips into arcadian rhetoric to describe its effect. The approximate vocabulary of her 'strange, sweet, crude, absurd, enchanting improvisation' becomes ordered through the more specific images of the 'young prophetess' and 'passive maiden', but the strain of containment produces the more uncertain 'half-bedizened damsel'.[1] Here, the red of her fan acts as a reminder of vampiric draining,[2] while Ransom attempts a conclusion for his feelings: 'It was simply an intensely personal exhibition, and the person

81

making it happened to be fascinating.' But that 'personal' has
difficulties in maintaining itself as Ransom proceeds to what is to
be his typical response, the evacuation of the performance by
dissociating Verena's utterance from the 'inanities she muttered',
a procedure which culminates in a further arcadian image:

> It made no difference; she didn't mean it, she didn't know what
> she meant, she had been stuffed with this trash by her father,
> and she was neither more nor less willing to say it than to say
> anything else; for the necessity of her nature was not to make
> converts to a ridiculous cause, but to emit those charming notes
> of her voice, to stand in those free young attitudes, to shake her
> braided locks like a naiad rising from the waves, to please every
> one who came near her, and to be happy that she pleased.

Ransom's evacuation is accomplished further by the masculine
reduction of the female to the realm of pleasure, and by again
invoking the insubstantiality of music, 'regarding her as a vocalist
of exquisite faculty, condemned to sing bad music' (p. 54).

At their next encounter, in Monadnoc Place, Ransom's linguistic perception of Verena extends his evacuation of her material
context. She 'irradiated' and 'made everything that surrounded
her of no consequence', dropping upon 'the shabby sofa with an
effect as charming as if she had been a nymph sinking on a
leopard skin'. Her 'fantastic fairness' reminds him of 'unworldly
places' which he conceptualises speculatively and confusingly as
'convent-cloisters or vales of Arcady' (pp. 193–4). His confusion is
occasioned by a change in Verena, her present radiance replacing
her former 'brightness', and whereas his earlier image of Verena
at Miss Birdseye's had struggled to maintain the idea of the
'personal', here his image is forced by 'her air of being a public
character' (p. 195), where 'public' is qualified by ovation: It was
not long before he perceived that this added lustre was simply
success; she was young and tender still, but the sound of a great
applauding audience had been in her ears; it formed an element
in which she felt buoyant and floated' (p. 193). Water is as
dispersive as music in Ransom's scheme of things; 'No wonder
she was a success', he muses, 'if she speechified as a bird sings!'
(p. 196). Nevertheless his confusion still requires an attempt to
objectify the change through his by now familiar images:

> At that other time she had been parti-coloured and bedizened,
> and she had always an air of costume, only now her costume

was richer and more chastened. It was her line, her condition, part of her expression. If at Miss Birdseye's, and afterwards in Charles Street, she might have been a rope-dancer, today she made a 'scene' of the mean little room in Monadnoc Place, such a scene as a prima donna makes of daubed canvas and dusty boards.

(p. 194)

From rope-dancer to prima donna is a large enough step, but it remains insufficient for Ransom's negotiations of this new factor in Verena. The uncertainty of the 'unworldly places' he began with is tested by the resort to theatricality where that resort itself is inadequate; so, pressurised further by the embarrassing need to explain the motive for his visit, he returns to the dispersive possibilities of the 'unworldly' to describe Verena's smile as 'innocent' in the 'Arcadian manner' and the tone of their conversation as 'the tone in which happy, flower-crowned maidens may have talked to sunburnt young men in the golden age' (pp. 194, 195). He chooses to underline the cosiness of his imagery on behalf of their conversation for a good reason. It is precisely Verena's conversational manner which lies at the core of his confusion because it exhibits so clearly her new 'public' air. In other words, the change in Verena involves a naturalising of 'public' style: Ransom notes her 'drop into oratory as a natural thing' and wonders 'did she take him for a full house? She had the same turns and cadences, almost the same gestures, as if she had been on the platform.' He enters a kind of blindness here, domesticating the change in an assumption of 'how the lecture-tone was the thing in the world with which, by education, by association, she was most familiar' which flattens, most unsatisfactorily, the confusion of 'an astounding young phenomenon' (p. 196). His blindness is partly calculated, just as his theatrical and arcadian languages are calculated in their efforts to dispossess Verena of her natural properties, but it is prompted in particular here by the absolute collision and subsequent mixing of personal and public worlds, expressed in the seemingly jocular and throw-away remark that Verena makes at this point: 'They tell me I speak as I talk, so I suppose I talk as I speak' (p. 197). It is Ransom who insists throughout on maintaining the schisms that the novel attempts to negotiate at a critical stage in their history: the schisms of male and female, work and home, personal (private) and public. What affronts him in Monadnoc Place is specifically Verena's elision of the separation between private and public, between speaking and talking. The context itself is revealing here. Not only is it the first time that Ransom is alone with her and the only time in the novel that they are substantially together indoors for conversational purposes (and is thus textually originative), but the name 'Monadnoc' itself, literally a single indivisible entity, and its environment (a 'sightless, soundless, interspaced, embryonic region': p. 203) pose questions of origination, reproducibility and generation that it is Ransom's design to resist. Its promise, paradoxically, of the reproduction of a single self free from social relationships goes directly against all Ransom's strategies for emptying Verena by the discourses he uses for her and by his schismatic perception which separates an assumption of a 'real' Verena from the attributes of her performances.

For Ransom, access to Verena depends absolutely upon exhausting her of her relationships whilst at the same time maintaining her illusory essence: he is both deeply embedded within the habits of spectacle that he despises, and 'reactionary' (as the narrative insists) enough to engage a wilful blindness towards the impossibility of any essential self under consumption. He is a vivid figure for the distortion of relations imposed by consumer culture at large, sceptical of the separations that come of its draining yet himself colluding with those effects in his schismatic handling of Verena. Ransom's most direct display occurs in the scene in Central Park (itself a clear landscape of release from civic turmoil), where overtly he disengages Verena from all history and all experience on behalf of the illusion of her uniqueness: 'You stand apart, you are unique, extraordinary; you constitute a category by yourself. . . . I don't know where you come from nor how you come to be what you are, but you are outside and above all vulgarizing influences' (p. 292).

The narrative itself wonders 'how she came to issue' (p. 68; compare p. 255) to ensure that we read Ransom's disengagement as extending beyond an individualistic quirk to reveal a cultural symptom. Olive, too, shares its disposition, convincing herself in the early stages of the novel that Verena's 'precious faculty' had 'dropped straight from heaven, without filtering through her parents' (p. 73), and proclaiming 'the wonder of such people being Verena's progenitors at all' (p. 100). Here, in an unusually extended passage of Olive's pondering on the 'perpetual enigma', the narrative again seems to participate in proposing the exceptionality of Verena by extracting her from all systems of relationship:

> She had explained it, as we explain all exceptional things, by making the part, as the French say, of the miraculous. She had come to consider the girl as a wonder of wonders, to hold that no human origin, however congruous it might superficially appear, would sufficiently account for her; that her springing up between Selah and his wife was an exquisite whim of the creative force; and that in such a case a few shades more or less of the inexplicable didn't matter. It was notorious that great beauties, great geniuses, great characters, take their own times and places for coming into the world, leaving the gaping spectators to make them 'fit in', and holding from far-off ancestors, or even, perhaps, straight from the divine generosity, much more than from their ugly or stupid progenitors. They were incalculable phenomena, anyway, as Selah would have said. Verena, for Olive, was the very type and model of the 'gifted being'; her qualities had not been bought and paid for; they were like some brilliant birthday-present, left at the door by an unknown messenger, to be delightful forever as an inexhaustible legacy, and amusing forever from the obscurity of its source.
>
> (pp. 100–1)

Just as Ransom's argument vibrated beyond individualistic quirk, so Olive's incorporates more than class prejudice. The extent of her collaboration with the world of publicity may be seen further here in the paradoxical authenticity she claims for Verena's 'qualities'; having divorced them from familial history (revealingly, the most detailed genealogy the novel presents) and social relationship, Olive naturalises them. They are 'superabundantly crude', which presents 'happily' the opportunity for Olive to 'train and polish' their virginity for her own design, but they are also 'as genuine as fruit and flowers, as the glow of the fire or the plash of water' (p. 101).

Such reconstructed and highly self-conscious naturalism (another of publicity's illusions) does not feature in Ransom's design in Central Park; in fact the converse is true of his imagery for Verena in its reliance on artifice which prompts the decisive and transformative figure of the 'preposterous puppet' on behalf of his final separation of Verena from those very qualities naturalised by Olive: 'It isn't *you*, the least in the world, but an inflated little figure (very remarkable in its way too), whom you have invented and set on its feet, pulling strings, behind it, to make it move and speak, while you try to conceal and efface yourself there' (p. 293). It is a potent figure not least because it orchestrates Verena's final choice between Ransom and Olive. It not only terminates the conversation in Central Park but forces Ransom's most explicit separation of 'public' and 'private' in terms of gender that we have seen so far. To Verena's query about the 'inferior' function for women, Ransom picks up his recent schematisation of 'public', 'home' and 'private life' (p. 291) and responds with the schismatic core of his entire philosophy: 'For public, civic uses, absolutely – perfectly weak and second rate. . . . But privately, personally, it's another affair. In the realm of family life and the domestic affections' (p. 294). We should not allow the broadness of this familiar 'reactionary' stand to conceal the difficulties of its central terms. The alliance of 'civic' and 'public' (a rare occurrence in the novel) registers the strained meaningfulness of the latter under publicity, while the qualification of 'privately' by 'personally' exposes the extent to which publicity renders both terms virtually interchangeable. Ransom's simultaneous divisions and mergings mark a further, crucial emptying: the suppression of any proper responsibility between the worlds he opposes to each other in their absolutist separation.

His arcadian language for Verena itself thus supports the spectacle of Verena it is designed to resist. In effect one spectacle, one version of publicity, simply replaces another. The same is true of Olive who is also willing (although to a lesser extent) to see Verena in arcadian terms. She pictures her voice as 'magical', as that of 'the pure young sibyl' (p. 137), and Verena's early presence at Olive's meetings after her move to Charles Street is 'not active'; it anticipates delicately Ransom's 'puppet', engineered by Olive to be 'like some gently animated image placed there for good omen' (p. 152). Olive's principal language for Verena is religious rather than arcadian, but it has a similar effect in draining Verena of relationships. It is significant that its first occurrence, Olive's stress that their shared project 'demands of us a kind of priesthood' (p. 119), is in the context of celibacy ('Priests

– when they were real priests – never married'), a context which belongs to the wider evacuations in Olive's general philosophy of sacrifice and renunciation, summarised in her quotation from Goethe's *Faust*: 'Thou shalt renounce, refrain, abstain!' (pp. 75–6). Olive's compliance with Verena's image of herself as Joan of Arc (pp. 74, 106, 126, 127) is thoroughly in keeping with her own hopes for martyrdom (pp. 13, 127), hopes which themselves are seen as an economic resource: 'the prospect of suffering was always, spiritually speaking, so much cash in her pocket' (p. 97). Again the narrative seems to collaborate in this language of 'holy office', 'unction', 'ecstacy', the 'sacred', the 'altar of a great cause', and the 'temple in which votaries of their creed could worship' (pp. 135, 137, 138, 146, 147, 155) and again, as we see with the pattern of Ransom's language its most potent occasion includes the difficulties of 'public' and 'private'. The moment is that intense scene in the New York hotel where, while trying to persuade Olive that 'I *have* renounced', Verena talks as she speaks in much the same manner as that which disturbed Ransom in Monadnoc Place: 'The habit of public speaking, the training, the practice, in which she had been immersed, enabled Verena to unroll a coil of propositions dedicated even to a private interest with the most touching, most cumulative effect' (p. 261). Olive is 'completely aware' of the tactic, but she avoids Ransom's discomfort at Verena's elisions and projects herself specifically into the role of audience, stilling herself into 'the same rapt attention she was in the habit of sending up from the benches of an auditorium'. At one of the most intimate points of the novel which demands above all the stability of 'personal' expression and response and the equality of dialogue, publicity forces Verena into spectacle and Olive into spectator. The effect is to produce again a damaged authenticity. Olive feels that Verena 'was stirred to her depths', that she 'was exquisitely passionate and sincere', and she expresses her feeling of authenticity through a climactic image which is simultaneously religious and arcadian: 'she was a quivering, spotless, consecrated maiden'.

The final image of Arcady in the novel renders the metaphor as almost literal. It is the natural landscape of Marmion where Ransom and Verena enjoy their final conversations:

Here all the homely languor of the region, the mild, fragrant Cape-quality, the sweetness of white sands, quiet waters, low promontories where there were paths among the barberries and tidal pools gleamed in the sunset – here all the spirit of a ripe summer-afternoon seemed to hang in the air. There were wood-walks too; they sometimes followed bosky uplands, where accident had grouped the trees with odd effects of 'style', and where in grassy intervals and fragrant nooks of rest they came out upon sudden patches of Arcady.

(p. 331)

This literalisation, especially in its quiet emphasis on pastoral rather than mythical qualities, potentially confirms the promise of liberation from publicity and its urban venue that is implicit within Ransom's ambition for his arcadian language. Its release seems confirmed also by our awareness that this is the period of most acute worry for Olive, and hence of her most acute pressure. But we have seen already how that language effectively serves to render Verena as much a spectacle as the entrepreneurship of Olive, Matthias Pardon and Selah Tarrant. We recognise the domestic limitations of Marmion: again, Ransom and Verena are forced out of doors, out of social context, and the periodicity of their excursions is severely demarcated to match its topographical constraints.

We realise too that Marmion's present tranquillity is in fact the peace which follows the activity of previous industry: the place was 'a good deal shrunken since the decline in the shipbuilding interest'. There were 'shipyards still', but their presence is marked only by their past where 'you could almost pick up the old shavings, the old nails and rivets'. They are 'grass-green now' and 'the water lapped them without anything to interfere'. Ransom is obliged to agree with the straightforward accuracy of Dr Prance who 'didn't say the place was picturesque, or quaint, or weird; but he could see that was what she meant when she said it was mouldering away'. Even under the 'mantle of night', Ransom has 'the impression that it had had a larger life, seen better days' (p. 304). His putative transposition of aesthetic terms for the pragmatic 'mouldering away' prompts our awareness of his willingness to conceal the memory of industrial wastage.

We have been shown, early on, that 'The artistic sense' in Ransom had 'not been highly cultivated', and he has resorted already to the bland inappropriateness of terms such as 'picturesque' and 'romantic' for the view of the Back Bay from Charles

Street (p. 15). Nevertheless, although he 'had seen very few pictures, there were none in Mississippi', his aestheticism is aware of its definite capacity for suppression. The view from the back garden of Olive's house in Marmion thus suggests to him 'a land of dreams, a country in a picture' that is congruent with his general hopes for art's transformativeness: 'he had a vision at times of something that would be more refined than the real world, and the situation in which he now found himself pleased him almost as much as if it had been a striking work of art' (p. 310). Marmion residually declares the first phase of American industrial activity, that which prepared the way for the present phase of consumption. It is entirely appropriate that it should be also the site for another death, that of Miss Birdseye whose own 'heroic' reformism was shaped by the impositions of that first phase. Marmion as it is experienced through Ransom's art functions as a literal reminder of what the spectacle of consumption suppresses; its wastage exposes the productivity of its own generation.

II

The literalisation of Ransom's arcadian metaphor is troubling. Its immediate occasion is to reveal the collaboration of the metaphor with the tactics of the consumptive vision, its avowed object for resistance. But something else is suggested here which has to do with the larger design of a novel with ambitions for the 'typical'. Those ambitions, particularly for the James influenced by Balzac, inevitably include an attention to place, to setting; and James is careful to present all the novel's settings through the engaged perspectives of his characters. There is one exception to this pattern, and it is a very odd exception: the New York of Second Avenue where Ransom's rooming-house is located. The oddity is twofold. First of all the location marks the only place in the novel outside the scenes at Marmion where the idea of the pastoral applied to landscape is invoked, and it is an invocation that is utterly extraneous to its context: amongst the disparate items of the scene, we find that:

a smart, bright waggon, with the horse detached from its shafts, drawn up on the edge of the abominable road (it contained holes and ruts a foot deep, and immemorial accumulations of stagnant mud), imparted an idle, rural, pastoral air to a scene otherwise perhaps expressive of a rank civilization.

(p. 160)

Such is the separation here between 'pastoral', the topography it designates, and its opposition to a 'rank civilization' that we might begin to suspect an element of playfulness on James's part. This is confirmed when we note the second aspect of the scene's oddity as James moves on to describe briefly the 'Dutch grocery' where Ransom lives, and he comments: 'I mention it not on account of any particular influence it may have had on the life or thoughts of Basil Ransom, but for old acquaintance sake and that of local colour.' His disconnection between character and setting is absolute, and he continues: 'besides which, a figure is nothing without a setting, and our young man came and went every day, with rather an indifferent, unperceiving step, it is true, among the objects I have briefly designated' (pp. 160–1). James then explicitly refuses the opportunity of his Balzacian occasion: 'If the opportunity were not denied me here, I should like to give some account of Basil Ransom's interior. . . . But we need, in strictness, concern ourselves with it no further than to gather the implication that the young Mississippian . . . had not made his profession very lucrative' (p. 161).

Whatever the mysterious demands of this 'strictness' may be, the passage is, in David Howard's excellent description, simply irrelevant; the setting 'seems to exist not for Ransom but for no purpose at all . . . it is almost wilfully irrelevant and indifferent. Setting and figure and author are liberated.'[3] Howard does not pursue this liberation; but clearly James's joke about one of the most crucial of novelistic procedures, particularly given his later literalisation of Ransom's pastoral and arcadian metaphors in Marmion, requires some attention. James had recognised the importance of this procedure in his essay of 1875 on Balzac, where, in terms that are directly relevant to the typicality of *The Bostonians*, Balzac's 'overmastering sense of the present world' was seen as a 'superb foundation for the work of a realistic romancer'. Primarily, this 'sense' provided the unmatched 'solidity' of Balzac's *mise en scène*:

The place in which an event occurred was in his view of equal moment with the event itself; it was part of the action; it was not a thing to take or to leave, or to be vaguely and gracefully indicated; it imposed itself; it had a part to play, it needed to be made as definite as anything else.

James goes so far as to say that 'we often prefer his places to his people' as he writes of Balzac's habit of lodging his characters in houses which are reproduced 'even to their local odours'.[4] *The Bostonians'* disposal of 'local colour' extends James's joke about his Balzacian proclivities by picking up on this final phrase: more is going on in this particular instance than the nostalgia of 'old acquaintance sake' for New York that we would find, for example, in *Washington Square*. What James's playfulness registers, in short, is the transience of the French novelist's relation between figure and setting, the very relation which his joke disrupts. Plainly the opportunity to give an account of Ransom's interior is not denied him save by his own volition, the volition which has already pointed the 'indifferent' feature of Ransom's relation to his surroundings and the problematical 'pastoral air' imparted by the waggon. This is not to ignore the novel's general preoccupation with domestic interiors as feminised space. No male has an interior (and neither has the problematical gender of Dr Prance), but James's interest here lies clearly in the furnishing of composition. Setting or place is destabilised as much as figure in the form of an assumed intrinsic self is shown to be dispersed by the machinations of publicity.

It matters that James chooses to place his concern about the relation of figure to setting in New York rather than in Boston. The cosmopolitan liveliness and glamour of the former, the world of 'infinite possibilities', renders it as the most appropriate location for consumer energy: as we have seen, it is where Verena emerges as a much more active figure in response to its 'vastness and variety', attending to her appearance, and alert for the first time to the benefits in talking as she speaks. James's structuring of his joke about setting is thus instructive for the location of the novel itself. If the novel is about publicity, then why does James choose to set it in Boston rather than in the New York that would yield more visibly to his design? The answer is that it is a simple lesson in presentation. It is precisely because New York is so appropriate for his design that he refuses it (despite the fact that he places there the major scene for the transformation of the relationship between Ransom and Verena); New York provides too blatantly (and hence, for James, too reductively) the location of publicity when what James needs is to emphasise the full effects of consumption in an arena which might otherwise (through its 'earnestness', its provinciality) be assumed to be somehow more innocent of those effects.

James's joke is concerned with the transience and instability of people and places under consumption; but it is also informative about James's historicism at the level of novelistic practice as well as at the level of novelistic detail. Facts, we know, are interesting to James only as they are experienced within a given consciousness, and this holds true also for the shifts of historical process: his interest is in the ways in which characters behave within the changing conditions of that process. To render consumerism rather than the reformism of the women's movement as the ostensible subject of the novel would be to sanitise consumerism's effective force, to imply it mechanically as an objective item whose mechanicalism would offer it as available only for the most obvious of criticisms whilst simultaneously concealing its real capacity for restructuring consciousness and behaviour, its unspoken machinations for entering perception unacknowledged. It is not difficult to be reductively hostile towards the criteria of publicity that are deliberately flattened out in Matthias Pardon and Selah Tarrant; but the more complex and less apparent operations of those same criteria in Olive and Ransom, because they are not so flatly offered, present the more germane difficulties of appreciating the experiencing of those criteria, and opening them to a genuine critique. With these considerations in mind, we may return to the settings that the novel provides for publicity itself.

These settings involve not only the temporariness of newspapers (designed to present the novelty of news, dramatising it as the event of a given day to be replaced by some fresh item the next day), but the site of the hotel, counterpointed to the home and exhibiting in clear form the transience of social action and intercourse. The hotel is an integral part of the worlds of both Selah Tarrant and Matthias Pardon. Tarrant is an inveterate lurker in not only 'the offices of the newspapers' but 'the vestibules of the hotels', and the latter present a more alarming distortion of human behaviour:

the big marble-paved chambers of informal reunion which offer to the streets, through high glass plates, the sight of the

American citizen suspended by his heels. Here, amid the piled-up luggage, the convenient spittoons, the elbowing loungers, the disconsolate 'guests', the truculent Irish porters, the rows of shaggy-backed men in strange hats, writing letters at a table inlaid with advertisements, Selah Tarrant made innumerable contemplative stations. He could not have told you, at any particular moment, what he was doing; he only had a general sense that such places were national nerve-centres, and that the more one looked in, the more one was 'on the spot'.

(p. 91)

The grating of 'national nerve-centres' against being 'on the spot' underlines neatly publicity's disguise of individual accident within common consensus, a grating enhanced by the disparate items for observation displayed in the passage and the uncomfortable image of 'the American citizen suspended by his heels'.

This distortive world is matched by that of Pardon for whom Tarrant's 'nerve-centres' become an even more grotesque twisting of responsibility:

he had begun his career, at the age of fourteen, by going the rounds of the hotels, to cull flowers from the big, greasy registers which lie on the marble counters; and he might flatter himself that he had contributed in his measure, and on behalf of a vigilant public opinion, the pride of a democratic State, to the great end of preventing the American citizen from attempting clandestine journeys.

(p. 108)

James's repetition of the 'American citizen' here underlines the specific nature of this twisting; it proposes the divorce of 'civic' from 'public' which is one of publicity's major dismantlings of the novel's lexicon. Entirely appropriate, then, is the account of Ransom's nocturnal wandering immediately prior to the glaring display of Verena at the Boston Music Hall; an account which lists neutrally all the major arenas of publicity and then culminates in an extensive description of the hotel itself. Significantly, the description of the hotel here is utterly free from the distortions of the place we see in the hands of Tarrant and Pardon:

The shop-fronts glowed through frosty panes, the passers bustled on the pavement, the bells of the street-cars jangled in the cold air, the newsboys hawked the evening-papers, the vestibules of the theatres, illuminated and flanked with coloured posters and the photographs of actresses, exhibited seductively their swinging doors of red leather or baize, spotted with little brass nails. Behind great plates of glass the interior of the hotels became visible, with marble-paved lobbies, white with electric lamps, and columns, and Westerners on divans stretching their legs, while behind a counter, set apart and covered with an array of periodicals and novels in paper covers, little boys, with the faces of old men, showing plans of the playhouses and offering librettos, sold orchestra-chairs at a premium.

(p. 370)

The non-committal presentation, intermingled with the neutrality of the passers-by and the street-cars, marks the extent of an unquestioning acceptability: without the earlier distortions of Tarrant and Pardon, we would be unaware entirely of the hotel's resonance.

It is not until *The American Scene* that James overtly castigates the world of publicity at length and in detail, emphasising its corruption of the equation between public and private through the interchangeability of market and home, and finding in the hotel the most potent image for publicity's interference.[5] Twenty years earlier, at the time of *The Bostonians'* composition, the hotel is not so visible as the site for publicity. Just as, in a different version of the novel, its setting would have been New York rather than Boston, so the site for publicity would have been not the hotel but the department store. By the 1880s, as Trachtenberg has noted, of all city spectacles 'none surpassed the giant department store, the emporium of consumption', which stood as 'a prime urban artifact of the age'. Here was not only a 'new world of goods' but 'the world itself newly imagined as consisting of goods and their consumption', where goods were presented 'as if they represented something other than themselves, some touch of class, of status, of prestige' and thereby 'staging grounds for the making and confirming of new relations between goods and people'.[6] In short, the department store becomes pre-eminently the arena where the fissures of publicity may be imaged most vigorously; for Rachel Bowlby, the shop-window smashes the illusion that there is a meaningful distinction 'between illusion

and reality, fact and fantasy, fake and genuine images of the self'
as part of the general instability of consumer culture: 'The
boundaries of subject and object, active and passive, owner and
owned, unique and general, break down in this endless reflexive
interplay of consumer and consumed.'[7] To Bowlby's list, we
might add the fissure of the boundary between public and private
and the general disturbances of male and female space in a novel
which takes 'the situation of women' as 'the most salient and
peculiar point in our social life'.[8]

James resists this potent resource, however; as New York is to
Boston in the unwritten version of the novel, so the department
store is to the hotel. While the store may mark a more immediate
intervention in the home, that intervention is simply too firm for
the purposes of a narrative which reveals its suspicions about the
very stability of setting itself. Hotels, in one sense, are located in
that interstitial area between home and the store and thus begin
to convey the more intimate uncertainties of publicity; indeed,
after the opening sequence of events which do occur in homes
(those of Olive, Miss Birdseye and the Tarrants), the home
virtually disappears in favour of hotels, rented rooms, the theatrical palace of Mrs Burrage and the mysterious hiding-place of
Olive and Verena (which we never even see) prior to the Music
Hall lecture. By deploying the hotel rather than the store as the
site for publicity, James effects a displacement which imparts a
singular accuracy to the novel's design: he avoids the mechanicalism of rendering the self as merely prey to the new glamour and
exhibits a concern with the *experience* of publicity's uncertainties,
experience from which his own practice is not exempt.

III

James establishes a common world between Matthias Pardon and
Selah Tarrant, but that world incorporates important differences.
Pardon has an undeniable air of the temporary about him: he is
vulgar, aggressive, impertinent and insensitive, but he is
ultimately rather brittle. His insistence on spectacular newness
not only confirms the centrality of that concept for consumer
culture, it also underlines his own fashionableness; he has all the
clumsiness of youth (the insistent detail of his white hair project-
ing an internal urge to keep up with things) which is always

prepared to be seduced by some fresh novelty. His energy provides the glamorous aspect of the new industry to which Verena in particular is subject (he is, in one sense, an appropriate suitor for her), the aspect that can be disarmed as easily as new novelties replace old novelties. Tarrant, by comparison, is a much more insidious character, 'carnivorous' and bat-like (p. 41), and not only because, in the marketplace of the novel, he is the only one actually to sell anything in his purveyance of Verena to Olive (his capacity for her marketability is limited, reminiscent of the older system of production, but he can recognise the larger potential of Olive's entrepreneurship). His predilection is not for the 'new' but for the other aspect of publicity, 'fame' and 'renown' (pp. 90, 91); and as opposed to Pardon's temporariness, his interest is in that which is much more permanent: for Tarrant, hotels are 'national nerve-centres', whereas for Pardon they are the site for 'clandestine journeys'.

We might graph these differences by saying that while Pardon's general attitude is impersonal, lacking in any volition rather than the fashionable, Tarrant's is personal: it is *his* name and that of Verena he wants to see advertised and, in the early stages, it is *his* hand which instigates her 'inspiration'. James's separation here belongs to the novel's pervasive questioning of ways in which ideas about the self are being reconstructed by the strategies of publicity. The hyperbolical language James uses to provide our first picture of Tarrant's 'vision' of publicity is in keeping with his subject's own inflated rhetoric:

> He was incapable of giving an off-hand answer or opinion on the simplest occasion, and his tone of high deliberation increased in proportion as the subject was trivial or domestic. If his wife asked him at dinner if the potatoes were good, he replied that they were strikingly fine (he used to speak of the newspaper as 'fine' – he applied this term to objects the most dissimilar), and embarked on a parallel worthy of Plutarch, in which he compared them with other specimens of the same vegetable.
>
> (pp. 88–9).

This glamorising vocabulary not only matches that of the spectacles produced by publicity; it marks a further element in Tarrant's 'sacrifice' of the home as it transforms the deliberately commonplace items of domestic intercourse, and its failure of discrimination registers very clearly the extent to which the terminology of publicity depends upon the increasing gap between word and object whereby goods are promoted beyond their immediate use.

Broadly speaking, exaggeration of language predicates an exaggeration, an inflation of self; and the novel has in mind here a model that is specifically announced in the opening portrayal of Tarrant. His 'habitually sacerdotal expression' is itself formed in large part by the success of Verena's performance at Miss Birdseye's, and his priesthood is elaborated by the narrative to include two crucial characterising images:

> He looked like the priest of a religion that was passing through the stage of miracles; he carried his responsibility in the general elongation of his person, of his gestures (his hands were now always in the air, as if he were being photographed in postures), of his words and sentences, as well as in his smile, as noiseless as a patent hinge, and in the folds of his eternal waterproof.
>
> (p. 88)

It is a striking testimony (to be joined with the detail of Verena's anaemia) to publicity's intimate disarrangements at the level of physiognomy; but it involves also, through the characterising images of the smile and the waterproof which invariably occur in tandem at Tarrant's every appearance, a model of an inflated self that is to be associated with Whitman.

Of the two images, Tarrant's smile is always the most vivid, verging upon the fantastic,[9] but here it approaches – unusually for James – almost Dickensian proportions. When James reviewed *Our Mutual Friend* in 1865, he noted not only that 'the fantastic has been his great resource', but that Dickens's 'extravagances' usually had a 'comparative consistency' in that 'they were exaggerated statements of types that really existed'. When such consistency failed, it was apt to produce 'nothing but figure' which 'added nothing to our understanding of human character'.[10] By comparison with the other descriptions we are given of Tarrant's smile, this is exactly what happens here: its portrayal as being 'as noiseless as a patent hinge', grotesquely engineered, effectively detaches it from character, even character which disports itself habitually as a performance. Not only is the smile detachable, but it contrasts violently with James's views on another smile in 1883, that of Alphonse Daudet. Tarrant has an unctuous wish to be agreeable, an impoverished version of Daudet's 'wish to please' which has an entirely opposite effect, being 'the quality by which Daudet persuades his readers most; it is this that elicits from them that friendliness, that confession that they are charmed'. It is Daudet's 'charm' that lies at the centre of James's admiration, a charm that James expresses in the figure of the smile: 'in nothing is he more modern than in this expressive and sympathetic smile – the smile of the artist, the sceptic, the man of the world – with which he shows us the miseries and cruelties of life'.[11]

These are the terms in which Tarrant's smile demands particular attention; and we can begin by noting that its determining figuration, 'as noiseless as a patent hinge', puns heavily on the title of Whitman's 'A Noiseless Patient Spider', idiomorphically a poem of the Whitmanian 'soul' exaggerating the spider's spinning out its affiliations through 'measureless oceans of space'.[12] Whitman's spider invokes the 'bat' which is suggested by Tarrant's smile earlier, again as an image of extent (p. 41; compare p. 381), and on another occasion of the smile – the negotiation of the sale of Verena – Tarrant employs a Whitmanian 'metaphor' in his advice: 'Don't shut down the cover, Miss Chancellor; just let her overflow'; this 'metaphor' is 'illuminated' by the 'strange and silent lateral movement of his jaws' (p. 144). The 'waterproof' which accompanies the smile is no ordinary item of apparel; it is 'eternal' (p. 88) and 'immemorial' (p. 354), not only continuing the image of Tarrant as 'priest'[13] but acting as an emblem of Tarrant's wilful and obstinate permanence through change.[14] And, in conjunction with its echo of the '*waterproofs plein de boue*' (mud-covered waterproofs) worn by the followers of Madame Autheman in *L'Evangeliste*,[15] it is, again, a Whitmanian garb, part of the list of accoutrements he provides for his projected role as guide to the entire range of humanity in 'Song of Myself', where 'My signs are a rain-proof coat, good shoes, and a staff cut from the woods.'[16] The nature of such a guide is to be limitless ('I was never measured, and never will be measured'), elaborating the extent of the spider to an assumption of absolute authority.

A range, an extent, of human sympathy is admirable, but its exaggeration into the determinant power of an inflated self is profoundly worrying in terms that are both moral and aesthetic (Whitman's conjunction of the soul and the spider, even within the correspondences of his transcendental romanticism, verges on the banal) as Ezra Pound, the most Jamesian of Whitman's successors, noted.[17] In general terms, Whitman offers himself as suitable for the concerns of *The Bostonians* – through his role as a newspaperman, for example, or through his commitment to the 'Union' that is both political (James, in his review of *Drum-Taps* in 1865, quotes as evidence for Whitman's 'pretensions' the entirety of 'From Paumanock Starting I Fly Like a Bird', with its ambition to 'sing first' the 'idea of all, of the Western world one and inseparable'[18]) and metaphysical in its pervasive relation of the 'I' and the 'En-Masse' (Whitman's 'word of the modern' in 'Song of Myself'[19]), or even through Whitman's well-known interests in the pseudo-sciences of phrenology and mesmerism[20] but we are not concerned so much with Whitman as a specific source; rather, let us suggest that, for James, he can be seen as a moment of focus whereby the dangers of the inflated self can be considered. In one sense, those dangers were endemic to the Swedenborgian atmosphere of the Jamesian household where egotism was associated with capitalistic enterprise;[21] clearly, they take on additional colouring in an age of publicity where everything, from goods to language and imaginings about one's own identity, is held in thrall to the inflation of spectacle.

James's thoughts on Whitman, unsurprisingly, are not extensive. Substantially, they appear in print in two places separated by a period of over thirty years: the review of *Drum-Taps* in 1865 and, more briefly and less systematically, as part of James's 'American Letters' series for *Literature* in 1898. By the time of the latter, James was able to respond warmly to 'The good Walt', to the 'natural' expression of 'natural' feeling in the 'Calamus' sequence. Here, James feels confident in wielding the problematical terms of *The Bostonians*, admiring the humility of Whitman's 'gift of sympathy', his 'extraordinarily delicate personal devotion, exercised wholly at his own cost and risk', which produced pages containing 'not a single bid for publicity'.[22] But the situation is reversed in James's earlier commentary where he confronts fully the antithesis of this humility, the Whitman who is 'very fond of blowing his own trumpet'.[23] 'For a lover', accuses James, 'you talk entirely too much about yourself', outlining a self-preoccupation which anticipates the imagery of religion he is later to use for Tarrant ('you seem to identify yourself with the third person of the Trinity') and which incorporates a bruising of James's ideas of art itself:

art requires, above all things, a suppression of one's self, a subordination of one's self to an idea. This will never do for you, whose plan is to adapt the scheme of the universe to your own limitations. You cannot entertain and exhibit ideas; but, as we have seen, you are prepared to incarnate them.

Furthermore, this self-preoccupation, James continues, results in a disabling separating out of words and ideas which in itself marks a betrayal of the public: 'It is for this reason, doubtless, that when once you have planted yourself squarely before the public, and in view of the great service you have done to the ideal, have become, as you say, "accepted everywhere," you can afford to deal exclusively in words.'

The fact of this betrayal is rendered more urgent by the occasion of Whitman's volume: the war itself which is to hover so powerfully within *The Bostonians*. For James, the public 'has sustained a monstrous war, and practised human nature's best in so many ways for the last five years', and it is 'not to put up with spurious poetry afterwards'. Whitman's separation of words from ideas renders as 'sublimity' what otherwise would be 'bald nonsense and dreary platitudes', and denies proper public responsibility at the level of poetic practice: 'To become adopted as a national poet, it is not enough to discard everything in particular and to accept everything in general, to amass crudity upon crudity, to discharge the undigested contents of your blotting book into the lap of the public.' We have here not only a failure of public 'refinement', but a distortion of 'democratic' fact in a proclaimed 'voice of a people' (Olive Chancellor's quasi-Whitmanian 'romance of the people' – pp. 31, 96 – similarly generalises enormously at the expense of particulars) where the authoritarian inflation of the self's incarnations is seen ultimately to deny meaningful public compact:

> You must respect the public which you address; for it has taste, if you have not. It delights in the grand, the heroic, and the masculine; but it delights to see these conceptions cast into worthy form. It is indifferent to brute sublimity. It will never do for you to thrust your hands into your pockets and cry out that, as the research of form is an intolerable bore, the shortest and most economical way for the public to embrace its idols – for the nation to realize its genius – is in your own person.

That 'person' as it becomes 'personal' is what marks finally the Whitmanian distortion: 'It is not enough to be rude, lugubrious, and grim. You must also be serious. You must forget yourself in your ideas. Your personal qualities – the vigor of your temperament, the manly independence of your nature, the tenderness of your heart – these facts are impertinent.'[24]

James's review of *Drum-Taps* is prior to the onset of consumerism which so preoccupies *The Bostonians*, and its implications for literary history (its assumptions about art, democracy, experience, and nationalism) are spread too widely to be included here. Nevertheless, its concerns with the literature of a war which shadows the novel so heavily, its unusual deployment of gender-based evaluative terms and its worries over the inflated self sketch out issues which are profoundly embedded in the novel. We may note, parenthetically, the rare directness of the review, its address to Whitman in the first person; a directness that indicates the strength of James's feelings on these issues which underline a distinction between the authoritarian and the democratic self, the hyperbolical 'personal' self and the self persuaded of genuine 'public' allegiances. The distinction is one to which James returns in his thoughts about Emerson and Carlyle at the very moment when he begins the composition of *The Bostonians*.

Both figures are invoked with characteristic brevity in the novel itself; but the slightness of their explicit textual tenure does not disguise their vibrancy for the novel's concern with the personal and public operations of the self. Miss Birdseye is a reminder to Olive Chancellor of the earlier 'heroic age of New England life', the age of Emerson which was 'the age of plain living and high thinking, of pure ideals and earnest effort, of moral passion and noble experiment' (p. 157). The narrative's ambivalence towards Miss Birdseye, despite its affectionate slant, inhibits us from the illusory comfort of reading this reminder of the Emersonian 'age' as nostalgic. James regrets here, certainly, that with the death of Miss Birdseye the age 'would effectually be closed' (a regret which is given added poignancy by Emerson's death in 1883), and in 1887, shortly after the publication of *The Bostonians*, in reviewing James Elliot Cabot's *A Memoir of Ralph Waldo Emerson*, he acknowledged that age as having 'the brightness of a society at once very simple and very responsible'.[25] But we do not have here the kind of critical act whereby one period of history (the past) is privileged over another (the present). James renders his hesitations about the present age abundantly clear, but his distaste for contemporary reformism and publicity is not expressed through any nostalgia for a cleaner, clearer past. Such an act would itself be as 'reactionary' as any principle held by Basil Ransom, a figure who habitually invokes the past to the detriment of the present. In fact James plays a joke here to dissuade the reader from such reductive historicism. The joke occurs in James's choice of surname for Ransom. His review of Cabot's *Memoir* approves of the portrayal of Emerson as 'by no means one of the professional abolitionists or philanthropists – never an enrolled "humanitarian" '. To sustain his approval, James quotes a passage from Emerson's journal as a true image of the reformist impulse which, revealingly on behalf of a novel where words and deeds have an uneasy alliance and where talkativeness is condemned unequivocally, finds its potency in a form of quietude:

> We talk frigidly of Reform until the walls mock us. It is that of which a man should never speak, but if he have cherished it in his bosom, he should steal to it in the darkness, as an Indian to his bride. . . . Does he not do more to abolish slavery who works all day steadily in his own garden, than he who goes to the abolition meeting and makes a speech? He who does his own work frees a slave.[26]

Immediately he goes on to say that 'even while I transcribe these words', he recalls his own attendance at the 'great meeting in the Boston Music Hall' (the site for the final action of the novel) in 1863 to celebrate Lincoln's Emancipation proclamation. It is a recollection not so much of the 'momentousness of the occasion' itself, but of the 'tall, spare figure of Emerson' reading his 'Boston Hymn', and James continues:

> I well remember the immense effect with which his beautiful voice pronounced the lines –
> 'Pay ransom to the owner
> And fill the bag to the brim.
> Who is the owner? The slave is owner,
> And ever was. Pay *him*!'[27]

Testimony to the memorable strength of these lines for James is provided by the fact that they are not actually quoted by Cabot:

he records only the delivery of the poem.[28] In acknowledging them as containing the source for Ransom's surname we recognise the thrust of James's joke against too unquestioning an assumption of his own idealism. No one could be further from Emerson than Ransom, but he does share a fondness for Carlyle as well as a distrust of reform's expression through mere talk; he may be reactionary in the human and social sense, but he is also clear-headed in his opposition to the 'talkative'. Simultaneously, then, James's joke maintains a truth to this aspect of Ransom's temperament whilst underlining Ransom's distance from a more honourable context. And for both James and Emerson, the act of talking about the age, despite their own willingness to do exactly that, is itself a sign of the age's talkativeness in its tendency towards generalisation (a tendency which James stresses in his critique of the Whitmanian inflated self).

In 1883, James reviewed an edition of the correspondence between Emerson and Carlyle; and it is in the figure of the latter that Ransom himself authorises his distaste for an age he describes as 'talkative, querulous, hysterical, maudlin, full of false ideas, of unhealthy germs, of extravagant, dissipated habits'. He shares Carlyle's suspicions of 'the encroachments of modern democracy' (p. 164), is 'sick of all the modern cant about freedom', and finds 'the spread of education a gigantic farce – people stuffing their heads with a lot of empty catchwords that prevented them from doing their work quietly and honestly' because the 'right' to education depends upon 'intelligence' which is 'a very rare luxury, the attribute of one person in a hundred' (p. 284). Ransom's Carlylean views inform the most strident expression of his schismatic perception in Central Park with Verena:

> The whole generation is womanized; the masculine tone is passing out of the world; it's a feminine, a nervous, hysterical, chattering, canting age, an age of hollow phrases and false delicacy and exaggerated solicitudes and coddled sensibilities, which, if we don't soon look out, will usher in the reign of mediocrity, of the feeblest and flattest and the most pretentious that has ever been.
>
> (p. 290)

His masculine and aristocratic fear of the new and of feminised space within the rhetoric of 'an age of unspeakable shams, as

Carlyle says' then resorts to his more habitual separations of 'public', 'home' and 'private life' (p. 291) as an antidote to 'this modern pestilence' (p. 292) of female reforms.

James's review of Carlyle's correspondence with Emerson provides ample testimony to the source of Ransom's rhetoric,[29] but that is not quite the point. The narrative itself stresses Ransom's notions as 'narrow' and out of tune with the world of the contemporary periodicals (p. 290). We are told of Verena at this point that 'she didn't suppose you could hear any one say such a thing as that in the nineteenth century, even the least advanced' (p. 284). In other words, it is the extreme nature of Ransom's Carlyle that is insisted upon as one of those further distortions of the age of publicity which force judgement into such violent schisms. Olive, too, for example, condemns contemporaneity in quasi-Carlylean terms, but in a much less vitriolic manner, seeing it as 'relaxed and demoralized' (p. 109) and recognising its 'feebler passions' (p. 267). And the reliable Dr Prance 'thought they all talked too much' (p. 37) while she herself 'didn't need any caution in regard to making vain statements' (p. 305). Carlyle is, of course, easily available for the kind of exaggerated use that Ransom makes of him, as James was well aware;[30] but Ransom's inflation is only part of Carlyle's resonance for *The Bostonians* since, as James's review makes clear, he provides an important occasion for James's meditations on the difficulties of private and public spheres within the reformist impulse itself, albeit the impulse of an earlier period where reformism had not the contemporary interchangeability with publicity which organises James's novel.[31] That period may be 'historical', belonging to 'a past that is already remote',[32] but James's reconsideration of it on the very eve of the novel usefully informs his present preoccupations.

James's admiration for the Emerson who was 'by no means one of the professional abolitionists or philanthropists' is echoed in the review's account of Carlyle's disdain for 'the American "reforming" class at large'. The quotation he uses to illustrate this disdain is appropriate for Emerson in principle as it is appropriate for Ransom in the articulation of that principle:

These people and their affairs seem all 'melting' rapidly enough into thaw-slush, or one knows not what. Considerable madness is visible in them . . . I am terribly sick of all that; – and wish it would stay at home at Fruitland, or where there is a good pasture for it . . . [a] bottomless hubbub, which is not at all cheering.

There is of course an immense difference between reforming the situation of women or slaves and reforming the vegetable diet for healthy living. It is easy enough to satirise one who is 'all bent on saving the world by a return to acorns and the golden age', but the ease of the jibe does not conceal the issue of egotism that for Carlyle, Emerson and James is so often associated with the reforming temperament. Carlyle lays this charge against Margaret Fuller. She is amongst those who have shared the danger of which he accuses Emerson, the danger of 'soaring away', of having attempted 'the flight of the unwinged' (an image which anticipates closely Verena's sense – see pp. 69, 276 – of being 'taken up' by both Olive and Ransom) where her egotism is seen in terms that are reminiscent of James's distrust of Whitmanian incarnations: 'Such a predetermination to *eat* this big Universe as her oyster or her egg, and to be absolute empress of all height and glory in it that her heart could conceive, I have not before seen in any human soul. Her "mountain *me*" indeed.'[33] Although James is careful here to stress how Carlyle is 'affectionate' as well as 'discriminating' towards his subject, it is inevitable that it is the image of the self's size which remains vivid in the memory.

Despite the utter disparity of their views on most issues, James sees Emerson and Carlyle as united by one overwhelming attitude: 'Both of them had the desire, the passion, for something better, – the reforming spirit, and interest in the destiny of mankind.' His sense of this 'reforming spirit' produces a central disquisition on *The Bostonians'* main evaluative vocabulary: 'Their Correspondence is to an extraordinary degree the record, on either side, of a career with which nothing base, nothing interested, no worldly avidity, no vulgar vanity or personal error, was ever mingled – a career of public distinction and private honor.'[34] James effects a vital dissociation here whereby the 'private' is meaningfully opposed to the 'public' exactly by means of its disengagement from the 'personal'. It is a dissociation that James maintains in his review of Cabot's *Memoir*, in which he praises Emerson's 'serenity' as 'that absence of personal passion' where his 'modesty' is 'that of a man with whom it was not a question of success, who has nothing invested or at stake'. For James,

Emerson's 'freedom from all wish for any personal share in the effect of his ideas' accounts for the absence of 'personal avidity', for 'the curious generalised way, as if with an implicit protest against personalities, in which his intercourse, epistolary and other, with his friends was conducted'.[35] Under publicity, no such dissociation is possible; indeed, it is precisely the effect of publicity to render 'private' and 'personal' interchangeable, and hence impoverished in their relation to 'public'.

5

The Peculiarity of Social Life: Reform and Gender

James's choice of reform as the substantial subject of publicity in *The Bostonians* bears strongly in mind the properly civic resonance of the dissociations discoverable in Emerson. For the wider issue of James's historicism, we should remember that Emerson's handling of the equation between private and public occurs in the context of that earlier period of radical commercial change during the 1830s and 1840s. This period had already provided a focus for James's attention at the end of the 1870s when he chose it as the setting for the action of *Washington Square* and *The Europeans*, texts where (especially in the latter) again we find Emerson's informative presence. The concerns with the changing nature of ideas about the self and with the fiscal instability that engage the main preoccupations of these novels are concerns which characterise the major shifts in the American economic history of the nineteenth century – the shifts from the sphere of accumulation to the sphere of reproduction where the latter begins its visible ascendancy towards the end of Reconstruction. The publicity of *The Bostonians*, examined through the issue of reform, marks the approaching dominance of the sphere of reproduction; and, by its Emersonian dissociations, serves to continue the story (begun in those earlier novels) of the self's changing shapes within the culture of consumption.

I

For Emerson the issue of reform itself is entangled with the new ways of trade. He begins 'Man the Reformer' (1841) by claiming that 'In the history of the world the doctrine of Reform had never such scope as at the present hour', at a time when 'The ways of trade are grown selfish to the borders of theft, and supple to the

107

borders (if not beyond the borders) of fraud'.[1] Trade panders to a particular distortion of Emersonian individualism, the inflation of the self, by its material encouragement of 'selfishness', the worst of Emersonian sins, as a 'system of distrust, of concealment, of superior keenness, not of giving but of taking advantage', a system which is 'a compromise of private opinion and lofty integrity'.[2] Emerson's lecture applauds manual labour as a means of resisting the abuses with which trade infects the world (James's review of Cabot's *Memoir* is to give its own approval to the proposition that 'He who does his own work frees a slave'). It is a means not only of establishing man's 'primary relations' with the world, but of resisting both the forgetfulness of commodity production and the prison of accumulation which follows on from that forgetfulness.[3] Here, Emerson's reminder of human productivity as a counter to trade's suppression of that very feature provokes a pun which underlines the particular operation of 'reform' itself in its entanglement with trade: 'What is a man born for but to be a Reformer, a Re-maker of what man has made.'

The pun incorporates a further major Emersonian principle, a version of self-reliance in which the main promise of reform is 'to clear ourselves of every usage which has not its roots in our own mind'.[4] This conjoining of reform and originality marks the potential of reform for its own debasement. As a general philosophy, what is 'excellent' is what is 'done the first time' but which 'loses all value when it is copied', and such a fate, in the lecture of 1844 on 'New England Reformers', is especially true of reform: 'Every project in the history of reform, no matter how violent and surprising, is good when it is the dictate of a man's genius and constitution, but very dull and suspicious when adopted from another.'[5] The loss of originality is the loss of self-reliant individualism, the loss of the sense of one's own productivity; but, following Adorno and Benjamin, the privileging of such individualism in the shape of the 'original' or the 'unique' (the evaluative categories of publicity for Verena Tarrant) is itself a reflex of the new commercial practices, a marketing illusion of authenticity in an age of mass-production which is to become not an alternative to that age but complicit with those very strategies of marketing which will encode publicity in *The Bostonians*. James is not able to enjoy the certainty of Emerson's faith in originality;[6] its distortion in the service of the spectacular marks yet a further strand in the debasement of the 'heroic age' in New England life.

The later lecture again puts the issue of reform within the issue of trade, here to show the latter's disturbance of social intercourse:

> This whole business of Trade gives me time to pause and think, as it constitutes false relations between men; inasmuch as I am prone to count myself relieved of any responsibility to behave well and nobly to that person whom I pay with money; whereas if I had not that commodity, I should be put on my good behaviour in all companies, and man would be a benefactor to man, as being himself his only certificate that he had a right to those aids and services which each asked of the other.[7]

These false relations which distort the proper equation of private and public are countered by reformism's 'great activity of thought and experimenting', the 'new spirit' of enquiry in which 'there was a keener scrutiny of institutions and domestic life than any we had known; there was sincere protesting against existing evils, and there were changes of employment dictated by conscience'. The result is 'a tendency to the adoption of simpler methods, and an assertion of the sufficiency of the private man', a tendency which summarises the 'affirmative principle of the recent philosophy' in its 'indication of growing trust in the private self-supplied powers of the individual.'[8] Nevertheless, Emerson's lecture is also sceptical about reform. It refers to 'this din of opinion and debate', and recognises its occasion for 'plentiful vaporing, and cases of backsliding',[9] symptoms which Emerson disdains along with Carlyle, Basil Ransom and James himself; but most importantly the lecture stresses reformism's narrowness of scope, a narrowness which emerges as a version of that form of selfishness already discerned in the infection of trade by the lecture on 'Man the Reformer'. Again we see the extent to which reform, advertised as an antidote to commercial practices, colludes with the effects of those practices.

Reform's narrowness, its 'partial' activity, is thus seen to share the project of trade in encouraging the vanity of the inflated self:

> The criticism and attack on institutions, which we have witnessed, has made one thing plain, that society gains nothing whilst a man, not himself renovated, attempts to renovate things around him: he has become tediously good in some

particular but negligent or narrow in the rest; and hypocrisy and vanity are often the disgusting result.

Emerson is opposed to any 'sally against evil by some single improvement, without supporting it by a total regeneration' and he instructs:

> Do not be so vain of your one objection . . . No one gives the impression of superiority to the institution, which he must give who will reform it . . . When we see an eager assailant of one of these wrongs, a special reformer, we feel like asking him, What right have you, sir, to your one virtue?[10]

The reduction of reformism to vain and selfish ends preoccupies his 'Lecture on the Times' where the idealism of reform lies in the 'sacredness of private integrity' and in the strength of being 'private and alone'. It is 'sacred' in origin but 'timid and profane' by 'management, by tactics and clamor'; its organisation produces 'a buzz in the ear'. Again, the 'partiality of character' reduces the 'private' to the 'personal' by the exaggeration and vanity of the reformers:

> They mix the fire of the moral sentiment with personal and party heats, with measureless exaggerations, and the blindness that prefers some darling measure to justice and truth. Those who are urging with most ardor what are called the greatest benefits of mankind, are narrow, self-pleasing, conceited men, and affect us as the insane do.[11]

To the 'defect' of 'partiality' Emerson adds, in 'New England Reformers', the 'reliance on Association' which grows out of the sense that 'the revolt . . . did not appear possible to individuals; and to do battle against numbers they armed themselves with numbers, and against concert they relied on new concert'. Such 'Association' is defective because it marks a diminution of the self, an 'asylum' for concealing individual anxieties about failure: 'I have failed, and you have failed, but perhaps together we shall not fail'. To the illusory 'concert' of 'Association' Emerson opposes the notion of union which, by implication, registers the public arena of the private self. In the former, the individual becomes 'cramped and diminished of his proportion' by a surrender of the self to collectivity in which a man 'mortgages' himself through the 'compromise' of surrender to become 'fractions' of himself. By comparison, union depends upon privacy:

> But leave him alone, to recognise in every hour and place the secret soul; he will go up and down doing the works of a true member, and, to the astonishment of all, the work will be done with concert, though no man spoke. Government will be adamantine without any governor. The union must be ideal in actual individualism.[12]

Emerson's anxieties about the fragmentation of the self are a response to the new industrial conditions which will later encourage the performativeness of the self, that artfulness of manner which James will explore in Baroness Munster and Serena Merle. His distrust of the allied consequences, whereby the self becomes paradoxically inflated, 'partial' and vain simultaneously, belongs to his recognition of the infections of both trade and reform, its illusory antidote. All these features are accommodated in *The Bostonians*, as are the implications of Emerson's telling opposition of 'Association' and 'union' whereby the 'personal' is allied to specious collectivity and the 'private' provides the ground for what is meaningfully 'public'.[13] James, however, is unable to rely upon the resource Emerson finds in integrated selfhood, in the absoluteness of self-reliance because, within the advancing conditions of trade where the publicity of the 1880s supplants the more straightforward mercantilism of the 1840s, it is that very selfhood which becomes increasingly impossible as it is dispersed by the spectacular marketing of desire. James's review of the correspondence between Emerson and Carlyle acknowledges the historical difference when he notes, in language very reminiscent of his study of Hawthorne, that Emerson's letters are 'especially interesting for the impression they give us of what we may call the thinness of the New England atmosphere in those days – the thinness, and, it must be added, the purity'. James finds this 'almost touching lightness, spareness, transparency' of the social scenery to be not only, by implication, a register of what has been lost in the contemporary world, but an important lesson in the size of the self. He is reminded, as he is reminded by Hawthorne's *American Notebooks*, of 'the importance of the individual in that simple social economy – of almost any individual who was not simply engaged in buying and selling'; he is careful to avoid nostalgia here (by the qualificatory 'almost' and the play on 'simple' and 'simply') and to suggest that despite historical difference, he wants to maintain Emerson's idea of the individual for the present age, the idea where 'every one had a kingdom within himself – was potential sovereign, by divine right, over a multitude of inspirations and virtues'.[14]

This is an important notion of the self in the commercial age; and, clearly, Emersonian self-reliance is to be distinguished from the omnivorous self James had found in Whitman and from the 'mountain *me*' of Margaret Fuller which he quotes from Carlyle a few pages previously. The Whitmanian self (conditioned to a significant degree by *his* reading of Carlyle) was for James, in his review of *Drum-Taps*, authoritarian rather than democratic; and here James's thoughts on the Emersonian individual recognise the 'hospitable attitude' of the latter and succeed in establishing a final distinction between the 'democratic ' optimism of Emerson and the 'aristocratic' pessimism of Carlyle. He contrasts Emerson, as 'the perfection of a listener' who 'stood always in a posture of hopeful expectancy', with Carlyle, who 'thought *all* talk a jabbering of apes'. James's sense of democracy is indeed 'simple' in keeping with those rather 'chilly' New England ethics he always associates with Emerson and Hawthorne:

> In a genuine democracy all things are democratic; and this spirit of general deference . . . was the natural product of a society in which it was held that every one was equal to every one else . . . Nothing is more striking in Emerson's letters than the way in which people are measured exclusively by their moral standards, designated by moral terms, described according to their morality.

His simplicity, in an age of exaggeration, is a calculated rhetorical tactic, and capable of restoring the 'personal' to its literal meaning within the general span of Emerson's democratic, optimistic individual who 'regarded such delivery of a personal view as a new fact, to be estimated on its merits'.[15]

It is equally 'natural' that Carlyle's philosophy 'should have aristocratic premises, and that he should call aloud for that imperial master, of the necessity for whom the New England mind was so serenely unconscious'.[16] James's choice of 'imperial' here prepares us for the third order of imagery (alternating with that of his theatrical and arcadian discourses) which Ransom's Carlylean temperament uses on behalf of Verena: the imagery rooted in the vocabulary of his disdain for the public which is patrician in the high Roman manner of a Shakespearean Coriolanus.[17] This comparison is not chosen idly. Just as Coriolanus is shown to be affronted above all by the people conceived as a mob, the stench of whose breath voices his name out of stature,[18] so Ransom exhibits a similarly patrician anxiety for the imagined abuse of Verena by her audience. In both cases, voice itself is crucial: for Coriolanus and for Ransom, name is defined and defiled by the voices of others. Where Ransom is concerned, the situation is compounded by the fact that Verena's name (for the purposes of publicity) is made through her own voice, and it is that which arouses the first expression of his disdain during his second visit to Charles Street. Olive Chancellor attends to the materiality of Verena's voice: its sound is 'pure' and not to be 'hushed'; it requires a 'public' occasion. Even Ransom cannot disagree with this ('it's too sweet for that'), again attending to its material quality and worrying about the effect of such an occasion on that very quality: 'But not raised to a scream; not forced and cracked and ruined. She oughtn't to become like the others. She ought to remain apart.'[19] His worry is about the 'show' of Verena, her 'exhibit' before a 'multitude' (p. 84) whose voice will physically destroy her own. For Ransom, the fame conferred by the voice of the audience will not only infect the body which he wishes to keep 'apart', but it will ravage the principal organ of that body. The Coriolanian character of his temperament is made clear later on their way to the Memorial Hall when he imagines the reception Verena received at the convention where 'I am told you made an immense sensation . . . that you leaped into fame' (p. 204). Such 'fame' is conferred by 'flushed women, with loosened bonnet-strings, forcing thin voices into ineffectual shrillness', and Ransom is angered by the thought of this distortion of utterance in which Verena herself is imagined as 'conjoined with them in emulation, in unsightly strainings and clappings and shoutings, in wordy, windy iteration of inanities'. Both her body and her name become subject to the rapine of voice where her desired apartness is submerged into the name that voice creates for her: 'Worst of all was the idea that she should have expressed such a congregation to itself so acceptably, have been acclaimed and applauded by hoarse throats, have been lifted up, to all the vulgar multitude, as the queen of the occasion' (pp. 205–6). Ransom's patrician stance is prompted by the publicity of a figure like Matthias Pardon.

He has not the 'slightest doubt' of her 'power to produce a sensation' by her Music Hall lecture, that it will be 'to the acclamations of the newspapers 'and that it was 'palpably in the air that she would become "widely popular"' (pp. 339–40), but the dramatising of this publicity that his patrician imagery effects has to be recognised (in concert with his theatrical and arcadian imagery) as emptying Verena of her 'natural properties' in the same manner as that of any newspaper paragraph. It provides not an opposition to that paragraph but simply a further spectacle in which Verena may be exploited; it is not an alternative but a collaboration. As he approaches the Music Hall through Boston's arenas of publicity (shop-fronts, evening papers, theatres and hotels) and sees 'Verena immensely advertised' (p. 370), he casts himself in the individualistic role he wishes for Verena's apartness. This is his version of the uniqueness celebrated by publicity for the sake of her novelty: 'He was not one of the audience; he was apart, unique, and had come on a business altogether special' with his 'vision of wresting her from the mighty multitude' (pp. 370–1). The imperial slant of his imagination transfigures the venue itself as having 'a kind of Roman vastness' where the swinging of the doors on the upper balconies by the passage of spectators 'reminded him of the *vomitoria* that he had read about in descriptions of the Colosseum' (p. 371).

Ransom's transfiguration reads the venue as a vulgar democratic spectacle, staged for the pleasure of the despised mass of the people: the choice of *vomitoria* economically summarises his stance, carrying visibly the etymological root it shares with the ejection of unaccommodated matter. Again he stresses the distortive effect of the voices and images which sustain the spectacle, the 'Photographs of Miss Tarrant – sketch of her life' and 'Portraits of the Speaker – story of her career' which are proclaimed by 'vociferous little boys' whose voices 'sounded small and piping in the general immensity'. Ransom's patrician language assumes a more contemporary vernacular ('there was a catch-penny effect about the whole thing' and the 'overture' from the organ seems also 'a piece of claptrap' on a par with 'this exhibition of enterprise and puffery'), but invariably it dominates his colouring of the scene as, literally, Olive's role in the new commerce, her 'new system of advertising', becomes translated into a political question. He sees her as 'making every sacrifice of state for the sake of the largest hearing, and conforming herself to a great popular system', a system which he translates into the Roman show of a battle between privacy and the vicious mass: 'He had a throb of uneasiness at his private purpose of balking it of its entertainment, its victim – a glimpse of the ferocity that lurks in a disappointed mob' (pp. 372–4). Ransom's translation of publicity and entrepreneurship[20] into a patrician social vision shows very clearly how publicity's re-alignments of 'public' and 'private' may be recruited into the discourse of politics which itself is required to acknowledge the new commerce. Inevitably the idea of theatre, one of Ransom's chief metaphorical sources when thinking of Verena, establishes an expressive arena for the debate[21] but here it is extended to question the basic tenets of American democracy itself: the meaningful relationship between an individual and the community. So Ransom returns to the rhetoric of Carlyle to pit his 'manhood' against 'the mighty multitude', 'that roaring crowd' (p. 382), the 'raving rabble' (p.385) and 'senseless brutes' (p. 387), and asks Verena, 'What do they care for you but to gape and grin and babble? You are mine, you're not theirs' (p. 382).

The text achieves more here than simply registering one voice's diminution of community because it poses as a counterpoint to the violence of Ransom's terms a series of other terms which attempt to specify a human collectivity. The narrative refers to 'the public' (pp. 381, 384, 389), 'the multitude' (p. 388) and 'a Boston audience' (p. 390). Matthias Pardon continually invokes 'the public' (pp. 367, 368, 369, 378). Mr Filer, the agent at the top of the entrepreneurial hierachy of 'the lecture business' (p. 378) – who echoes Selah Tarrant's earlier 'sacrifice' of 'home' by setting 'our domestic affairs' against the expenditure of spectacle (p. 381) – pleads the case of 'the public' (pp. 380, 383) as 'the most magnificent audience ever brought together! The city of Boston is under this roof!' (p. 382). For Verena, there is 'the great, good-natured, childish public' (p. 384) and 'the people' (p. 387), while Mrs Tarrant is forced into referring to 'the mob' in the face of Ransom's 'selfishness' (p. 383). As for Ransom himself, on the two occasions he refers to 'the public' he intends it solely as the 'audience' (pp. 376, 378). With confidence drawn from his seeming triumph at the end, Ransom is able to recast the direction of his imagery by an oblique generosity and to see Olive as a 'heroine' in her putative confrontation with 'the multitude'. The narrative on his behalf resorts to portraying her by grander sacrificial allusions than any we have had before: for example, 'She might have suggested to him some feminine firebrand of Paris revolutions, erect on a barricade, or even the sacrificial figure of Hypatia, whirled through the furious mob of Alexandria' (p. 388); and Olive projects herself as victim of the debasing voice of the audience's breath: 'I am going to be hissed and hooted and insulted!' It is at this precise moment that Ransom effects his final and literal emptying of Verena, thrusting her hood over her head 'to conceal her face and her identity', to leave behind 'the great public' which for him is now no longer a threat as 'even when exasperated, a Boston audience is not ungenerous' (pp. 389–90). The result of the interference of these competing terms is not only to reduce the 'public' to a gathering of spectators but to display a cacophony of meaning where 'public' is rendered irrevocably unstable. That instability is clearly worrying for a conservative temperament (hence the violence of Ransom's language which the comfort of his more confident rhetoric cannot elide), but in a more important sense it suggests not only an elitist fear of social disorder but a fear of a more radical kind: if 'public' is shorn of its human, civic meaning, then how will any form of social commentary be possible?

Wee are not allowed the ease of dismissing Ransom's patrician stance as merely a register of aristocracy's aversion to democracy. As the expression of his own striving for Verena, his own publicity for maintaining her apartness, it belongs too intimately to the manners of the new spectacularity which occasion James's deepest anxiety. And indeed, one of the major lessons of that anxiety is exactly to resist such schismatic oppositions which themselves are most fully promulgated by Ransom. It would be a mistake, for example, to assume that James's review of the correspondence between Emerson and Carlyle, one of the richest 'sources' for the novel, presents an unproblematical ground for reading Ransom's politics simply in terms of 'aristocrat' versus 'democrat'. James employs this distinction in discriminating between Carlyle and Emerson to the political credit of the latter, but he uses it also as the basis for important observations on style where the judgement is reversed. The ideas of 'color' and its concomitant capacity for specification and feeling are used to applaud the style of Carlyle, while their general absence is used to deprecate that of Emerson.[22] The review quotes Carlyle far more extensively than it quotes Emerson and although, as we have seen, Ransom's style is deployed to manipulative ends, it is the most colourful of any in the novel. This is not to defend that style, but to note the complexity of James's arrangements which dissuade us from, first, assuming that Ransom's languages proffer a real alternative to the world of publicity, and second, colluding with those forms of schismatic perception he himself invokes on every issue.

The complexity of James's dissociation of Emerson and Carlyle for a reading of Ransom might be best illustrated by one of the most crucial moments in his persuasion of Verena. It occurs during one of their walks at Marmion where, in 'sportive' and 'light' mood, they continue the debate on the privatising of her public life that had begun in Central Park. In a playful version of Selah Tarrant's 'sacrifice' of 'home' to publicity, Verena speculates 'Perhaps you intend to have a platform erected in our front parlour', and Ransom responds: 'the dining-table itself shall be our platform'. More is going on here than a joke about a pernicious invasion. Their mood locates an air of control over a deeply troubling issue, a control which we note not only as illusory but as preparing the way for Ransom's most insidious domestication. The final stage of his argument is to suggest that her gift will take on a new venue:

> It won't gush out at a fixed hour and on a fixed day, but it will irrigate, it will fertilize, it will brilliantly adorn your conversation. Think how delightful it will be when your influence becomes really social. Your facility, as you call it, will simply make you, in conversation, the most charming woman in America.
>
> (p. 337)

Ransom's slippage of 'social' into 'sociable' is one of the most alarming infections of publicity. It shadows the lightness of the mood from our point of view but, more importantly, it obliges the narrative to insist (twice) that Verena is 'easily satisfied' by the notion that 'there are lovely, neglected, almost unsuspected truths on his side' (pp. 336–7). The narrative is forced to be patronising at this point because of the intimacy of Ransom's appeal which, although blatant and, in one sense, familiar in its argumentation, is decidely effective in its emotional resonance.

It is Ransom's purveyance of 'conversation' that returns us to the complication of Emerson's place in the novel. In 1855, Emerson delivered a lecture on 'Woman' before the Women's Rights Convention in Boston, a lecture which remained unpublished until the Riverside edition of Emerson's works in 1883. Here, women are admired broadly for their delicacy, sentiment, sympathy and magnanimity, but always in the sense that these qualities function to serve male activity. Emerson's appreciation is wide, but it is always expressed for a supporting and beneficent influence rather than direct action in its own right; an appreciation of the female which is exactly that of Ransom in his less vitriolic moments in the tranquillity of Marmion. And it is above all conversation that for Emerson marks the proper arena for female influence:

> But there is an art which is better than painting, poetry, music, or architecture – better than botany, geology, or any science; namely, Conversation. Wise, cultivated, genial conversation is the last flower of civilisation and the best result which life has to offer us, – a cup for gods, which has no repentance. Conversation is our account of ourselves. All we have, all we can, all we know, is brought into play, and as the reproduction, in finer form, of all our havings.

Woman are 'by this and their social influence, the civilisers of mankind'. He asks 'What is civilization?' and answers 'the power of good women'.[23] Emerson is willing, in his oblique way, to allow women's rights (the rights to education, property and the vote), but he hedges his bets carefully on their role in the civil sphere and he is definite in his resistance to an organised movement on behalf of those rights: 'let us deal with them greatly; let them make their way by the upper road, and not by the way of manufacturing public opinion, which lapses continually into expediency and makes charlatans'.[24] At the same time, however, he sees the antagonism to slavery as an important step in the social progress of the female, giving 'Women a feeling of public duty and an added self-respect', and he is dismissive of the male charge against their temperament, the argument used by Ransom himself (p. 289), that 'They are more personal. Men taunt them that, whatever they do, say, read or write, they are thinking of themselves and their set.'[25]

The point here is that James's use of Carlyle, and particularly of Emerson, resists the temptation to schismatic perception that besets Ransom. And we as readers need to be alert also to this temptation in our response both to the novel and to its history. Emerson's lecture on 'Woman' provides a good test-case if we can envisage Ransom as its reader. He would respond positively, for example, to the 'finish' that Emerson celebrates as a major feature of women: 'They finish society, manners, language. Form and ceremony are their realm. They embellish trifles . . . Their genius delights in ceremonies, in forms, in decorating life with manners, with proprieties, order and grace.' But his response would be positive for the wrong reasons; understanding these decorative powers as essentially trivial when in fact Emerson, probably with the famous conversations of Margaret Fuller in mind, intends them as indications of potent human creativity which extends beyond the drawing-room: 'man invents and adorns all he does with delays and degrees, paints it all over with forms, to please himself better; he invented majesty and the etiquette of courts and drawing-rooms; architecture, curtains, dress, all luxuries and adornments, and the elegance of privacy, to increase the joys of society'. It is in just this 'department of taste or comeliness' that 'woman is the prime genius and ordainer'. Ransom's imagined misreading, whereby the first of these quotations would be understood in ignorance of the second, is aided by Emerson's argument about proportion and women which intervenes between the two:

> They are, in their nature, more relative; the circumstance must always be fit; out of place they lose half their weight, out of place they are disfranchised. Position, Wren said, is essential to the perfecting of beauty; – a fine building is lost in a dark lane; a statue should stand in the air; much more true is it of woman.[26]

Arguments for proportion lend themselves easily to assumptions about conservatism where we might consider ourselves to be on safe ground as far as Ransom is concerned. But, again, we need to be wary of such absolutist preconceptions. There is something odd, and distinctly un-Jamesian, about the way in which the narrative continually stresses the 'reactionary' nature of Ransom, and it is surely disingenuous in claiming so stridently that his ideas on 'minority rights' (leaving irony aside) are 'about three hundred years behind the age' (p. 163). As Alfred Habegger has argued skilfully, 'the omniscient narrator, with his critical eye, sound heart, and sane mind, operates as a satirical persona', and although the satire is directed primarily against 'the Boston radicals and the Mississippi reactionary'[27] it makes particular demands also on our roles as readers. We cannot share Habegger's early faith in the narrator's good sense (which leaves us precisely with radicals and reactionaries: further schisms) but the satiric thrust obliges us to question the judgements it presents: for example, here on the question of Ransom's conservatism. It has its essentialist cast, certainly dividing the human race, for instance, into 'the people who take things hard and the people who take them easy' (p. 11), and women into those 'who are unmarried by accident, and others who are unmarried by option' (p. 17); and his 'conception of vice' is 'purely as a series of special cases, of explicable accidents' (p. 18).

Such essentialism promotes both a form of intellectual fixity and schismatic perception and it is not confined to Ransom; Olive shares this tendency in her generalised rhetoric of 'human progress' (p. 19) and 'the coming of a better day' (p. 22), and where she is concerned, the narrative chooses not to intervene with its own commentary. She is happier with types than individuals (pp. 132–3) and, 'thanks to the philosophic cast of her mind', she is 'exceedingly fond of illustrations of laws' (p. 141; compare pp. 95–6). The inadequacy of the narrator's charges against Ransom as 'provincial' (p. 11) and 'reactionary' (p. 164) can be seen by their proximity to Verena's naïve reading of his diatribe against 'all the modern cant about freedom' where 'she didn't suppose you could hear any one say such a thing as that in the nineteenth century, even the least advanced' (p. 284). Carlyle, of course, did say such a thing, as the narrative itself tells us in condemning Ransom as 'reactionary'. Despite her naïveté, however, Verena does mark one advance on the narrative's judgement in recognising that Ransom does not belong to that order of conservatives who are 'only smug and stubborn and self-complacent, satisfied with what actually existed', but her terminology for his politics then slips into language that defines things with only an awkward approximation, relying upon words such as 'perverse' and 'cynic' (p. 284).

III

The experience of *The Bostonians* persuades us that the true nature of Ransom's conservatism is found precisely in his urge for the major separations in the novel, predominantly those of private and public worlds which he then casts into gender terms. Here lies the real meaning of his reactionary temperament, not only because it freezes possibilities for change (in preparation for the immobilisation that is the condition of any commodity), but in the sense also that these differentiations themselves are shifting contemporaneously: he is literally out of date, as we see by comparison with the gender differentiations advanced by Olive. A crucial aspect of the novel's greatness can be seen in its interrogation of such schisms: by its Hawthornesque anxieties about its own narrative power,[28] by its questioning of the idea of union in its application to both social and political relationships as a seeming solution to a divided world,[29] and by its presentation in the figure of Verena of the suffering that ensues from living within such a world.[30] We can see this interrogation in more detail by looking at the curious affair of Dr Prance where, in a novel which takes the ideational reform of gender as its ostensive theme, we witness what amounts to virtually a literal re-forming of assumptions about gender itself. This argument is premised on the proposal that we need to attend to Dr Prance's dispersive function, her disruption of the antinomies which structure the other characters and provide the problematical locus for the novel's concerns in general. Her role, specifically, requires us to question again the absolutist separations of work and release from work, sites of labour and those of relaxation, public and private behaviour, and the range of gender-based perceptions which condition and perpetuate those separations. Dr Prance provides telling access to one of James's most powerful preoccupations: his antipathy towards those modes of seeing and understanding which freeze the world into intolerant binary structures and thereby threaten its relational practices.

The presentation of Dr Prance is marked by an almost total absence of those 'personal' details we expect in a novelistic expression of 'character', an absence which is singular in a work which James himself describes as 'something like Balzac'.[31] Her first appearance is as a name on a sign (p. 24), and this is one of only two occasions where she is accorded the colour of a Christian name; on the second occasion, that name is distanced from the text by parenthesis (p. 36). Her intimacy with Miss Birdseye circumscribes her main activity in the novel, and that is marked by the details of a shared absence of physical feature (compare pp. 24 and 37) and a shared bespectacledness (see pp. 28 and 31). In fact her physical presence is characterised only by her cropped hair, the detail which enables Ransom to recognise her in the dusk at Marmion (p. 301). Ransom is the sole person with whom she converses, and he recognises at their first meeting that her profession renders her 'incapable of asking him a personal question' (p. 38). Here, 'personal' is set against what Ransom calls the 'private lecture' they see Olive receiving from Mrs Farrinder, a privacy which, Dr Prance notes, will not obviate the necessity for payment. Ransom's phrase conjoins two disparate terms, and it is left to Dr Prance to reveal that disparity in her reminder of the commercial world which structures reformist performance and where publicity ensures that nothing is for free; nothing is 'private'. The moment is prepared for by the narrative's distinctions between two forms of the 'public' world and by the lecture itself.

These two forms are shaped by the vivid contrast between Miss Birdseye (pp. 25 and 27) and Mrs Farrinder (pp. 27–28), whose differences are carefully plotted point for point. The ultimately affectionate portrayal of Miss Birdseye is of a public life which has suppressed the 'personal', while the frightening picture of Mrs Farrinder is of a public life where the 'personal' is not present even to be dismissed. Physiognomically, they are formed by the shared lecture-hall in which the former is the audience and the latter is the performer (pp. 25–8). In Mrs Farrinder, 'public' partakes of the qualities of her eye, 'large, cold, and quiet', and the non-diaological dominance of her conversation. The shapelessness of the old, where Miss Birdseye has 'no more outline than a bundle of hay', is opposed to the mathematically smooth intolerance of the new (Mrs Farrinder's 'fine placid mask' and her 'terrible regularity of feature'). The older body of reform is constantly shifting (and hence losing its singularity of face) due to the variety of spreading sympathies, while the new body is narrowly fixed by its more limited concerns and by the demands of an audience, acquiring an 'exposed reticence' and 'the air of being introduced by a few remarks' (a brilliant satiric thrust). 'Public' becomes the frozen face of a publicity poster as we see, again, human physicality literally being re-formed by the effects of the new culture (pp. 27–8).

It is Mrs Farrinder's 'eye of business', recognised by Dr Prance as the real meaning of the 'private lecture' she witnesses with Ransom, which presents to Olive a 'picture of the part Miss Chancellor might play by making liberal donations to a fund for the diffusion among the women of America of a more adequate conception of their public and private rights'. The unquestioning conjoining of 'public and private' is the rhetoric of 'the speaker's most successful public efforts' and it imposes a mesmeric influence over Olive, placing her 'under a spell' and making her feel 'almost inspired'. It transfigures Olive's view of the 'serious, tired people' in the 'barren' room into an image of the 'glow' of 'a company of heroes' and instigates a vision of the women's movement as a 'crusade', a vision that becomes increasingly exaggerated and generalised to conclude with a romanticisation of Miss Birdseye as 'martyr'. This final image prompts Olive to distinguish her from the general charge that had been brought against the female cause since the mid-century: 'And yet people said that women were vain, that they were personal, that they were interested!' (pp. 33–4). In short, public rhetoric shores up an individualistic vision which, while proclaiming disinterestedness for the female cause, in fact deeply personalises it (we know that the idea of martyrdom is central to Olive's image of herself) by an unquestioning, generalising rhetoric of its own; and embedded within Olive's vision is a concern with 'names' and 'the tables of fame' which marks, again, the proximity of 'public' to 'publicity'.

With a marvellous economy, James chooses this very moment, immediately following Olive's observation on the 'personal', to insert a detail which concludes his preparation for the word on behalf of Dr Prance: Olive fastens Miss Birdseye's 'small battered brooch' which had become partly detached. It is an act of simple tenderness that is genuinely 'personal' in an unproblematic sense, placed against its more general misuse within the new rhetoric where it proposes mainly self-interest. Gently, the detail corrects the stress in Olive's vision of Miss Birdseye never having 'a thought or an impulse for herself' by providing the brooch with a brief history within Miss Birdseye's earlier reformist activity. That history quietly suggests her naïveté, but it also restores a proper human warmth to the 'personal'. Dr Prance's 'personal' is then set apart from Olive's rhetorical usage, given meaning by her 'tough and technical' involvement with the profession of her authentically public role as doctor (p. 38). At the same time, the discrepancy between word and deed in Olive's vision and her tender act is restored by the larger, pervasive tenderness of Dr Prance's care for Miss Birdseye, a care in which the 'personal' is seen to mediate between the selfless and the selfish. She is incapable of asking a 'personal' question to the extent that, as we are told later at Marmion, she is incapable of asking 'any question with a social bearing' (p. 305); as a dealer in facts (p. 307), where words and deeds are absolutely entwined, she has an aversion to generalisation (p. 28) which renders the vocabulary of 'public', 'private', and 'personal' virtually unnecessary. She is the only character in the novel who is free from this vocabulary; the implication is that such freedom is a release from an inadequate shorthand for describing relationships. Dr Prance is not only a straight talker but one who, by comparison with the varieties of loquaciousness which surround her, talks very little at all.

She fulfils Ransom's expectations of the 'Yankee female' but, more importantly, she fulfils also the expectation of an absence of the feminine in that image; 'Spare, dry, hard, without a curve' (p. 36), she not only goes fishing (p. 312) and seems a suitable candidate to receive a cigar (p. 303), but she shares his specific irritation with the women's movement: his general Carlylean disapproval of an age that is too talkative (p. 37). It is appropriate, then, that the narrative, on behalf of Ransom's perspective, disperses gender categories altogether in presenting Dr Prance:

> She looked like a boy, and not even like a good boy. It was evident that if she had been a boy, she would have 'cut' school, to try private experiments in mechanics or to make researches in natural history. It was true that if she had been a boy she would have borne some relation to a girl, whereas Doctor Prance appeared to bear none whatever.[32]
>
> (pp. 36–7)

The privacy of her experiments suggests an honourable truancy from institutional schisms of gender education, but at the same time implies that such transgressions involve a sacrifice which cannot be accommodated by a community's consensus: for the sake of her profession (her public role) her sexuality is obliged to remain problematically tacit. When we are told a little later, again at a moment where the narrative colludes with Ransom's point of view, that 'it was certain that whatever might become of the movement at large, Doctor Prance's own little revolution was a success', it is in the context of her boredom with 'being reminded that she was a woman – a detail that she was in the habit of forgetting, having as many rights as she had time for' (p. 43). By comparison with the 'movement' Dr Prance's 'success' is private and individualistic, making no demands upon others (a main source of its attractiveness for Ransom); but it is based upon her professional, public activity. The slippage of one concept into another is matched here by the dispersal of her gender, a dispersal which she maintains herself in remarking drily: 'Men and women are all the same to me . . . I don't see any difference. There is room for improvement in both sexes' (p. 37).[33]

Allied to the dispersal of gender we witness in Dr Prance is the way in which she acts as a reminder of the productivity which is suppressed by consumer culture. This is the world of use, established by her profession generally, and registered specifically by the telling detail of the name-plate which first introduces her into the novel: it has 'a peculiar look of being both new and faded – a kind of modern fatigue – like certain articles of commerce which are sold at a reduction as shop-worn' (p. 24). Her activity is advertised in the very language of consumption itself where it is precisely the world of use ('faded' and 'shop-worn') that is suppressed by the pristine, virginal world of exchange ('new' and 'modern'). Equally used and worn are the physical features of Miss Birdseye, the only figure with whom Dr Prance enjoys any association. Miss Birdseye is equally the reminder of a world of action, delusive perhaps, but remaining a public action which is now overtaken by publicity; a world of the 'hands' rather than the 'tongue', which are precisely the terms of Dr Prance's disapproval for Selah Tarrant's charlatanry that defines to such a large extent the new world of consumption. As Guy Debord has summarised, the abstractions of exchange's suppression of use are as symptomatic of consumption as they are of commodities in general:

The spectacle is the other side of money: it is the general abstract equivalent of all commodities. But if money has dominated society as the representation of the central equivalence, namely as the exchangeable property of the various goods whose uses remained incomparable, the spectacle is its developed modern complement, in which the totality of the commodity world appears as a whole, as a general equivalence for what the totality of the society can be and do. The spectacle is the money which *one only looks at*, because in the spectacle the totality of use is already exchanged for the totality of abstract representation. The spectacle is not only the servant of *pseudo-use*, it is already in itself the pseudo-use of life.[34]

Debord writes on behalf of our own stage in the history of consumption, but his reading is pertinent to the shift from accumulation to reproduction that is witnessed by *The Bostonians*.

James's simile of shop-wornness is especially appropriate to the wider dispersal which Dr Prance imagises. While proposing the suppression of material production by the spectacle of display, the simile is anxious that it suggests nothing so reductive as the replacing of one order by another. This is where the illuminating parenthesis, 'a kind of modern fatigue', comes in as an enabling ground for the simile. The point about 'shop-worn' is that it belongs completely to neither of the two orders it proposes: too faded to be of value for full exchange, equally it is the victim of another form of 'pseudo-use' in that it has not been used in any real sense at all but has suffered the ravages of display itself; it has been 'worn' only by spectacle. In other words, the simile registers acutely an interstitial moment of transition as one order of commercial activity is witnessed in the process of change. Here, again, we find Dr Prance's crucial dispersal of available or established worlds and her vital place within the novel's general concern to confront the instabilities, always attendant upon transition, that are a consequence of such dispersal. The fake 'use' implied by 'shop-worn' then prepares us for Debord's category of 'pseudo-use' that is so stridently discovered in Verena as an image relating to a more developed stage in commercial change.

The only use to which Verena is put by both Olive and Ransom is that of display, in concert with what Richard Godden has described as the general fate of the female in the new economy: 'The woman, at the centre of her drawing room, becomes the medium through which the man forgets labour and transforms consumption into sentimental privacy and art.'[35] For both, the nature of Verena's display is determined by her most immaterial feature, her speaking voice: it is designed by Olive for the oratory of the public platform and by Ransom for the conversation of the private parlour, and both attend to its oracular performativeness at the expense of its ideational expression according to their differing notions of entrepreneurship. The immateriality of Verena's voice is only one aspect of the spectacle she becomes as a result of the various evacuations effected by her admirers, and it lends, paradoxically, a material element to the abstractions of display. If, again following Debord's distinctions, the first phase of the domination of the economy over social life (the phase of accumulation) had degraded 'being' into 'having', then the second phase (that of consumptive reproduction) involves the further 'sliding' of 'having' into 'appearing' which provides the new prestige and function for possession in general.[36] In other words spectacle, emptied of use by exchange for the new desires of consumption, involves a distinctive impairing of whatever solidity might be ascribed to the objects which confer value or status to their possessor. Appearance underlines the paradox of consumption by advertising itself simultaneously as the real thing and its disguise, along the lines of Veblen's diagnosis at the end of the nineteenth century of the 'make-believe' deployment of the 'instinct of workmanship'.[37] *The Bostonians* plots the shift from 'having' to 'appearing' in the respective financial resources of Olive and Ransom. Olive has the real wealth to purchase Verena, but Ransom has not; it is only the limited success of publication (the sole area of publicity he acknowledges openly) in *The Rational Review* that enables his justification for purchasing Verena[38] as a substitute for a sounder resource: in short, 'appearing' robs 'having'.

To read *The Bostonians* as a novel that is about publicity as an analogue for the disturbances of consumption is to read its choice of 'the situation of women' as 'the most salient and peculiar point in our social life' beyond the confines of reformist agitation. As the recent work of Lears and Bowlby has shown,[39] it was predominantly women who constituted the main body of the advertisers' audience and who were consequently the main consumers; it was through women in the first instance that the effects of the new commerce were made visible. The equation is straightforward: to write 'a tale very characteristic of our social conditions' is to write about consumption which in turn is to write about women, and consumption, as it applies to women, enforces rigid categorisations of public and private. Lears summarises it in a way that describes exactly Ransom's strategy for male hegemony:

> Feminist political claims were deflected into quests for psychic satisfaction through high-style consumption. The emphasis on self-realization through emotional fulfilment, the devaluation of public life in favor of a leisure world of intense private experience, the need to construct a pleasing 'self' by purchasing consumer goods – these therapeutic imperatives helped to domesticate the drive toward female emancipation.[40]

James is not Howells or Dreiser, who present this strategy in more materially-based forms; Ransom cannot offer the glamour of goods, but his case for 'conversation' in the limited sociability of the parlour clearly employs its tactics on behalf of his gender-based oppositions of public and private.

It is within these oppositions that Dr Prance emerges so decisively. She 'dealt in facts' and sees publicity as an established social category, uncoloured by the patrician fantasies of Ransom; Verena's lecture at the Music Hall will be simply 'on a great scale' and will cause 'a big sensation' (p. 307). 'Objective' is perhaps the term we can use for the professionalism of her perception which is modestly accurate and presented as free from contemporary foolishness, the product of (as David Howard puts it) 'real and quiet work'.[41] Despite the fact of Ransom's collaboration with the narrative's dispersal of her gender (his capacity to appreciate the doctor certainly qualifies what is otherwise a predominantly pejorative presentation of him), that dispersal requires us to question the very oppositions the new commerce cultivates and relies upon. It is partly a question of the difficulty in assimilating the new, her 'modern' qualities (the figuration of Verena, as we have seen, poses a similar difficulty); but more importantly she disrupts notions of work and leisure, office and home (her apartment is the site of both), public and private, and all the sexual assumptions which support and promote those divisions. As neither male nor female, and not permitting that very dissociation, she resists standard gender-based appropriations, encouraging us to reconstruct these absolutist categories. She is an expression of one of James's most strongly held beliefs, held in conjunction with Howells, as Alfred Habegger has noted:

Howells and James were alike in their deep opposition to their culture's central gender roles. Their uncompromisingly competitive, hard-driving men . . . are never seen sympathetically. Their idealistic women . . . are apt to be misguided and occasionally destructive. And both writers would be obsessed most of all with the sensitive outsider, male or female, who cannot find a satisfying niche in the social order.[42]

We can go further to connect this account with James's equally deep hostility to schismatic perception: his interest in the 'outsider' figure of Dr Prance is in a figure who not only enables an interrogation of the existing order but who herself blurs schismatic divisions. These divisions are unacceptable to him because they belong to the concealed absolutes whereby the new commerce intolerantly promotes itself and, above all, because they inhibit the relational nature, the sympathy, of human intercourse that is James's greatest discovery as a novelist: the relational nature he expresses most famously in 'The Art of Fiction' at the moment of beginning *The Bostonians*: 'Experience is never limited, and it is never complete; it is an immense sensibility, a kind of huge spider-web of the finest silken threads suspended in the chamber of consciousness, and catching every air-borne particle in its tissue.' Against such 'tissue' what he calls the 'clumsy separations', the 'series of blocks', the artificiality of 'frontiers' whereby fiction and its procedures are categorised, have at best 'little reality or interest' for the producer of fiction. What is true for novelistic practice (the categories of 'incident', 'character', 'dialogue' and 'description' are those he itemises) is true also for experience and behaviour: 'People often talk of these things as if they had a kind of internecine distinctness, instead of melting into each other at every breath, and being intimately associated parts of one general effort of expression.'[43] For James, generally, any separation out of events or people is an arbitrary affair, a matter of boundaries and categories for the sake of epistemological conveniences. Schismatic perception is the most problematical of such conveniences because, as the most ingrained of our habits of looking, it is the least likely to be questioned; and it is especially intrusive when it is gender-based, since one's sense of one's self and its relationships is invariably most intimately bound up with notions of maleness and femaleness.

For Dr Prance to carry out the role outlined, she has to do so in a deliberately drab way; the way, perhaps, of the 'laconic and inexpressive speech' of the 'pared-down' and 'pinched' New England mentality (Alfred Habegger's description in a private communication) that we associate more with, say, the Wentworths in the Jamesian canon. And although she is productive as an 'outsider', she can scarcely be described as 'sensitive' because we are not presented with any evidence either to support or deny such an epithet. But her diminished novelistic presence has its own point to make, a point which is fully congruent with her function for dispersal. She has none of the donative pzazz we usually find in James's off-centre females (in Henrietta Stackpole, for instance), and we cannot ascribe to her the suffering that might otherwise underwrite rare-spokenness (as it does in Catherine Sloper). Equally, despite her 'likeable anomalousness' (again, a useful phrase from Habegger), she cannot be seen to exemplify the complex rational perspective schematised by 'The Art of Fiction'. Dr Prance's *effect*, however, is profoundly disturbing for the reader; a disturbance mirrored in the difficulty all of us share in accounting for her. In a novel that is so pervaded by strategies of consumption and spectacle (strategies which are not to be divorced from the displays of character and situation engaged by fiction), a substantial part of her presentation is to resist the temptation to the gorgeousness that is the feature itself of spectacle. At the same time, that presentation has also to resist the established categories of novelistic practice: she pertains towards the possibilities of sensitive outsider and relational consciousness, but she cannot inhabit them. Her potency has to remain tacit enough to avoid full presence but likeable enough to register an impact. The very anomalousness of her presentation as character mimes closely both the design of her dispersal and the pattern of dispersal's relational effect, a pattern which manages to do without the 'immense sensibility' that elsewhere, and in a different kind of novel, James would rely upon. Dr Prance's eluding of *The Bostonians'* schisms provides a signal lesson for the relational sense that is always threatened by the intolerance of schismatic perception.

6

The Personal, the Private and the Public

There is a term missing from the chapter title. It is 'publicity': the world of spectacle, promotion, advertisement, calculation and construction of desire, which may be taken as characteristic of the industrial and marketing shifts graphing the consumer culture that began to structure American ways of seeing in the 1870s. The terms the title does contain are those which are most threatened by 'publicity', and some of the ways in which that threat is manifested in *The Bostonians* will be suggested.[1]

The argument will be that James invokes a model for the relationship between 'private' and 'public' discoverable in Sainte-Beuve and in Emerson. That relationship constitutes a direct equation where the 'private' denotes a form of self-expression which is free from the avidity of self-centredness and from any urge towards appropriation. In this sense, 'private' has a compact with 'public' by recognising its civic role and bears an aura of proper responsibility to the external sphere of events by acknowledging their necessary otherness. The world is not to be soaked by individualistic design. At the same time, of course, such design cannot be ignored as a function of human perception, and this is why the compact James envisages involves both Emerson and Sainte-Beuve. James finds in Emerson a temperament where 'nothing interested, no worldly avidity, no vulgar vanity or personal error, was ever mingled', where the absence of self-centredness guarantees 'a career of public distinction and private honour'. In Sainte-Beuve, he discovers a notion of the 'personal' (for the purposes of this argument such a notion, despite the difference in nomenclature, is parallel for James to the Emersonian 'private') which, paradoxically, relies upon that same absence of mere self-interest. The size and extent of the Sainte-Beuvean 'personal' is such that its homogeneity produces disinterest. James is able to note simultaneously that 'no writer was ever more personal, more certain, in the long run, to infuse into his judgements of people and things those elements out of which an image of himself might be constructed', and that 'There is very little overflow of his personal situation, of his movements and adventures, of the incidents of his life.'

In these contrasting views of the Sainte-Beuvean 'personal', we have a striking example of one of the main slippages which the present analysis will explore: the shift from a disinterested self-expression that commits itself wholly to the homogeneity of its public role to a self-expression that bears an appropriative interest towards the world. It is a shift from the civic to the advertisable, from 'public' to 'publicity', and, following Jean Baudrillard's invaluable schematisation, an acknowledgement of how, simultaneously, the notion of 'person' becomes dissolved into 'personality' within the structures of consumer culture: that is, the process whereby the self moves from the integrity of the Sainte-Beuvean 'personal' and the Emersonian 'private' to become a cluster of attributes, effects and performances. Here, 'publicity' (the world of Matthias Pardon and Selah Tarrant) is regarded as a disarrangement of 'public' in that it presents an illusory image of collectivity, of civic responsibility, and panders to the desire of the second meaning of 'personal' which James's consideration of Sainte-Beuve locates: the parochialism of self-centredness. It is that notion of the 'personal' as self-interested desire which disarranges the selflessness of 'private' as 'publicity' debases the social community of the 'public'. In short, it will be the parochial sense of 'personal', the world of appropriative desire, which for James will distort the responsibility owed by the 'private' to the 'public'.

Verena Tarrant, the novel's object of desire, is never allowed to exist outside the relationships established by the manipulations of desire.[2] Her presence is as spectacle, the product of the competing publicities fashioned by Olive and Ransom where neither is more attractive than the other: James's critique of publicity offers nothing so simplistic as an alternative to its infections. Publicity is understood as the projection of images and roles, and while the entrepreneurship of Olive and the commodification of Verena present clear instances of publicity's effects, we should not ignore the extent to which Ransom's persuading of Verena shares effects which are strikingly similar to those engineered by Olive. Ransom thus has a slighter role than the women in the argument, but the

theatrical vocabulary he employs on behalf of Verena commodifies her just as much as do the advertisements and publicity
posters. Both wish to place her on a platform, but while Olive's
platform is situated in the Boston Music Hall, Ransom's is in the
parlour. Olive's strategy is to persuade Verena into an image of a
public role, while Ransom's is to envelop her in an image of a
private role, and for their respective personal appropriations both
are forced into negotiations with the seemingly impersonal tactics
of publicity: respectively, the advertising of reformist responsibility and of domestic consanguinity.

What both sets of images achieve is to force perception (importantly, for the reader as well as for the inhabitants of the novel)
into an absolute schism of public and private. This schism,
accompanied by all its freezing of choice and possibility, is not
allowed to remain stable. Paradoxically, it constitutes the strident
shape of the new world of desire which, in Walter Benn
Michaels's words, is 'an involvement with the world so central to
one's sense of self that the distinction between what one is and
what one wants tends to disappear'.[3] Rachel Bowlby, taking the
shop-window as the emblem of the new world, puts the case
more forcefully: 'The window smashes the illusion that there is a
meaningful distinction in modern society between illusion and
reality, fact and fantasy, fake and genuine images of self.'[4] It is
precisely Verena's fate not only to be incapable of choice in the
final scene of the novel, but to be confronted by the failure of the
opposing terms which have structured the novel throughout. The
schismatic perception of publicity not only paralyses the self but
in the process disengages the divisions of its own programme;
and it is on this double front that *The Bostonians* constructs its
campaign, fearful simultaneously of both schism and of what
follows when schism is dissolved.

The words 'public', 'private' and 'personal' are by far the most
common in the novel's evaluative vocabulary, occurring with a
frequency that is probably unmatched anywhere else in James's
fiction. What is striking is not simply the frequency of these
words' occurrence, but the frequency of their occurrence together,
within either the same conversation or the same moment of a
particular scene. It is this latter frequency which registers both the
instability of their traditional compact within the new world of
publicity *and* a frantic yoking against that world as a fragile
reminder of the more measured period when their compact was

felt to mark a more purposive connection between the individual and society. The novel tests each word against the other within a continually shifting relationship in respect of not only their interaction but of their own assumed stability. It is not intended here to describe each shift (simply on the grounds of length), but from the examples to be offered shortly it will be clear that they establish no consistent pattern (a pattern that would, in any case, be untrue to the novel's general resistance to pattern) save that of a pervasive worry about the difficulties of connecting 'public', 'private' and 'personal' within the regime of publicity. Even the authoritarian schisms of Ransom and, to a lesser extent, Olive, display their own slippages.

We may begin to exemplify these shifts by noting how James's criticism on the art of writing exposes the epithet 'personal' (the first of our three terms to be introduced in the novel) to its awkward variousness in those two essays, 'The Art of Fiction' and 'Alphonse Daudet', which are contemporary with his planning of *The Bostonians*. The former proclaims famously that, 'A novel is in its broadest definition a personal, a direct impression of life' but the value of that impression is then seen to depend upon a 'freedom to feel and say' and this freedom takes James's argument beyond the fact of the impression to the form of a writer's execution which attracts the same epithet: 'The execution belongs to the author alone; it is what is most personal to him, and we measure him by that.' Within the space of a dozen lines then, 'personal' is applied to both 'impression' and 'execution'. And within a further couple of pages, James remembers an English novelist who, on the basis of one brief glimpse of French Protestant youth, 'had got her direct personal impression, and she turned out her type'.[5] The essay on Daudet of the previous year expands on the difficulties James associates with 'personal' as a critical term. He takes his cue from a comment by Zola on *Numa Roumestan*: 'a work which I regard as one of those, of all Daudet's productions, that is most personal to himself'. Here, 'personal' is allied to the writer's temperament, as Zola goes on to note that 'He has put his whole nature into it, helped by his southern temperament, having only to make large draughts upon his innermost recollections and sensations.' This is perhaps not too far from the 'personal' quality of James's 'direct impression' but, nevertheless, James feels that the Gallic resonance of the word is not possible in English. He registers his own response to

Daudet as 'an irresistible impulse to express a sense of personal fondness', and immediately he seems to feel an embarrassment in making such a judgement:

> This kind of feeling is difficult to utter in English, and the utterance of it, so far as this is possible, is not thought consistent with the dignity of a critic. If we were talking French, nothing would be simpler than to say that Alphonse Daudet is adorable, and have done with it. But this resource is denied me, and I must arrive at my meaning by a series of circumlocutions. I am not able even to say that he is very 'personal'; that epithet, so valuable in the vocabulary of French literary criticism, has, when applied to the talent of an artist, a meaning different from the sense in which we use it. 'A novelist so personal and so penetrating,' says Emile Zola, speaking of the author of *Numa Roumestan*. That phrase, in English, means nothing in particular; so that I must add to it that the charm of Daudet's talent comes from its being charged to an extraordinary degree with his temperament, his feelings, his instincts, his natural qualities.[6]

James's embarrassment is that of self-expression conceived as self-exposure, the quality with which the French mind feels no discomfort,[7] and he resorts to the French version of the word to summarise his subject's Provençal features: 'To be *personnel* to that point, transparent, effusive, gushing, to give one's self away in one's books, has never been, and will never be, the ideal of us of English speech; but that does not prevent our enjoying immensely, when we meet it, a happy example of this alien spirit.'[8] Clearly more than Anglo-Saxon critical decorum is involved here, since self-exposure, in different hands, might come perilously close to self-aggrandisement; to, for example, Whitmanian inflations of the self[9] and the contemporary exaggerations of consumptive publicities. Nevertheless James's criticism, three years earlier, does manage to sustain a firm use of 'personal' when considering the work of a Frenchman whom he always regards as the model for the critical act, Sainte-Beuve.[10] In his review of Sainte-Beuve's *Correspondance* in 1880, James acclaims: 'no writer was ever more personal, more certain, in the long run, to infuse into his judgements of people and things those elements out of which an image of himself might be constructed.' Sainte-Beuve is thus 'personal' as, in a not dissimilar way, Emerson is 'private': that is, in the homogeneity of their personality and in the paradoxical disinterestedness of their self-expression. James continues: 'The whole of the man was in the special work – he was *all* a writer, a critic, an appreciator. He was literary in every pulsation of his being, and he expressed himself totally in his literary life. No character and no career were ever more homogeneous.'

Sainte-Beuve's work offers 'a singularly complete image of his character, his tastes, his temper, his idiosyncrasies' because 'It was from himself always that he spoke – from his personal and intimate point of view.' James admits that praise of a man's work as 'in a peculiar degree the record of a mind, the history of a series of convictions and feelings, the reflection of a group of idiosyncrasies' does not, in itself, constitute the value of the work. It all depends, of course, on the quality of the mind concerned, and 'It so happened that Sainte-Beuve's was extraordinary, was so rich and fine and flexible, that this personal accent, which sounds everywhere in his writings, acquired a superior value and an exquisite rarity.' And the expression of that mind is additionally valuable to the degree that it is free from the 'personal' in its more limiting, parochial sense: 'There is very little overflow of his personal situation, of his movements and adventures, of the incidents of his life.'[11] In other words Sainte-Beuve, like Emerson, presents the 'personal' without the 'personality' where, as James admires in his review of the *Correspondence* between Emerson and Carlyle, 'nothing interested, no worldly avidity, no vulgar vanity or personal error, was ever mingled – a career of public distinction and private honor'.[12] The Sainte-Beuvean 'personal' and the Emersonian 'private' share a meaningfully 'public' expression against which the excesses and slippages of those terms in *The Bostonians* are tested to display the distortions of publicity.

It is fitting then, that 'personal' is the first of those terms to enter the novel; fitting because, as James's critical writing shows, intrinsically it is the most problematical of the three, particularly in its relations to the self's projections. Olive, on her initial meeting with Ransom, becomes subject to one of her 'fits of tragic shyness' and her discomfiture is exacerbated by Mrs Luna 'becoming instantly so personal' in her remarks about Olive's mode of dress. We are told: 'There was nothing in the world so

personal as Mrs Luna' (pp. 10–11), where 'personal', predominantly, is a synonym for frivolous, a connection which Olive
reiterates later when she views Mrs Luna as 'given up to a merely
personal, egotistical, instinctive life', a view which excludes
specifically any public engagement: 'and as unconscious of the
tendencies of the age, the revenges of the future, the new truths
and the great social questions, as if she had been a mere bundle
of dress-trimmings, which she very nearly was' (p. 139). Such a
view is slightly unfair to Mrs Luna since for all her foolishness she
is capable, as here in her observations on Olive's attire, of
accurate perception. But the point is that her accuracy becomes
overlaid by what is ultimately a masculine term of disparagement[13] which instigates the first announcement of the position
that Ransom is to maintain throughout the novel: the schematisation of private and public worlds on the basis of gender, where
the male sphere of civic responsibility is opposed to the inactive
female sphere of privacy. He contrasts Olive's 'morbidness' with
the women of 'his own soft clime' and concludes:

> That was the way he liked them – not to think too much, not to
> feel any responsibility for the government of the world, such as
> he was sure Miss Chancellor felt. If they would only be private
> and passive, and have no feeling but for that, and leave
> publicity to the sex of tougher hide!
>
> (p. 11)

The narrative's insistence that Ransom is 'very provincial' here
pertains most forcefully to the schismatic nature of his perception
rather than to the ideational content of its utterance. He slips
from one term to another: 'private' is modified not only by
'passive' but by the 'personal' feature of Mrs Luna which instigates Ransom's speculation in the first place. And although he
opposes this sphere to governmental 'responsibility', a clear
version of the 'public', he ends by using the term 'publicity' as the
other pole of his antithesis. These slippages are compounded by
the grammar of Ransom's expression: 'private and passive' are
adjectival while 'publicity' is nominative – the grammar refuses
equality of weight to the items of Ransom's equation, despite its
declared ambition (in keeping with the temperament of one who
will write for *The Rational Review*) for measured, bilateral
judgement.

These slippages reveal more than the bias of Ransom's position. They display very clearly the instability of a terminology which structures the entire novel, a terminology which itself insists upon its schematisations at the moment when publicity both elides the earlier compact between 'private' and 'public' and perpetuates that compact for the purposes of its own practices. At the simplest level, 'private' becomes transformed into 'personal' and the public arena of civic 'responsibility' into 'publicity'. The persistent competition between those terms produces not only instability but a decided vacating of the ground whereby they may sustain any prescriptive value at all; their continual opposition results only in artificial fixity in which our questioning of them becomes virtually paralysed. The first clash between Verena and Mrs Farrinder, for example, is presented as being between new and old; the spontaneity and enthusiasm of 'personal purity' and 'atmosphere' against an 'eminently public manner' on the basis of 'the collective heart of her sex' and 'hard facts' (pp. 46–7). But the clash presented in this way produces only an immaterial voice in the first instance and silence in the second. In the spectacular world of 'accepted and recognised wonders natural in an age of new revelations' (p. 48), where 'everything is remarkable nowadays; we live in an age of wonders' (p. 302), everything is reduced to the remarkable, the wonderful for the sake of its marketability, and Olive's cry, on the occasion of this clash at Miss Birdseye's, 'A voice, a *human* voice, is what we want' (p. 50, my emphasis), proclaims ironically exactly what is lost in such a world.

Verena's early judgement of Olive shows what difficult company 'personal' has to keep: 'how nervous and serious she was, how personal, how exclusive, what a force of will she had, what a concentration of purpose' (p. 69). This difficulty is detailed in Olive's use of 'personal'. She compares Mrs Farrinder to Verena: 'she was not personal enough – she was too abstract. Verena was not abstract; she seemed to have lived in imagination through all the ages' (p. 75). Her invocation of Wilde's 'critical spirit' and Pater's version of the 'Mona Lisa' here not only expresses her sense of Verena's modernity, but lays the foundation for a move from personal to personification, as Verena notes a little later when she describes Olive's ambition for her: 'She says it's a great advantage to a movement to be personified in a bright young figure . . . She says I ought to have a wide influence, if I can obtain the ear of the public' (p. 88). We know that Olive sanitises emotions towards 'individuals' by arguments for the 'public' category of 'type' (pp. 95–6), but at the same time she recognises that her philosophy is deeply personalised:

> Miss Chancellor would have been much happier if the movements she was interested in could have been carried on only by the people she liked, and if revolutions, somehow, didn't always have to begin with one's self – with internal convolutions, sacrifices, executions. A common end, unfortunately, however fine as regards a special result, does not make a community impersonal.
>
> (p. 98)

This is not only a fine diagnosis of Olive's class-position, but exposes vividly the contradictions of the movement and the self, the people one 'liked' and the necessary 'impersonal' feature of the community. The text's display of Olive recognising her capacity to personalise the public arena, to drench the seemingly objective play of feminist principles with her own idiosyncrasies, shows that special knowingness James revealed in deploying the two meanings of 'personal' when considering Sainte-Beuve: the tendency of the appropriative self-centred 'personal' to displace the self-expressive 'personal' in its responsibility to the 'public' sphere. When Olive reverses her inital comparison of Verena with Mrs Farrinder to find the girl 'abstract, platonic' in her views on 'the cruelty of man' (p. 106), her claim is that female detestation does need to be personalised ('she [Verena] didn't detest him in consequence'), but this is in the context of her worries over potential suitors for Verena, and so her prescription itself is recognisably personal in its own impetus. Olive oscillates widely in any case: it is not too long, for example, before she finds Verena 'too rancourless, too detached from conventional standards, too free from private self-reference' to take offence (p. 151).

James's word-play can have fun with his deepest preoccupations. We are told, for example, on behalf of Ransom who would not acknowledge a 'public' arena in this instance anyway – that Verena's speech at Miss Birdseye's 'was simply an intensely personal exhibition, and the person making it happened to be fascinating' (p. 54).[14] The pun reminds us of the human base for the term and its distance from the rhetorical exploitation which more usually characterises its deployment, but it also prepares us for the odd remark Verena makes, twice, about Ransom's interest in her: 'The interest you take in me isn't really controversial – a bit. It's quite personal!' (pp. 207 and 275; compare pp. 280–1). Of course that interest is 'personal', and so is that of Olive, Pardon and everyone else who circulates around Verena (despite obvious differences in motive: Olive's is sexual while Pardon has an eye to fame, for example); but why is it given to Verena to state this truism, and why does she apply it only to Ransom?

Part of the answer lies in Verena's own naïveté (her general blindness towards Olive's motives, for example), but the oddity of her remark lies in the choice of 'controversial' against 'personal'. It is prompted by the weighty sententiousness of Ransom's play on Verena's 'use' (precisely that which is suppressed in the world of commodities). 'I have a great use', proclaims Verena on behalf of 'the brilliancy of her success at the convention', to which Ransom replies with a knowingly aphoristic pomposity: 'The use of a truly amiable woman is to make some honest man happy' (pp. 206–7). Again, here, we discover James's dexterity: Ransom returns, as it were, Verena's 'use' from a public to a private sphere, alerting us to the capacity of 'controversial' itself for other forms of turning. Its looser meaning of 'disputatious' rests upon the more literal, and accurate, meaning of its etymology where it signifies a 'turning against'. Verena's choice of 'controversial' thus mimics, indeed *uses*, Ransom's turning of 'use', and it does so by a turning in its own right, by exploiting the etymological literalness of 'controversial' and so disorientating Ransom's posture of male complacency as he is forced to stutter, 'My interest in you – my interest in you' and then stop. When he begins again, it is to attempt to salvage his position by claiming of his 'interest' that, 'It is certain your discovery doesn't make it any less!' The attempt fails to work, and Verena is able to conclude the conversation with a final turning by re-invoking the more general meaning that 'controversial' carries: ' "Well, that's better," she went on; "for we needn't dispute" ' (p. 207).

A few pages later, James's play is extended in Ransom's remark on Miss Birdseye's ambition for them: 'She believes you are going to convert me privately' (p. 213). His rhetoric of self-dramatisation here ('so that I shall blaze forth, suddenly, out of the darkness of Mississippi, as a first-class proselyte: very effective and dramatic') renders the whole reform issue purely individualistic: where Miss Birdseye would, on Emersonian lines, dissociate 'private' from 'personal', would separate the responsibilities of the disinterested self from the appropriations of self-centredness, Ransom clearly intends 'privately' as a strategic substitution for 'personally' in order to persuade Verena that his interest is indeed 'controversial', a persuasion which in turn depends upon a further etymological salvation through the similar histories of 'controversial' (to turn against) and 'convert' (to turn about). If it is to be argued that these moments might exemplify, in David Howard's words, Verena's awareness that Ransom provides her with 'a private identity, a sense of self other than the continuously public self of her upbringing and life, a self, predictably of a genuine domestic and familial vocation' where 'Ransom stands for personal values against the world of publicity',[15] then we have to recognise how that argument assumes the very stability, mirrored in a conclusion that sees Verena being offered 'the private life of a public man', which the novel everywhere disavows. The pithy axioms in which Howard's position is expressed are themselves too susceptible to the schismatic schematisations of Ransom's own arguments. Furthermore, while Verena's attribution of 'personal' to Ransom may well incorporate her own image of release from her public role, the experience of the novel powerfully informs us that it is a strictly limited affair; a contraction rather than an extension of the self's relationships, an isolation of the 'personal' realm into the 'private' realm projected, like the 'public' realm, by publicity. Ransom may appear to oppose more vigorously the 'publicity' into which the 'public' has degenerated than is the case with Olive, but that is only because it is more immediately in her interests to retain the proximity between the two terms.

Howard's essay on *The Bostonians* is one of the most perceptive we have, but its argument at this point seems to be productively misleading in one further direction. Its phrasing of Ransom's offer to Verena of 'the private life of a public man' echoes that of a letter from James to Mrs Humphry Ward on 9 December 1884 while he was in the midst of writing the novel.[16] The letter comments upon *Miss Bretherton* in terms that are directly related to his own composition: 'The private history of the public woman (so to speak), the drama of her feelings, heart, soul, personal relations, and the shock, conflict, complication between those things and her publicity, her career, ambition, artistic life – this has always seemed to me a tempting, challenging subject.' The parenthesis alone suggests James's hesitancy about his own sententiousness and about the comfort of his schisms. He goes on to suggest that Ward has 'seen that concussion too simply' in not recognising how the actress in the novel would have been 'carried away' by 'the current of her artistic life, the sudden growth of her power, and the excitement, the ferocity and egotism' of her 'success'. By diminishing the potency of that success, the ending of the novel 'has a little too much of the conventional love-story',[17] a convention subtly resisted by James's own ending.

The distance between James's account of *Miss Bretherton* and *The Bostonians* emphasises the distance between the latter and the cultural perspective which relies upon too limited a posing of 'The private history of a public woman', and the distance is to be explained by precisely the intervention of publicity which deranges exactly such axiomatic judgements. One of the most disturbing effects of the novel is not only that 'private' and 'public' are refused, under publicity, a meaningful equation, but that they are revealed themselves as equally the products of that very publicity and so rendered equally distorted. When Verena finds the decisive conversation in Central Park to be an 'ordeal' that is 'so personal and so complete' (p. 285), it is because it obliges her to recognise her own factitiousness. Ransom's image of the 'preposterous puppet' (p. 293) is a figure which engineers her 'transformation' (pp. 331–2) by separating an assumed self from its performances, and it comes to be shared by Verena; she begins to repeat, for example, 'I don't loathe him – I only dislike his opinions' (p. 321; compare pp. 324, 364). The immediate impact of Ransom's image is that Verena, noted for her 'serenity' while 'exposed to the gaze of hundreds', is now 'unable to endure the contemplation of an individual'.

Verena's discomfort here is occasioned by her displacement from the ease of the public world ('the gaze of hundreds') to the experiential awkwardness of the private ('the contemplation of an individual'), and her reaction is to reverse the order, to 'detach him, to lead him off again into the general' by asking 'I am to understand, then, as your last word that you regard us as quite inferior?' Ransom's reply offers the clearest demarcation in gender terms of public and private that he has given so far:

For public, civic uses, absolutely – perfectly weak and second-rate. I know nothing more indicative of the muddled sentiment of the time than that any number of men should be found to pretend that they regard you in any other light. But privately, personally, it's another affair. In the realm of family life and the domestic affections

at which point Verena's discomfort is such that she can respond only with 'a nervous laugh' and an interruption, 'Don't say that, it's only a phrase!' (p. 294). That 'phrase' is Ransom's invocation of 'family life' and 'domestic affections', the gender-based arena of privacy's slippage into the personal which Verena always finds so threatening. Ransom's demarcation again anaesthetises the world of choice; he has 'made the idea of giving herself to a man more agreeable to her than that of giving herself to a movement' (p. 334), an idea whose schisms freeze possibilities whilst, by the glamour of publicity, seeming to offer choices. It is instructive that, just as the first 'personal' is given to Mrs Luna, so its last occurrence is on behalf of publicity itself: the twilight world of Matthias Pardon's *Vesper*, seeking 'any little personal items', not to invade privacy so much as to exploit it for the purposes of spectacle.

In commenting upon *The Bostonians*, it is difficult to avoid constructing our own discourse without relying upon the divisions that are so integrally embedded within it: male and female, personal and impersonal, private and public (even this listing displays a whole range of hierarchical preconceptions). And, indeed, such reliance is necessary since they provide such powerful items within our social vocabulary. But the experience of the novel is not only to expose the tendency to confuse these terms or to point their general disarrangements; their destabilisation is such that it becomes precarious, under the conditions of the new commerce, to see them meaningfully as opposites at all: that is, they are themselves shown to be part and parcel of publicity's reconstructions of human life, of its interventions in the changing categories whereby the self and the self's relations may be estimated. To subscribe to these oppositions, the novel tells us, is to subscribe to the stultifying fixation of the world that is concealed by publicity's promises of choice: human growth is stunted equally by Ransom and Olive.[18] David Howard has claimed, rightly, that Ransom and Verena are 'two performers in a performing world', and this captures exactly the world of the novel, although Olive's role should be added to the performative exercise.[19] Performance becomes the principal, and possibly the only, activity in a culture where the self and the reality upon which it depends become removed from their earlier autonomy by the physical liberations of the new technology and by the glittering world of choice offered by publicity. Here, the self becomes not so much disarranged as reconstructed through the manipulations of desire; becomes, as Jackson Lears puts it, 'an empty vessel to be filled and refilled according to the expectations of others and the needs of the moment'.[20] Under such conditions, the 'private' and the 'personal' are revealed as the most sustaining fictions for the self's return to substantiality, for inner-directed choice, and the irony is of course that they too are firmly enmeshed within the very system they are designed to resist: as resources for the 'real' they share publicity's deceit in disengaging product from production, relations from relation, word from object, in much the same way as any 'story of the speaker' or any advertisement.[21] Ransom's masculine persuasion of privacy, for example, clearly invokes fictions of solidity, an authenticity of experience that itself is becoming increasingly precarious in the world of consumption, the world which in turn exploits the guarantees of autonomy and integrity of earlier notions of selfhood in the interests of sale and exchange. Despite his opposition to Pardon, Ransom's promise of the 'personal' to Verena shares exactly the form of the newspaperman's search for 'any little personal items' that are demanded by his story's fiction of authenticity. In its most important sense, *The Bostonians* displays through its system of frozen choices (for the reader as well as for Verena) just how difficult it is under publicity to determine not only what one *really* wants but also what one *really* is: the 'private' and the 'personal' are shown to be as much the distortive products of spectacle and 'publicity' as is 'public' itself.

Part III
Romancing the Past:
The Europeans and the Design of Desire

7

Sincerity and Performance

'It is impossible you should be sincere; you live in the latter part of the nineteenth century', complains Wilfred Athel to Beatrice Redwing in Gissing's *A Life's Morning*. The complaint is expanded:

> Look at the position in which you stand. One moment you are a woman of the world, the next you run frantic with religious zeal, another turn and you are almost an artist, at your piano; when you are tired of all these, you become, or try to become a sort of *ingénue*. In the name of consistency, be one thing or another.[1]

Caught here is the shadow of a major nineteenth-century debate about sincerity of feeling and behaviour, authenticity of representation, the self and its presentations. This debate had engaged James half a decade earlier in *The Europeans*, in the presentation of Eugenia: its occurrence in Gissing's novel provides several of the main terms and strategies we need for an analysis of James's treatment. Gissing locates the debate as an issue of gender, opposing male singularity against female variousness. Athel continually narrows things down. He equates sincerity with consistency and instructs that 'the conditions of your birth and education' in fact forbid Beatrice's philanthropic ambitions. But, paradoxically, on behalf of his notion of sincerity, he effectively prescribes for Beatrice only a choice of roles[2] rather than a range of possibilities: giving up everything to work in the slums, surrendering herself entirely to 'the life of society', or pursuing a musical career. All these roles are conceived as mutually exclusive rather than interactive. The consistency of Athel's idea of sincerity depends on nothing more than choosing a role and sticking to it; performing that role to the exclusion of others. It is that consistency which guarantees the sincerity of the self:

147

Follow any one of these courses, and you will make of yourself a true woman. By trying to be a bit of everything you become insignificant . . . There is a self in every one of us; the end of our life is to discern it, bring it out, make it actual.

Athel's male perception of sincerity and self distorts female variousness and alterability by freezing relational possibilities into discrete roles. Beatrice's response reflects this freezing. Under the pressure of Athel's loquaciousness, she is forced into the virtually silent simplicity of a single repeated statement, 'I am sincere' which, although uttered 'with more passion than he had ever imagined her capable of uttering',[3] fails to effect diaological contact between them and only persuades Athel into an embellishment of his original position. Her variousness is forced into a single vision as, to proclaim her own sincerity, she is obliged to assume a role that is declarative and that permits none of the leeway of true conversation.

What emerges from this moment in the novel is not simply the instability of sincerity itself (within a further paradox, Athel begins by claiming 'we shall be friends none the worse for ingenuousness on both sides'), but the mingling of sincerity and performativeness, of the self and its roles, a mingling that is compounded by the assumptions it includes about gender. Such a mingling is characteristic of the new structuring of desire within a culture of consumption; in Walter Benn Michaels's words, 'an involvement with the world so central to one's sense of self that the distinction between what one is and what one wants tends to disappear'.[4] The involvement is with a world of spectacle where ideas about role, appearance and, crucially, surface and performativeness, radically reconstruct notions about self and about the sincerity which underwrites the episteme of self. James's handling of the idea of surface, through the character of Eugenia, poses important questions concerning contemporary reconstructions of self and sincerity; questions about our ingrained assumptions towards issues of artifice, the opposition between surface and depth, the dangers of the superficial and the essentialist problem that surface is all we ever honestly see. These questions have resonance for both the historicising strategies of *The Europeans* and the larger issue of James's concerns with writerly representation: they are both epistemological and aesthetic within James's understanding of history.

In *Washington Square*, James's only other novel to be composed during the late 1870s and to be set substantially in the 1840s, his concern was to track the effects of contemporary commercial and industrial activity through its initial flourishing. In *The Europeans* his concern is similar in that, again, he is engaged with the effects of the commercial world upon human behaviour and perception, but here that engagement has more to do with specific reconstructions and display of the self through the strategies of consumerism to which the late 1870s provide contemporary witness. What the novel displays is one of the great shifts in perceptions of the self experienced by nineteenth-century America, admirably and exhaustively documented most recently by Karen Halttunen:[5] the shift from the sentimental cult of sincerity during the 1830s and 1840s to a recognition during the latter part of the century of the necessity for performativeness in social manners and intercourse.

The act of setting a novel in the recent past inevitably poses a problem of potential nostalgia for a cleaner, clearer historical period. For James, as Richard Poirier and Tony Tanner have argued persuasively,[6] the 1840s were the era of Emerson and Hawthorne, and the common reading of James's *Hawthorne* or his 1877 essay on Emerson views that era as simple, pure and innocent. Such a reading has a strong element of truth, but it tends to forget, particularly in the case of Emerson, that arguments for self-reliance or moral integrity were powerfully encoded by their resistance to the developing tactics of America's first industrial revolution, to Jacksonian politics, to social unrest and to fiscal disorder. *The Europeans* itself would seem to collude in this forgetfulness; it certainly appears less available to political and economic resonance than *Washington Square* or its companion-piece, *The American*, and it is certainly difficult to conjure from the novel any specific historical cognisance. The innocence of earlier New England (with its attendant expression through the integrity of the self, of sincerity, the absolute conjunction of appearance and truth, and its distrust of what it saw as the hypocrisies of performance and surface) has an undeniable presence, but it is a considerably more complex issue than critics have allowed. James himself attests to this complexity in 1866 when he reviews the *Lettres d'Eugénie de Guérin*:[7]

Nowhere are exquisite moral rectitude and the spirit of devotion more frequent than in New England; but in New England, to a certain extent, virtue and piety seem to be nourished by vice and skepticism. A very good man or a very good woman in New England is an extremely complex being. They are as innocent as you please, but they are anything but ignorant. They travel; they hold political opinions; they are accomplished Abolitionists; they read magazines and newspapers, and write for them; they read novels and police reports; they subscribe to lyceum lectures and to great libraries; in a word, they are enlightened. The result of this freedom of enquiry is that they become profoundly self-conscious. They obtain a notion of the relation of their virtues to a thousand objects . . . and, owing to their relations with these objects, they present a myriad of reflected lights and shadows.[8]

This passage is a useful corrective to James's more familiar comments on the thinness of New England society, on its chilly morality and on the implications of these features for a writer's presentation of a society, particularly where, as we shall see, he seeks colour and the picturesque in his portrayal of *The Europeans*. We should note also the passage's resistance to a charge of parochialism on behalf of that society: it stresses an alertness to a wide range of public events, and from this alertness emerges a notion of self-consciousness that depends upon recognising relations. Here, James's final image is telling. The presentation of 'a myriad of reflected lights and shadows' bespeaks not only complexity, diversity and colour, but also a world that is potentially fragile: lights and shadows are attractive but simultaneously deceptive because their reflections belong above all to the realm of appearance, performance, mirror, surface, and social gambit which is the realm inhabited and exploited by Eugenia. In short, this is the realm of glitter which defines consumer culture. If the 1840s are in part for James the period of Emersonian sincerity, then they are also the period of all that sincerity structures itself against: a period of dazzle and deception which Emerson describes in the essay on 'Experience' in 1844. With striking prescience, Emerson's worries about the New England culture of the 1840s and its threat to the self's integrity anticipate directly the effects of consumption in the 1870s. We might note initially that the essay takes its main imagery from the operations of the eye. For a Jamesian character to 'see' is almost as important as it is to 'know'; and not only is the visual sense predominant for

Eugenia and Felix in a novel that seeks to be 'picturesque', but it is primarily to the eye that the spectacles of consumption appeal.[9] The world of Emerson's essay is a world of surface, a world which the advertising industry, the great department stores and the handbooks on etiquette of the 1870s will structure more vividly. 'All things swim and glitter. Our life is not so much threatened as our perception. Ghostlike we glide through nature, and should not know our place again', claims Emerson on behalf of a world where 'there is at last no rasping friction, but the most slippery, sliding surfaces'. Even the most intense experience, suffering, fails to find the sharp 'friction' which might claw such surfaces: 'There are moods in which we court suffering, in the hope that here at least we shall find reality, sharp peaks and edges of truth. But it turns out to be scene-painting and counter-feit . . . That, like all the rest, plays about the surface, and never introduces me into the reality'.[10] In one sense, we have here a familiar Emersonian story which opposes the relativity and sub-jectivity of the experienced world to the absoluteness of 'the great and crescive self',[11] but it would be a mistake to leave that opposition comfortingly within the realm of transcendentalist thought. When Emerson argues that 'intellectual tasting of life will not supersede muscular activity',[12] he offers an oblique reminder of the world of labour suppressed by the commodity relation which had already begun to inform perception during the 1830s.[13] This relation's emptying of content in both objects and persons for the purposes of exchange (James's major theme in *Washington Square*) constitutes the ground for the later, and more pervasive evacuations of consumption (the major theme of *The Bostonians*) which become evident during the 1870s and 1880s. The sincerity of self-reliance in the subjective world depicted in Emerson's essay ('Thus inevitably does the universe wear our color, and every object fall successively into the subject itself'[14]) veers alarmingly close to self-centredness which, as *The Bostonians* again demonstrates, is one of consumption's worst distortions.

Emerson is deliberately various about surface. As the quota-tions given above proclaim, surface, when it is opposed to depth, belongs to illusoriness; but that is only part of the story. First of all we may note that, bearing the hallmark of a universal applicability, any imputed opposition to depth becomes virtually irrelevant: 'Fox and woodchuck, hawk and snipe and bittern, when nearly seen, have no more root in the deep world than man, and are just such superficial tenants of the globe.' And not only is the opposition disavowed here, but surface itself is credited with a special reality of its own, sanctioned by modern science, as Emerson continues: 'Then the new molecular philosophy shows astronomical interspaces betwixt atom and atom, shows that the world is all outside; it has no inside.'[15] This reconstructed reality of surface, which is illusory at the same time, is strengthened further by its alliance with the principle of change, with all that resists the additional illusion and danger of the permanent:

> The secret of the illusoriness is in the necessity of a succession of moods or objects. Gladly we would anchor, but the anchorage is quicksand. This onward trick of nature is too strong for us: *Pero si muove*. When at night I look at the moon and stars, I seem stationary, and they to hurry. Our love of the real draws us to permanence, but health of body consists in circulation, and sanity of mind in variety or facility of association. We need change of objects.[16]

Change, for Emerson, is associated with a sense of the alterability of things, a sense which takes cognisance of the fact that objects, institutions, laws, any of the governing factors of life, are *made*, are constructed by human agency at the very moment when such making is being disguised and beginning to be forgotten by the reifying practices of the marketplace. His conjunction of surface, change and alterability provides, in his lecture on 'Politics' of 1840, his most complete statement on the necessity for re-making as a means of disclosing the alterable design of the state, a re-making which insists upon a view of society as 'superficial' in the potent sense offered by 'Experience', as released by surface from the illusion of depth or root:

> Let us not politely forget the fact that [the state's] institutions are not aboriginal though they existed before we were born: that they are not superior to the citizen: that every one of its institutions was once a man: that every one of its laws and usages was a man's expedient to meet a particular fact: that they are all alterable; all imitable; we may make as good; we may make better. All society is an optical illusion to the young adventurer. It looks to him massive and monumental in its

repose with certain names, men, institutions rooted like oak trees to the centre round which all arrange themselves the best they can and must arrange themselves. But the fact is Society is fluid; there are not such roots and centres but any monad there may instantly become the centre of the whole movement and compel the whole to gyrate around him.[17]

Surface is a key term for James's presentation of Eugenia and, in the Emersonian context that has been described, for the historical tactics of *The Europeans*. In the late 1870s consumption accentuates surface as part of the dazzle of spectacle and, simultaneously, surface is authorised as an agency for social and business intercourse. In the Emersonian 1840s it is recognised as the new reality of commercial and industrial practices through its suppression of labour and the systems of production. Simultaneously, through its alliance with notions of things being manufactured and consequently of their alterability, it is an important instrument for resisting the 'monumental' permanence of the new industrial age. These paradoxes are exploited by *The Europeans* as a testimony to, and anxiety about, the reconstructed authenticity of artifice.

The argument of 'Experience' is summarised in a single phrase: 'We live amid surfaces, and the true art of life is to skate well on them.'[18] Within James's critical vocabulary, 'surface' belongs to that range of terms to do with the registration and recording of his material,[19] and it applies not only to the texture of the producing temperament but also to the art-product itself. In this latter context, we find James reworking Emerson's aphorism in his preface to *The Wings of the Dove* as part of his argument for an 'attention of perusal':

> The enjoyment of a work of art, the acceptance of an irresistible illusion, constituting, to my sense, our highest experience of 'luxury', the luxury is not greatest, by my consequent measure, when the work asks for as little attention as possible. It is greatest, it is delightfully, divinely great, when we feel the surface, like the thick ice of the skater's pond, bear without cracking the strongest pressure we throw on it.[20]

The 'work' itself and the reader's necessary acceptance of its 'illusion' become virtually synonymous with the 'surface' that supports the reading experience. This is the sturdy resilience we have to confront: there is no question of that unnecessary illusion, 'depth'. James has a joke about precisely this issue in *Washington Square*. In Chapter 21, Sloper, in conversation with Mrs Almond, reiterates his conviction that Catherine will 'stick' to Townsend. Mrs Almond asks 'shall you not relent?' and the conversation continues:

> 'Shall a geometrical proposition relent? I am not so superficial.'
> 'Doesn't geometry treat of surfaces?' asked Mrs Almond . . .
> 'Yes, but it treats of them profoundly. Catherine and her young man are my surfaces; I have taken their measure.'[21]

James's play of 'superficial', 'profoundly' and 'surfaces' has a local interest for his presentation of the man of science, but it has also a clear capacity for disestablishing the notion of depth. To put it schematically, the opposition of surface and depth is a reliable index to a limited imagination. In *The Ambassadors*, for example, Strether's early confusions are summarised in his famous image of Paris:

> It hung before him this morning, the vast bright Babylon, like some huge iridescent object, a jewel brilliant and hard, in which parts were not to be discriminated nor differences comfortably marked. It twinkled and trembled and melted together; and what seemed all surface one moment seemed all depth the next.[22]

Parisian light does not permit the marking of difference, only that of resemblance, which was always, for James, a severe failing.[23] Strether's failure of dissociation is established early in the novel, during the visit to the theatre with Maria Gostrey, where he conceives his European task as dealing with 'types'. The only advance Strether is able to make is to recognise that Paris presents a greater variety of 'types' than had Woollett, and he employs an image of surface which is as unsophisticated as that of types:

> Here, on the other hand, apart from the personal and the sexual range – which might be greater or less – a series of strong stamps had been applied, as it were, from without; stamps that his observation played with as, before a glass case

on a table, it might have passed from medal to medal and from copper to gold.[24]

What is notable about Strether's judgement is not so much its 'superficial' quality ('It befell that in the drama, precisely, there was a bad woman in a yellow frock, who made a pleasant, weak, good-looking young man in perpetual evening dress do the most dreadful things'), as the limits of a discrimination which occasions one of the signal Jamesian sins, a confusing of the satisfactions of art and experience: 'the figures and faces in the stall were interchangeable with those on the stage'.[25] What counters the impoverishment of Strether's imagination in this scene is the 'freedom' of Maria Gostrey's 'extravagantly' guessing at things. Such guessing inevitably operates from the play of surfaces and performances, and its freedom has strong connections with the wider liberations from the illusions of the 'real' guaranteed by surface and artifice.

In 1883, James's essay on 'Alphonse Daudet' remembered again the argument of Emerson's 'Experience', which claimed 'We live amid surfaces.' Significantly, James's remembering occurs in the case he presents for finding Daudet 'peculiarly modern', and that modernity has as its hallmark a new consideration of the world of 'appearances', a consideration authorised by its up-to-dateness:

> Alphonse Daudet is, in truth, very modern; he has all the newly-developed, the newly-invented, perceptions . . . It is scarcely too much to say that (especially in the Parisian race), modern manners, modern nerves, modern wealth, and modern improvements, have engendered a new sense, a sense not easily named nor classified, but recognisable in all the most characteristic productions of contemporary art. It is partly physical, partly moral, and the shortest way to describe it is to say that it is a more analytic consideration of appearances. It is known by its tendency to resolve its discoveries into pictorial form . . . The appearance of things is constantly more complicated as the world grows older, and it needs a more and more patient art, a closer notation, to divide it into its parts. Of this art Alphonse Daudet has a wonderfully large allowance, and that is why I say he is peculiarly modern.

As Emerson in the 1840s had found the new reality of appearance and surface freshly confirmed at a moment of accelerated commercial change, so James in the early 1880s discovers a later confirmation in the very modernity of commerce's next major change, that from production to consumption. And both writers express their judgement in terms of perception: that is, they choose not to invoke a schismatic model of surface and depth. It is here that James recalls the argument of 'Experience', noting of Daudet that 'What he mainly sees is the great surface of life' and reiterating his point with aphoristic force: 'But life is, immensely, a matter of surface, and if our emotions in general are interesting, the *form* of those emotions has the merit of being the most definite thing about them.' Again, the play with surface is acknowledged as a liberating force; here by its resistance to the literal, its relational structure, and its 'pictorial' quality, those features which are so striking in *The Europeans*: 'His imagination is constantly at play with his theme; it has a horror of the literal, the limited; it sees an object in all its intermingled relations – on its sentimental, its pathetic, its comical, its pictorial side.'[26]

The idea of surface, imaged in *The Europeans* by the performativeness of Eugenia, provides access to the text's historicity. It is in this sense that Harry B. Henderson's judgement on the novel is instructively misleading: 'Superficially a holist historical novel written out of a critical but sympathetic understanding of Hawthorne, *The Europeans* reveals the tendency of the holist historical novel in one of its metamorphoses to become pure surface, with no effort to represent historical forces or movements at all.'[27] Henderson's opposition between 'surface' and history is itself superficial here. It invokes not only what is for James an illusory separation, but a notion of history which valorises the specifics of material at the expense of the representation that is the fullest Jamesian subject. Surface is itself an historical event; and for the age of consumption within which James is writing, it is *the* defining feature of the contemporary world in the forms of social etiquette and commercial spectacle. The spectacle engineered by the commodity relation under consumption displays, by its suppression of its own production, the surface that increasingly begins to govern social life in the 1870s. This is its new reality: this is how things are felt under the new commerce. But simultaneously surface is also a means of reconstituting essentialist, absolutist notions of the self and its behaviour which are gathered under the sentimental rubric of sincerity. Eugenia's performativeness, which is James's first major expression of the office of surface in its capacity for change and variousness, has its Emersonian accuracy as a design of the 1840s to dispel fixed social mores, and it exhibits also the main feature of contemporary consumption in the 1870s. This entanglement tests consumption and succumbs to its glamour at the same time.

Eugenia's performances belong to a further history; that of writing itself. Many of the issues generated by the social meaning of her artifice are pertinent to James's conception of composition. Richard Poirier has chosen a perfect title in 'The Performing Self'. Although his invigorating analyses of, predominantly, contemporary literature contain little that has to do with James directly, Poirier's understanding of performance is useful for some of the ways in which we can respond to the situation of Eugenia. Poirier recognises well the liberating agency of performance which operates through performance's sense of relation in its capacity for imagining alternatives,[28] but, crucially, he notes also its contradictory politics: 'Performance may, in its self-assertiveness, be radical in impulse, but it is also conservative in its recognition that the self is of necessity, if unwillingly, inclusive of all kinds of versions, absorbed from whatever source, of what that self might be.'[29]

The contradictory politics of performance, and of the surfaces whereby performance is effected, are determinant for understanding James's handling of these issues in *The Europeans*. Performance and surface are simultaneously radical and conservative in that they both threaten the advertised monumental solidity of the world of goods that is the marketplace, and are themselves the very feature of the display, the spectacle of those goods under consumption. While these contradictions need to be maintained, the present argument will be biased in favour of the more radical James not only because the conservative James has received more than a due share of critical airing, but because to do so raises further, instructive, issues on behalf of his modernity as a writer. The single most innovative characteristic of Eugenia's performativeness is its destabilising of the illusory relation between surface and depth. A useful concept here is the neo-Nietzschean critique of spatial metaphors conducted by Pierre Macherey. His analysis of what he calls the 'empiricist ideology of interiority'[30] serves as a general framework for our discussion of the novel, and reminds us of the particular intimacy between writing and criticism that is always present in James: that is, the way in which his presentation of ideas about the self through Eugenia informs his wider preoccupations with the problems of representation. The 'openness' of the text[31] eschews the pseudo-realistic notion of interiority in order to recognise the text as 'the site of an exchange',[32] a site which incorporates always otherness and alternatives. And as it is for text, so it is for the presentation of character where the concepts of relation and change enable us to question assumptions about the authenticity and integrity of the self as a social subject. Assumptions about autonomy and coherence (the commonly advocated features of the integrated self) become destabilised on the grounds of not only their suppressive but their excluding activities, thereby opening up the dialogical field of relation and exchange for its most urgent function: that of alteration.

II

Any discussion of Eugenia as a positive force in the novel still needs to take its cue from Richard Poirier and Tony Tanner. For Poirier, Eugenia is 'the lady of disguises, of manners, of artfulness', features which provide an expansion rather than a contraction of the self,[33] and it is Eugenia's performativeness that lies at the core of her social creativity.[34] She deceives, certainly, but here deception also presents occasions in which others may find liberation for their behavioural explorations: freed from a singleness of being or conduct, the variousness that is guaranteed by deception engineers a more patient field where the self's extent may be fully tested. Poirier falls short of recognising just how radical is the potential for his view of Eugenia's roles: he sees her performativeness simply as self-expression freed from the necessity of 'public self-justification' and its New England conflict as involving little more than the presence *versus* the absence of a creative imagination. Crucially, that performativeness requires the reader to recast notions of authenticity and sincerity, the very notions which are in the process of reconstruction by consumer culture as, paradoxically, the honesty of deception, the truth of artifice. We need to realise, with Poirier in a later judgement, that 'Eugenia is the kind of character in literature who is meant to escape our customary moral evaluations and to claim our admiration for her mode of being, her style, in the broadest sense of that word',[35] but such escape has to be acknowledged also as having profound implications for the new history of the self that the novel engages; as Tanner sees it, albeit rather blandly: 'Presentation of the self, "performance" of the self through "style", or a grave indifference to personal appearance in face of the world: these are some of the underlying controversies of the book.'[36]

Tanner extends his perception in noting an important exchange between Gertrude and Brand. In defence of the 'frivolous', of 'pleasure' and 'amusement', Gertrude proclaims: 'I am trying for once to be natural . . . I have been pretending, all my life; I have been dishonest; it is you that have made me so!'[37] Tanner comments:

> The Puritans' self-conceit was that their way of life represented something absolutely simple and natural, whereas the amoral Europeans were given over to concealment and pretence. But here is a spirited girl revealing that it is those honest, simple Puritans who have imposed a life of concealment and pretence on her, while it is with the adorned and eloquent Europeans that she feels most 'natural'. The paradox is potentially a deep one. Perhaps it is with the aid of art and style that we may most readily discover – and be – our most natural selves; while the attempt to deny and exclude art . . . in the interests of purity and radical integrity and godliness may involve a falsification of the self more destructive than the artifice in the flexible performances of the Baroness, for instance . . . Art might make for 'nature'.[38]

This comment is pertinently perceptive, but it wields too easily the very terms that are brought into question by the novel: natural and artifice. Tanner has a good sense of how these evaluative categories are beginning to be probed, but his context remains too local; too limited by the schema of a worldly Europeanism as opposed to a parochial New England, and hence lacking in historical specificity. Furthermore, his judgement remains caught within a schismatic perception (Europe and America, artificial and natural) that inevitably ends up by privileging one side of the opposition (here, the natural), despite its efforts to display how both sides continually interfere with each other. Much of James's early fiction plays with systems of opposites (which in another sense has to do with a concern for the choices of allegiance the reader is reqired to make), but precisely not to privilege either side. His project is threefold: to resist the anaesthetising of perception which is the result of looking at the world in binary terms (a feature, as Roland Barthes has argued, of the bourgeois temperament), to test the extent to which terms such as 'natural' and 'artificial' can be regarded as opposites in any case (hence the accuracy of Tanner's comment), and to acknowledge the reconstruction of these terms under consumption. I am thinking here of Jean Baudrillard's definitive argument that, within the codes of consumer society, 'natural' becomes displaced by the idea of 'naturalness', and, crucially for any debate about the self, 'person' becomes displaced by 'person-ality'.[39] It is in this way that the most sacred pillars of authenticity and sincerity are revealed as subject to design, to the intimate intrusions of consumption's artifice. Here, too, we see again the most fundamental paradox of the Jamesian enterprise: a commitment to the liberation of design (the manufactured art of the world which promises alterability) which is itself a function of design's system. This is why Gertrude's outburst to Brand is so pivotal for the historicity of *The Europeans*. Her opposing of the natural to pretence in the novel's setting of the 1840s properly invokes the cult of sincerity, the Emerson of 'Self-Reliance', but already, as the other Emerson of 'Experience' instructs us, that opposition is being threatened by the onset of consumption, and by the time of James's writing in the late 1870s the beginning of consumption's new and strident phase, it is rendered obsolete entirely. Art may indeed make for nature, but in the process nature is displayed as the product of design equally with anything else in the marketplace. And it is important to stress that James is not being nostalgic (not, as Tanner puts it, looking back across a certain 'shadow-line' to a mythical pre-war New England);[40] he is acknowledging a specific track of historical movement.

Gertrude not only sets the 'natural' against pretence, but she associates it with frivolity, pleasure and amusement: that is, against the obvious strands of solemnity in New England life we see focused in Brand. Her association reflects upon James's initial conception of the novel, outlined in his letter of March 1877 to William Dean Howells. He writes of the arresting possibilities of 'the tragedies in life' for his imagination, but, he continues, 'if I fix my eyes on a sun-spot I think I am able to see the prismatic colors in it'. The idea of colour suffuses James's projection of the novel, 'a very joyous little romance' on behalf of which a 'jocund muse' will offset his 'dusky fancy'. Its merit will be in 'the amount of *color* I should be able to infuse into it', and 'for the sake of the picturesque I shall play havoc with the New England background'.[41] Qualities of colour and the picturesque are invoked for not only his subject but his mode of writing. For Emerson, the picturesque was a means of resisting the deadened idioms of language and of tradition by its capacity for drama and, within the dramatic vision, for alterability.[42] James, in his 1879 study of Hawthorne, thinking back to the 1840s in general and to Emerson in particular, maintains a similar sense of the picturesque's capacity for alterability that is specifically conceived against the emerging commercial culture:

> In the United States, in those days, there were no great things to look out at (some forests and rivers); life was not in the least spectacular; society was not brilliant; the country was given up to a great material prosperity, a homely *bourgeois* activity . . . There was, therefore, among the cultivated classes, much relish for the utterances of a writer who would help one to take a picturesque view of one's internal possibilities, and to find in the landscape of the soul all sorts of fine sunrise and moonlight effects . . . To make one's self so much more interesting would help to make life interesting, and life was probably, to many of this aspiring congregation, a dream of freedom and fortitude.[43]

Gertrude seeks exactly the 'spectacular', the 'picturesque' and the 'interesting'. They are partly what she hopes for in the 'natural', and although her imagination is subject initially to the kind of dramatic foolishness (as evidenced by her reading of the *Arabian Nights*) we would find in a character like Mrs Penniman in *Washington Square*, for example (a character who shares a predilection for the 'picturesque'), she is transformed by the colour she discovers in Felix. The colour that James proclaims for the anticipated subject-matter of the novel in his letter to Howells is offered primarily on behalf of Felix (whose 'gayety and sweet audacity' produce a 'picturesque imbroglio'),[44] but in the finished version we surely associate colour more closely with Eugenia who is, indeed, 'spectacular'. Again, here, we find James's sense of history mingling with his ambitions for the style and subject of *The Europeans*.

To put it briefly, Felix's pastel colour belongs to the 1840s while Eugenia's more vivid primary colour is contemporary to the 1870s (this is one of the reasons for the respective acceptance and rejection of Felix and Eugenia in the ethos of the earlier period in New England culture). James's provisory sketch for the novel, which focuses entirely upon the figure who will become Felix and, revealingly, contains no inkling of Eugenia, employs a distinctive vocabulary to describe its character's transformative effects: under cover of the 'picturesque imbroglio' he engineers, 'the other maidens pair off with the swains who have hitherto been starved out'.[45] There is a whimsical air to James's use of pastoral terms here, but similar language appears with more direction in the novel itself on two resonant occasions. The first is our introduction to the Wentworth house in Chapter 2 where we find Gertrude's enjoyment in being alone on a Sunday morning: we are told that 'the front door of the big, unguarded home stood open, with the trustfulness of the golden age; or, what is more to the purpose, with that of New England's silvery prime' (p. 51). The second is the 'rosy light' flung by Felix's 'fancy' over the 'pastoral roughness' of New England in Chapter 4:

> He appreciated highly the fare that was set before him. There was a kind of fresh-looking abundance about it which made him think that people must have lived so in the mythological era, when they spread their tables upon the grass, replenished them from cornucopias, and had no particular need of kitchen stoves.
>
> (p. 80)

Felix's colour is simple. Here he sees the attention paid to him by the Wentworths as 'like a large sheet of clean, fine-grained drawing paper, all ready to be washed over with effective splashes of water-colour'. His colour is associated with the sincerity of his openness, his capacity for gaiety and pleasure, all of which contribute to a sense that James is seeking to modify a sense of nostalgic fondness for the pre-war era. The colour is 'rosy' (compare pp. 113, 153, 159), and we have had already Eugenia's view of Felix that 'his capacity for taking rose-coloured views was such as to vulgarise one of the prettiest of tints' (p. 59). Her view is accurate, and its accuracy may be underlined by the contrasting visual appropriations we are given in the novel's opening scene. Felix's juvenescent excitement over the new country prompts a forceful and exotic parallel for the Boston skyline: 'it shows how extremes meet . . . Instead of coming to the West we seem to have gone to the East. The way the sky touches the house-tops is just like Cairo; and the red and blue sign-boards patched over the face of everything remind one of Mahometan decoration.' (p. 41)

'The young women are not Mahometan' is Eugenia's reply, which points drily to the inappropriate terms of Felix's willingness to make connections. His exoticism, dependent upon his liking for the picturesque and local colour (p. 43), displays an artifice that is vividly estranged from its subject, estranged and inappropriate as artifice always is in unsophisticated hands. Eugenia at this point offers a visual perspective that is wholly in keeping with the reason for her visit ('to seek her fortune': p. 43): the late afternoon sunlight colours the landscape and makes it appear to her 'gilded as with gold that was fresh from the mine' (p. 42). For all her decorative powers, Eugenia's artifice is commensurate with its material, while Felix's is frequently at a considerable remove from his subject.[46] Eugenia shares his fondness for local colour, but in her design the 'colour' is in keeping with the 'local'; on the question of having a cook, for instance:

> An old negress in a yellow turban. I have set my heart upon that. I want to look out of my window and see her sitting there on the grass, against the background of those crooked, dusky little apple trees, pulling the husks off a lapful of Indian corn. That will be local colour, you know.
>
> (p. 84)

On the first occasion of James's pastoral language in the novel, we have already had Gertrude noting as part of her aloneness that 'there was no stout negress in a red turban, lowering the bucket into the great shingle-hooded well' (p. 51). This observation is offered neutrally, as a matter of fact, with no hint of exoticism. Eugenia's wish for a cook (who turns out to have a crimson turban and who shells peas: see p. 85) in this context exhibits similar features.

The point here is that while Eugenia's colour is decorative, it is more deeply embedded within the actuality of things than is Felix's, and that this distinction is bound up with the historicity of the novel, its dissociations between the Felix of the 1840s and the Eugenia of the 1870s. It is entirely appropriate that Gertrude's first sight of Felix should be as the Prince Camaralzaman from the *Arabian Nights* (she will shortly envisage Eugenia as 'the Queen of Sheba': see p. 56) and that this sight should occur at the moment of James's pastoral language which describes the 'trustfulness' of the Wentworth house (pp. 51–2). The particular form of exoticism here extends beyond an indication of the reading fantasies of a period to imply a commentary on the suitability, and consequent limitations, of Felix as a figure for the 1840s.[47] The appropriateness of Felix's figuration as Prince Camaralzaman lies in the removal of his imagination from what it perceives; the distance between the Boston skyline and his picturing of it which is so great as to render comparison itself almost absurd. Or, if not absurd, then approaching the kind of abstractness which, through its all-embracing manner (imaged otherwise through his perpetual geniality), in effect denies any meaningful correspondence between its terms and veers towards a form of absolute. The more decorative, and decorating, Eugenia is never guilty of such imagining. This is one of the reasons for the insistent literariness that James relies upon to describe Felix's impact upon Gertrude, the literariness that is presented not only by the obvious reductiveness of the *Arabian Nights*, but by more contemporary literature. When Felix narrates his picaresque history as painter, musician and actor to Gertrude, we are told of her response: 'While this periodical recital was going on Gertrude lived in a fantastic world; she seemed to herself to be reading a romance that came out in daily numbers. She had known nothing so delightful since the perusal of *Nicholas Nickleby*' (p. 94). The epithet 'fantastic' is carefully chosen to underline the distanced nature of the imaginative world Felix encourages. It refers to one feature of the later Dickens that James held reservations about when he reviewed *Our Mutual Friend* in 1865: 'In all Mr. Dickens's works the fantastic has been his great resource; and while his fancy was lively and vigorous it accomplished great things. But the fantastic, when the fancy is dead, is a very poor business.'[48] It is a feature that James notes in conjunction with an important observation on style: 'Seldom, we reflected, had we read a book so intensely *written*, so little seen, known, or felt.'[49] And this observation seems to be applicable to Felix but, again, not to Eugenia who is left clean of the kind of literariness James deploys on behalf of Felix.

Felix is a painterly version of the Dickensian 'written' in the sense James outlines. When Gertrude exclaims, much later, 'I shall never think you mean anything . . . You are too fantastic', at least he has sufficient self-knowledge to recognise 'that's a licence to say everything!' (p. 125). The indiscriminating rosy hue Felix casts over the novel's landscape belongs to that pastoral moment which embeds him within the 1840s.[50] It belongs also to the crucial lesson in perception which immediately follows that moment. We, are told that Felix 'was in love, indiscriminately, with three girls at once', and, in the midst of his fairly lumpen attempts to discriminate between them, the narrative presents our lesson:

> He had known, fortunately, many virtuous gentlewomen, but it now appeared to him that in his relations with them . . . he had been looking at pictures under glass. He perceived at present what a nuisance the glass had been – how it perverted and interfered, how it caught the reflexion of other objects and kept you walking from side to side.
>
> (p. 81)

Felix is making the distinction which grounds the novel's entire debate about perception: a distinction between an implied naturalness of looking, as direct, single, true, 'in the right light'; and the artifice of designed sight, as indirect and various, incorporating the otherness which always hovers on the margins of the eye's range. His image of the glass not only anticipates Lambert Strether's limiting reliance on a similar image in the theatre sequence of *The Ambassadors;* it also demands comparison with the image that opens and closes *The Europeans*: the mirror before which Eugenia manufactures her performances.

While Felix is discomforted by the variousness of the glass, Eugenia, in the novel's first scene, uses the mirror not only for self-decoration but for recognising the self as other through her changing moods; for precisely, in other words, the multiplicity that is to be a 'nuisance' for Felix:

> She never dropped her eyes upon his [Felix's] work; she only turned them, occasionally, as she passed, to a mirror suspended above a toilet-table on the other side of the room. Here she paused a moment, gave a pinch to her waist with her two hands, or raised these members – they were very plump and

pretty – to the multifold braids of her hair, with a movement half-caressing, half-corrective. An attentive observer might have fancied that during these periods of desultory self-inspection her face forgot its melancholy; but as soon as she neared the window again it began to proclaim that she was a very ill-pleased woman.

(pp. 33–4)

Eugenia's braids are the telling detail here as a constituent part of that more exotic otherness which stamps her style: her hair is 'always braided in a manner that suggested some Southern or Eastern, some remotely foreign, woman' (p. 35). Richard Poirier has rightly insisted upon the stylistic 'fanciness' of the novel's opening paragraph where the narrative matches the style of Eugenia herself. He notes that the appeal of such fanciness is 'largely to the enjoyment of fanciness itself, to the amusement offered by an extravagance of style'. In Eugenia, we are witness less to 'actual feelings' than to 'a performance about them', and Poirier recognises that our response to Eugenia's style is integral for our response to James's style.[51] For this alliance of style alone, we need to attend to the centrality of Eugenia's effects, her performances: the mirror which closes the novel is revealing, connected by Eugenia with a thespian simile (p. 192).

However James's opposition between Felix's glass and Eugenia's mirror, the triumph of otherness, variousness and performance over the assumedly natural sincerity of the 'right light', allows us to extend Poirier's recognition into the novel's historicism. We might begin by remembering another occurrence of the mirror in a context close to James's preoccupations: Hawthorne's reworking of Coleridge in 'The Custom-House' section of *The Scarlet Letter* at the end of the decade which provides the setting for *The Europeans*. There, Hawthorne makes his famous complaint about the atmosphere of the Custom-House being so little conducive to 'the delicate harvest of fancy and sensibility', an atmosphere where 'My imagination was a tarnished mirror.' His description of the imaginative faculty is dependent entirely upon images of reflection from bright surfaces through the play of diverse lights, and it concludes:

Glancing at the looking-glass, we behold – deep within its haunted verge – the smouldering glow of the half-extinguished anthracite, the white moonbeams on the floor, and a repetition of all the gleam and shadow of the picture, with one remove farther from the actual, and nearer to the imaginative. Then, at such an hour, and with this scene before him, if a man, sitting all alone, cannot dream strange things, and make them look like truth, he need never try to write romances.[52]

Hawthorne's mirror and its image of writing, its proclamation of light's variousness, is clearly resonant for the otherness discovered in Eugenia's mirror and it accentuates the limitations which accrue to the simple, straightforward sunlight sought by Felix's model of looking: a model which, in its turn, carries echoes of the 'broad and simple daylight' that Hawthorne both admires and regrets a little later in America.[53]

Eugenia's use of the mirror helps to establish her as a 'personality' in Baudrillard's sense, as an inhabitant of the consumer world. It is through the attractiveness and interest of Eugenia (for us as readers) that James reveals simultaneously his criticism of that world and the extent to which he is caught within it. It is here that Poirier's argument for an alliance between the styles of Eugenia and the narrative receives fresh importance. Most of the good recent readings of James in the context of consumption have tended to focus upon the later works of the turn of the century where that context is most vividly present. The richest of such readings is provided by Jean-Christophe Agnew, and he properly acknowledges the process of consumption's role throughout the range of James's fiction.[54] Most importantly, Agnew maintains that what James's characters actually produce are 'effects', effects which are 'always contrivable, alienable, acquirable' or, simply, manufactured and designed. His description of these effects may be applied directly to Eugenia:

And in the measure that social life approximates a traffic in effects, the social selves generated therein acquire the durable and resilient feature of goods. Over time, the ensemble of a person's effects – the product of the mutual effort to appropriate and to *be* appropriate – congeals into character. Character is, in turn, 'internalized as a possession,' that is, 'as something which can be either displayed or interpreted,' and the circle is completed – a circle that Raymond Williams describes, in his etymology of the word 'character' as 'an extreme of possessive individualism.'[55]

Performance, then, the calculation of effects, creates a 'sedimenta-
tion of cumulative effects', a 'mask or shell or collaborative
manufacture that solidifies with every representation'. And here
the sense of surface is revealed as the primary object of consumption: 'Theatricality and commerce mix themselves in James's
writing so as to suggest that conspicuousness itself – the exposure
of stage or shop window – burnishes its human objects.'[56]

We should not forget, however, the double project of James's
criticism and complicity, and the experiential fact that the glamour of Eugenia and James's narrative hospitality to her style *are*
undeniably attractive, partly because they involve a more sophisticated consideration of otherness. The design of 'effects' is inevitably calculated according to one's imagining of the responses of
others and it incorporates a more flexible range of human
understanding than, say, the sincerity of a character like Felix
who, for all his sunny charm, shows himself frequently to be
insensitive.[57] We need to acknowledge this more positive aspect of
James's handling of consumption on behalf of not only the
possibilities of his own art but our historical reading of that art.
The world of goods, the relations of consumption, are what we
live through, not merely what we observe (although observer
emerges as the role in which we are cast, 'just looking' at the
'society of the spectacle'); they are too embracing, too experientially intimate, to allow disengaged analysis. If Jamesian characters are given as observers rather than as experiencers, that is
their truly realistic function, and it is one of the great achieve-
ments of James's fiction to negotiate the discomfort of such
realism. The self as effect, not origin, recognises its place in a
world it has not made, but recognises also, by its ontology as an
effect, that it needs to maintain the possibility of further manufacture which may turn out to be transformative.

A further quotation from Agnew on James's general characterisation may serve to make the point:

> In place of human actors engaging one another in a material
> environment, James substitutes their properties or characteris-
> tics – fully materialized, fully animated, and fully prepared to
> take on a life of their own . . . A universe in which the
> 'properties' of goods and people imperceptibly mingle is a
> world of precarious substantiality. It is, to say the least,
> unsettling, defamiliarizing.[58]

The 'material environment' is that which is always suppressed in the consumer world as, analogously, it is always viewed with considerable hesitancy by the narrative 'fanciness' of James's style. At the same time, such suppression (and, again, this is a source of attractiveness for James) may be liberating. A world of 'properties' or 'effects' is indeed a world of 'precarious substantiating', but its 'unsettling, defamiliarizing' impact, by virtue of those very features, releases possibilities for alterability. A sense of the strangeness of things is a prerequisite for recognising the design of things and hence for realising their changeable nature. Paradoxically, then, the defamiliarizing impact of surface and performance may enable a return to the material world, the world of production, that is otherwise repressed by consumption and the commodity relation.

The difference between Felix's glass and Eugenia's mirror registers these possibilities. While Felix cannot accommodate himself to a barrier or surface of style he regards as intrusive and distortive for sincere, direct perception, Eugenia attempts to exploit that surface and its invitations to otherness and alterability for all its worth. The world of the 1840s where Felix's glass belongs, the world that images itself as one of openness, candour and sincerity, is of course neatly and familiarly captured by the volume of Emerson's *Essays* which lies in the sick-room of Mrs Acton (p. 109). Eugenia has already made the relevant comment on the Bostonians a few pages earlier: 'I am told they are very sincere; they don't tell fibs' (p. 101). It is especially striking, then, that the 'fib' she tells herself, the first one in which she is caught out, should occur in the presence of a person who is 'very ill', presided over by Emerson's volume. This is a very brief scene and one which is careful not to force itself upon our attention, but it schematises graphically the historical process that the novel registers. To Eugenia in the immediate local context, fibbing does not matter: 'who were these people to whom such fibbing was not pleasing?' she asks, and she is surely right. Her fib is a social pleasantry, designed to ease the progress of a sticky conversation, and would be a perfectly acceptable tactic of manners in the 1870s. It is not accidental that within less than a page, at the beginning of the next chapter, we are told that Felix was 'a decidedly flattering painter' (p. 111). In deciding between the fibbing of artifice and the flattering feature of candour on an ethical scale, we enter the novel's historicism; and we recognise the novel's paradoxical negotiations (as part of that historicism) of what may be assumed to be natural and sincere and what is conceived as artificial or artful and performative.[59]

The history that *The Europeans* negotiates is a history of manners, of the means whereby people conduct their intercourse in the social and commercial spheres at a time when such intercourse is being radically restructured by the habits encouraged by consumption. This history, in substantial part, has been excellently documented recently by Karen Halttunen, and the story she tells is indispensable for James's characterisation of Eugenia and for his use of the 1840s from the viewpoint of the 1870s. Drawing her evidence from fashion magazines, advice literature on etiquette and the rituals of mourning, and from domestic ceremonies such as parlour theatricals, Halttunen charts the shift (the break occurs during the 1850s) from what she terms 'sentiment' (which includes openness, candour, the cult of sincerity) as the presiding feature of manners to theatricality as a necessary social manoeuvre:

> By the 1850s and 1860s, the American middle classes were learning to distinguish between an evangelical Christian trust based on heartfelt sincerity, and bourgeois social confidence based on proper social forms; and they were deciding to rely upon the latter. They were learning to place confidence not in the sincere countenance but in the social mask; to trust not in simple dress but in elaborate disguise. Finally, they could rest secure in the knowledge that heart cannot meet heart in a world of strangers, and in the recognition that the uncloaked heart is the most dangerous acquaintance of all.[60]

The *Bazar Book of Decorum* warned in 1870 that, 'if every one acted according to his heart, the world would soon be turned upside-down'.[61]

The cult of sincerity, sentimentalism, flourished 'in its purest form'[62] between 1830 and 1850, the period James chose as setting for *The Europeans*. Its slippage into performance and the world of surface was not, of course, simply a matter of displacement. Felix, seen in the light of the Wentworth house (sincerity, 'trustfulness', prior to its cult) rather than that of Eugenia (achieved, burnished surface and performance), traces this slippage as he marks the moment where candour is obliged to construct a type, a manufactured face, of itself. It is Felix who locates the anxiety of Jacksonian America as the country experiences the accelerated industry and commerce witnessed by *Washington Square*, the anxiety of an intensely mobile culture whose inhabitants sense a placelessness in an open society where they are continually moving amongst strangers and confronting the problems of face-to-face contact, the difficulties of 'sincere' social intercourse in a world increasingly structured by the variousness (and hence, here, the deceits and hypocrisies) necessary to the new commercial forms. This anxiety expresses itself on the issue of sincerity by, paradoxically, cultivating appropriate or effective shapes for the display of candour, shapes which in turn enable subsequent performativeness.

What Felix accomplishes is to use his charm as a means of guaranteeing the effectiveness of these shapes. Eugenia acknowledges the commercial usefulness of that 'charming nature', regarding it as 'our capital' (p. 37), and Felix himself shares this sense of charm's capacities in the marketplace: 'the more charming a woman is, the more numerous, literally, are her definite social uses' (p. 132). If Felix's charm falls short of Eugenia's bright theatricality, then it does register (precisely because of that falling short) the cult of sincerity that renders the initial New England singleness of expression available for the later performances sanctioned by consumerism; a 'well-ordered consciousness' (p. 71) organises the Wentworth house where 'the simple details of the picture addressed themselves to the eye as distinctly as the items of a "sum" in addition' (p. 47). James's arithmetical analogy is entirely appropriate for a consciousness that is 'angular' (p. 186), as 'neat and well-dusted' (p. 174) as Wentworth's oddly-named office at home (the text draws our attention to the oddity) which matches, presumably, the office in Devonshire Street where (with what is, again, a telling pun) 'a large amount of highly confidential trust-business' is transacted (p. 88).[63] Terms such as 'confidence' and 'trust' are vibrant with duplicity in the 1840s, and Wentworth is certainly as capable as Eugenia and Felix, in a descending order of magnitude, of the language of commercial appropriation; there is, for example, his curious remark about Gertrude, late in the novel on the occasion of Felix's proposal: 'She has not profited as we hoped' (p. 184).

Felix inhabits that interstitial arena between, say, Wentworth and Eugenia, that cult of sincerity, where, for example, he can respond to Wentworth's assumption that 'moral grounds' are fixed and absolute by suggesting gently, 'It is sometimes very moral to change, you know' (p. 186). The cult developed styles of sincerity to compete with and to resist the styles of social performance, and in the process fell prey to the glamour of style itself. By the 1850s:

> middle-class Americans were beginning to break out of the vicious circle established by the sentimental ideal of sincerity and to embrace more avowedly theatrical cultural forms. Proper dress gradually came to be accepted as a legitimate form of disguise; proper etiquette was increasingly viewed as a means of masking and thus controlling unacceptable social impulses; and mourning ritual was coming to be a form of public theater, designed to display the perfect gentility of its participants.[64]

And during the 1870s, the period which Eugenia-Camilla-Dolores, the Baroness Munster of Silberstadt-Schreckenstein[65] and her successor Serena Merle emblematise, 'a new success literature was emerging that effectively instructed its readers to cultivate the arts of the confidence man in order to succeed in the business world'. The manipulation of others through artifice was coming to be accepted as a 'necessary executive skill', and whereas *ante bellum* advice literature had 'cautioned young men never to cultivate outward appearances at the expense of inner realities', *post bellum* success manuals 'advised their readers about how to manipulate appearances to their own advantage'.[66]

The history Halttunen documents provides clear empirical testimony concerning changing ideas of the self during the nineteenth century brought about principally by the designs of consumption, a change from what David Riesman has charted as a move from an 'inner-directed' to an 'other-directed' self, and revealing above all a sense of the body as a social construct. And it matters enormously that, in James's hands, the great stylists of the self and of the body are always female and not male.

8

The Self's Representations

I

Eugenia's mirror, strategically placed to enclose and reflect the entire novel, proposes not only the potential liberation of otherness but the place of the female within consumer culture. Rachel Bowlby has argued strongly for the connection between 'the figure of the narcissistic woman and the fact of women as consumers' in terms of the reflective/reflecting gaze:

> Seducer and seduced, possessor and possessed of one another, women and commodities flaunt their images at one another in an amorous regard which both extends and reinforces the classical picture of the young girl gazing into the mirror in love with herself. The private, solipsistic fascination of the lady at home in her boudoir, or Narcissus at one with his image in the lake, moves out into the worldly, public allure of *publicité*, the outside solicitations of advertising . . . Consumer culture transforms the narcissistic mirror into a shop window, the *glass* which reflects an idealized image of the woman (or man) who stands before it, in the form of the model she could buy or become. Through the glass, the woman sees what she wants and what she wants to be.[1]

And for the changing history of the self during the nineteenth century, from the singularity of sincerity to the variousness of performance, the mirror/window destroys the boundaries of subject and object in an 'endless reflexive interplay of consumer and consumed'. One should perhaps go further than Bowlby here and say that, instead of reading the mirror/window as smashing the 'illusion' that there is a 'meaningful distinction' between 'fake and genuine images of the self',[2] it is part of James's radicalism to recognise how consumption throws that very schism into question, how the 'genuine' is increasingly unavailable as an alternative to the 'fake'. Jean-Christophe Agnew's phrase for Serena Merle, an 'achieved market-place identity',[3] is appropriate also (albeit less vividly) to Eugenia. Both manufacture their effects (which are hence 'contrivable, alienable, acquirable')[4] and both are profoundly enigmatic.[5] Their enigmas are produced by their worlds of surface and are ultimately indecipherable within the common language of realism.

It is through the enigma of these two women that we may detect, again, James's double function of surface and performance under consumption as both liberation and imprisonment. The narrative of *The Europeans* provides two separate judgements upon Eugenia, which together graph the outlines of the shifting field we have to deal with. Early in the novel, we are told: 'nothing that the Baroness said was wholly untrue. It is but fair to add, perhaps, that nothing that she said was wholly true.'[6] That 'perhaps' and the evasiveness of 'wholly' offer due warning about assuming a reductive schism of 'untrue' and 'true', a warning (ultimately a lesson in the necessary flexibility of reading both signs and characters) reiterated later when we are instructed: 'There were several ways of understanding her: there was what she said, and there was what she meant, and there was something between the two, that was neither' (p. 156). That 'something' is undecidable, and we need to be careful not to sanitise it into being something like ambiguity or irony. It has to do with the play of performance, a play that cannot be reduced to oppositional terms such as saying and meaning, truth and lie, because it probes the practices of interpretation itself and the patterns of desire which inform those practices. Here again, we discover James's positive sense of a character's surfaces through Eugenia's special kind of openness, her availability for others in the marketplace. Leo Bersani has brilliantly expanded Poirier's reading of her 'dishonesty' as 'the margin she leaves for her own and for other people's absorbing possibilities' to see Eugenia as one who 'lives the novelistically dangerous life of a character whose reality depends on the willingness of other characters to expand their own natures by inventing one for her'. What Bersani fails to acknowledge is that Eugenia's function, as he so accurately describes it, is possible only within the simultaneous liberation and entrapment of the surfaces and signs through which consumption perpetuates itself. His account is, nevertheless, invaluable for the present argument in that it locates productively both the resistance of Eugenia's 'something' to those structures of apparent alternatives which in fact restrict perception (James's worry in *The Bostonians*), and the very attractiveness of surface and performance:

> If she lied, she would say the opposite of what she means, but 'between' her words and her meanings lies the *prospect* that the beneficently strenuous conjectures of another mind may offer some views of her meanings rich enough to make a relation seem appealing. With Eugenia, James dramatizes the possibility of an intentionality unsupported by motive, that is, of a desiring self so responsive and so indefinite that it is created entirely (but never limited) by the responses to its performances.

The lesson is to avoid the rigidifying response of, say, Charlotte, who, while having Eugenia's social practices explained to her by Gertrude, insists 'There can surely be no good reason for telling an untruth' (p. 83). Such a response, while meaningful in the 1840s, the period of the novel's setting, is clearly impossible by the 1870s, the period of the novel's composition, under the sway of that other form of truth, the truth of masks. Bersani's account enables us to see the figuration of Eugenia as exemplary for a crucial aspect of James's whole notion of character: 'She suggests the possibility of identifying character with the appreciation of character; the possibility, ultimately, of both limiting and infinitely expanding reality by defining it only *as* (and not merely through) an interested version of it'.[7] Such 'appreciation' is the major element in the project James shared with Hawthorne to liberate character from the confines of the objective world, from the illusion of 'going behind', and to liberate the reader from novelistic realism.[8] It is this element of appreciation that embeds James's writerly practice most profoundly within the issues of consumption which both structure that practice and occasion its critical attention.[9]

Eugenia is not appreciated by the New Englanders. Her foreignness, her morganatic marriage, her diffusion of origin (compounded by the associations of these features with a brother who is 'Bohemian' and 'amateur'), and her habit of doing things differently, all occasion both the fascination and distrust of the otherness which constructs spectacle and novelty. She is viewed by the Wentworths in those theatrical terms (always suggestive of inadequate apprehension) which anticipate Basil Ransom's attempts in *The Bostonians* to categorise and control that other major spectacle of James's early fiction, Verena Tarrant: 'Their attitude seemed to imply that she was a kind of conversational mountebank, attired, intellectually, in gauze and spangles' (p. 69). Oddly, in the novel which continues to negotiate the preoccupations with surface and performance focused on Eugenia, *The Portrait of a Lady*, it is left to Isabel Archer with her untutored notions of flexibility to voice the central lesson of appreciation: 'That is the great thing . . . that is the supreme good fortune: to be in a better position for appreciating people than they are for appreciating you.'[10] While Isabel's flexibility is naïve,[11] that close companion to flexibility, variousness, is exemplified in Madame Merle who is Eugenia's clear descendent.[12] Indeed the historical nexus of the 1840s/1870s, analysed in *The Europeans* through the relationship between Eugenia and Felix (where Eugenia is representative of the 1870s and Felix of the 1840s), is represented in *The Portrait of a Lady* through the relationship between Madame Merle and Isabel (who is visibly a transcendentalist figure, in alliance with the Emersonian Ralph Touchett).

Isabel is allowed to voice the lesson of appreciation because it is at this point in the novel that she begins to estimate the possibilities of Madame Merle as 'model', possibilities which include the recognition that 'I needn't be afraid of becoming too pliable; it is my fault that I am not pliable enough' (pp. 175–6). The naïve naturalism of Isabel's 'pliable' finds at this stage only one 'fault' in her model, 'that she was not natural' in the sense that 'her nature had been too much overlaid by custom and her angles too much smoothed. She had become too flexible, too supple; she was too finished, too civilized.' Isabel's judgement again invokes the opposition of the intrinsic self to the cultivated self, of sincerity to performance, of self-reliance to the self which is relational, mannered within the design of appreciation that, as we have seen, encodes both James's sense of social change and his presentation of character; 'Isabel found it difficult to think of Madame Merle as an isolated figure; she existed only in her relations with her fellow-mortals. Isabel often wondered what her relations might be with her own soul.' At least Isabel had escaped ('just sufficiently') the feeling that 'having a charming surface does not necessarily prove that one is superficial' (p. 178), but her escape does not modify her commitment to an essentialist self which is expressed most famously less than ten pages later in that central conversation with Madame Merle. Madame Merle makes the crucial case, so close to James's own practice, for the performative self (her term is 'expressive'), its surfaces ('appurtenances') and its relational nature:

> When you have lived as long as I, you will see that every human being has his shell, and that you must take the shell into account. By the shell I mean the whole envelope of circumstances. There is no such thing as an isolated man or woman; we are each of us made up of a cluster of appurtenances. What do you call one's self? Where does it begin? Where does it end? It overflows into everything that belongs to us – and then it flows back again. I know that a large part of myself is in the dresses I choose to wear. I have a great respect for *things*! One's self – for other people – is one's expression of one's self; and one's house, one's clothes, the books one reads, the company one keeps – these things are all expressive.[13]

Isabel's response is to reinforce her earlier (p. 48) testament to an Emersonian singleness of being:

> I don't know whether I succeed in expressing myself, but I know that nothing else expresses me. Nothing that belongs to me is any measure of me; on the contrary, it's a limit, a barrier, and a perfectly arbitrary one. Certainly, the clothes which, as you say, I choose to wear, don't express me; and heaven forbid they should! . . . My clothes may express the dress-maker, but they don't express me.
>
> (pp. 186–7)

Despite its fame, there is something odd about this conversation. It schematises the debate between performance and sincerity very cleanly but also rather reductively in that it inhibits a more productive, interrogative dialogue. Madame Merle's emphasis on 'expression' certainly reinvokes the category of 'appreciation' that is so necessary for performance generally within consumer culture, but the conversation, as it stands, feels undeniably flat and enclosed. The positions taken up here occur at the very end of the longest conversation in the novel; the narrative itself refuses them any further leeway. Their flatness suggests that they stand as formulae, as generalisations and – as is common in James – generalisations exist always to be tested and questioned. What the text wants is to persuade us to beware any schismatic separation of these notions of the self and to generate the interrogative dialogue refused by the conversation itself.

We may begin by noting Madame Merle's strategic choice of clothes as her principal metaphor. In an obvious sense, clothes belong to that catalogue of social rituals through which we may evidence the shifting nature of manners and the self under consumption. Clothes thus have that immediate appropriateness to the self outlined by Madame Merle; but they have also a satirical and more subversive resonance for her case in Thomas Carlyle's 'Philosophy of Clothes', published in 1838 as *Sartor Resartus*. This is not the place to debate the complex thrusts of Carlyle's text, or even James's reading of it, but its portrait of clothes is a preparation for the ways in which James opens up the seemingly closed conversation between Madame Merle and Isabel Archer for further questioning. Carlyle's ludic seriousness produces his philosophy's axioms: 'Society, which the more I think of it astonishes me the more, is founded upon Cloth', and (in a neat parody of Emerson) 'all Symbols are properly Clothes', so that 'all forms whereby Spirit manifests itself to sense, whether outwardly or in the imagination, are Clothes' where 'if the Cut betoken Intellect and Talent, so does the Colour betoken Temper and Heart'.[14] Clothes belong intimately to the construction of the self: 'For neither in tailoring nor in legislating does man proceed by mere Accident . . . In all his Modes, and habilatory endeavours, an Architectural Idea will be found lurking; his Body and the Cloth are the site and materials whereon and whereby his beautiful edifice, of a Person, is to be built.'[15] And at one point, Carlyle anticipates directly the frozen schism of the conversation in *Portrait*: 'Am I a botched mass of tailor's and cobbler's shreds, then; or a tightly-articulated, homogenous little Figure, automatic, nay alive?'[16] 'What is life without curtains?' we might be tempted to ask, remembering Eugenia as a great attender to interior design.

Carlyle's play on clothes, particularly in its gesture towards schismatic perceptions of the self, echoes through *Portrait*'s debate, alerting us to James's worries about the sealed positions on performance and sincerity, calculation and naturalness he offers in that crucial conversation. Much later, Ralph Touchett offers one of his acerbic dismissals of Gilbert Osmond, the novel's other great calculator, in terms which extend the arena of the public and the private assumed by the conversation:

> under the guise of caring only for intrinsic values, Osmond lived exclusively for the world . . . Everything he did was *pose*: – *pose* so deeply calculated that if one were not on the look-out one mistook it for impulse. Ralph had never met a man who lived so much in the land of calculation.
>
> (p. 364)

Ralph's schematisation of 'pose' and 'impulse' rehearses the earlier schisms, but the context of his judgement, as well as what we know of his temperament in general, again promotes wariness on the reader's part. He has just pictured the change in Isabel after her marriage: 'if she wore a mask, it completely covered her face. There was something fixed and mechanical in the serenity painted upon it; this was not an expression, Ralph said – it was a representation' (p. 362). There is a good deal of difference between Ralph's use of 'expression', relying upon sincerity, and Madame Merle's use which draws upon the encoding of 'appreciation'. The difference is a token of the larger shift in manners and social deployment occasioned by the changing nature of the marketplace, the shift from the valorisation of sincerity and singleness of self during the 1840s to the acceptance of performance and variousness of self during the 1870s. In other words, Ralph relies upon that earlier historical phase; and hence he misunderstands Isabel's changing shape, seeing the change pejoratively as a decline from natural and sincere 'expression' to calculated 'representation'. He is blind to historical process, shoring up his own nostalgic position here by sticking to the idea that 'Isabel had no faculty for producing calculated impressions'. He is simply wrong, since 'producing calculated impressions' is exactly what Isabel has to learn in order to live within the later historical phase,[17] as Ralph himself implicitly acknowledges when he continues his portrait: 'Her light step drew a mass of drapery behind it; her intelligent head sustained a majesty of ornament. The free, keen girl had become quite another person; what he saw was the fine lady who was supposed to represent something' (p. 363).

Ralph's opposition between the forms of Isabel, the 'free' and the 'representative', recapitulates the positions of her conversation about expression with Madame Merle. But we need to recognise how that earlier 'free' figure is just as much a product of Ralph's Emersonian leanings as her current 'representation' is, more visibly, a product of her perception of her role as Osmond's wife: the difference is that the latter is more clearly brought into the foreground and is less conducive to the reader's sympathy than the former. Ralph's Emerson is the Emerson of 'Self-Reliance' rather than 'Experience' or 'Politics'. His earlier instruction to Isabel is a direct lesson from the first of these essays, 'Judge every one and everything for yourself' (p. 231), and it matches Isabel's own temperament in assuming a singleness of self-presentation against the variousness of perspective offered by Madame Merle. The issue is not ontological solely, but extends into the matter of money. Ralph's attempted liberation of Isabel through financial gift distinctly puts into practice the precepts of the essay on 'Wealth' that Emerson published in *The Conduct of Life*, the volume of 1860 in which Emerson is acutely aware of the social and economic constraints besetting his ambitions for self-reliance and for, in Ralph Touchett's language, the 'free, keen' individual. Emerson's essay casts a different light upon the notion of 'representative', allowing us to see that Ralph's sense of the word as a pejorative term is deeply embedded within the debate about money which so concerned the historicity of *Washington Square*:

> Money is representative, and follows the nature and fortunes of the owner. The coin is a delicate meter of civil, social and moral changes. The farmer is covetous of his dollar, and with reason. It is no waif to him. He knows how many strokes of labor it represents. His bones ache with the days' work that earned it. He knows how much land it represents; – how much rain, frost, and sunshine. He knows that in the dollar he gives you so much discretion and patience, so much hoeing and threshing. Try to lift his dollar; you must lift all that weight.[18]

Representation here has all the concreteness of labour, assuming the most direct of relations between image and object, a relation where the value of a dollar bears the marks of its production. Emerson contrasts the weight of the farmer's dollar with the corresponding slightness of the speculative dollar: 'In the city, where money follows the skit of a pen or a lucky rise in exchange, it comes to be looked on as slight.' He concludes, 'I wish the farmer held it dearer, and would spend it only for real bread; force for force' on the assumption that while the farmer's dollar is 'heavy', the clerk's is 'light and nimble' and 'leaps out of his pocket; jumps on to cards and faro-tables'.[19] Emerson's metaphors ally weight to images of the real and the secure, and the absence of weight to images of social frivolity and hazard. These alliances enable his argument about the ethics of money's representative function: 'A dollar is not value, but representative of value, and, at last, of moral values . . . Wealth is mental; wealth is moral.'[20] This is not the place to invoke the full complexities of Emerson's notions of representation within his general commitment to a system of 'correspondence', but we do need to underline his insistence on the dollar's social and ethical mimetic force[21] and to recognise also that his illustrations for that force, the farmer and the clerk, clearly re-invoke the powerful debate about coined and paper money during the 1830s which had preoccupied the treatise on *Nature* in 1836[22] and which became again an urgent political issue in the years following Reconstruction. James himself had already given witness to that debate and to its resurrection in *Washington Square*.

The representation which Ralph decries in Isabel is, we may see with the aid of Emerson's essay, not simply that of Osmond's wife. It is also the representation of Ralph's money, the money which had created that social possibility in the first place. We do not know the source of the Touchett fortune, but what is clear is that its present use by Ralph corresponds less to the heavy coin of the farmer than to the light paper money of the clerk (money which, as Emerson claims, has a 'curious . . . susceptibility to metaphysical changes').[23] Such changes are not anticipated in Ralph's ambition to maintain Isabel as the 'free, keen girl', hence his disappointment at her 'susceptibility' to another mode of representation, the 'fine lady'. His historical naïveté which prefers 'expression' (the value of the farmer's dollar or coined money) to 'representation' (the clerk's dollar, or paper money) is partly the result of his fiscal confusion which, while wanting one portrait of the lady through one form of money's representative power, in fact enables its opposite. Ralph's attempted liberation of Isabel shares Emerson's faith in wealth's moral function, a faith which was reworked at the end of the decade by a figure who was thoroughly immersed in the practices of contemporary commerce: Andrew Carnegie published his essay on 'Wealth' in the *North American Review* in 1889. Both Emerson and Carnegie maintain the public responsibility of wealth. Emerson's opening argument claims that 'Everyman is a consumer, and ought to be a producer. He fails to make his place good in the world unless he not only pays his debt but also adds something to the common wealth',[24] while for Carnegie the 'ideal state' is one in which 'the surplus wealth of the few will become, in the best sense, the property of the many, because administered for the common good'.[25] Crucially, both men condemn the hoarding of wealth and insist on its dispersal. Carnegie maintains that 'Men who continue hoarding great sums all their lives, the proper use of which for public ends would work good to the community, should be made to feel that the community, in the form of the state, cannot thus be deprived of its proper share', and presents a strong argument for those sums to be distributed during the life of the distributor, not left until death, inducing 'the rich man to attend to the administration of wealth during his life, which is the end that society should always have in view, as being that by far most fruitful for the people'.[26] In more lyrical vein, Emerson presents the same case:

> Some men are born to own, and can animate all their possessions. Others cannot: their owning is not graceful; seems to be a compromise of their character; they seem to steal their own dividends. They should own who can administer, not they who hoard and conceal; not they who, the greater proprietors they are, are only the greater beggars, but they whose work carves out work for more, opens a path for all. For he is the rich man in whom the people are rich, and he is the poor man in whom the people are poor.[27]

Despite these central parallels, there are, of course, substantial differences between the positions of Emerson and Carnegie, too substantial for present attention, but Ralph Touchett both follows Emerson and anticipates Carnegie in his moral view of wealth and his strategic use of it prior to his death. Historically, he is poised at the moment where ethical notions of wealth, underpinned by metaphors of the organic and the natural, become transformed into the full force of business enterprise.[28] The transcendental liberation of money which Ralph essays through Isabel seeks the expressive representation of coined money where value has weight, but such a hope is historically destined to fix her within that other form of representation where value is light, where the social mask is a new economic necessity. Ralph's difficulties with representation and the extent to which he is caught by the very issues he seeks to avoid not only allow us to read in wider terms the seemingly closed positions announced by the conversation between Isabel and Madame Merle, but also enable us to question more radically the apparently schismatic notions of the self proposed by those positions. In short, Ralph's antagonism to Osmond's world of the 'pose' and to Madame Merle's world of surface is deeply suspect: at the very least, it encourages the reader's commitment to a polarity of sincerity and performance that the novel seeks to interrogate.

Osmond is clear in his ideal of the female, and it depends on the image of surface:

> What could be a happier gift in a companion than a quick, fanciful mind, which saved one repetitions, and reflected one's thoughts upon a scintillating surface? Osmond disliked to see his thought reproduced literally – that made it look stale and stupid; he preferred it to be brightened in the reproduction . . . this lady's intelligence was to be a silver plate, not an earthen one – a plate that he might heap up with ripe fruits, to which it would give a decorative value, so that conversation might become a sort of perpetual dessert. He found the silvery quality in perfection in Isabel; he could tap her imagination with his knuckle and make it ring.
>
> (p. 324)

His notion of conversation is not too distant from part of Basil Ransom's plans for Verena Tarrant, and the male patronage which dominates his ideal requires no further documentation. But these features should not disguise what else is going on here: the predilection for scintillation, brightness and decoration, and distaste for the staleness of forms of reproduction that are literal. Such qualities share the terminology James used on behalf of *The Europeans*, outlined in his letter of March 1877 to Howells, for 'color' and the 'picturesque',[29] and his acknowledgement in 1883 of Daudet's 'horror of the literal' and of his concern with the

'pictorial side'.[30] The silver reflection guarantees not only brightness but economic resource, a combination which allows that
reflection to be seen further as a version of the appropriative and
appropriated gaze into the shop window, registering again the
changing commercial and social habits which maintain a tacit
presence within James's general questioning of the self and its
representations.

Osmond's ideal is right in acknowledging as its object the Isabel
who admires the fact that 'Madame Merle was armed at all points;
it was a pleasure to see a person so completely equipped for the
social battle' (p. 370) and who, employing Osmond's language, is
alert to the value of 'the advantage of being like that – of having
made one's self a firm surface, a sort of corselet of silver' (p. 371).
Isabel's images are close to those of Osmond and Madame Merle,
but not indiscriminately so, as we see when she uses similar
images to describe Countess Gemini's spiritual vacuousness: 'The
Countess seemed to her to have no soul; she was like a bright
shell, with a polished surface, in which something would rattle
when you shook it' (p. 414). Isabel's developing capacity for the
necessary dissociations accompanying a sophisticated use of surface enables her to put the opposite argument in the case of Mrs
Touchett, 'a person whose nature had, as it were, so little surface
– offered so limited a face to the accretions of human contact'.
Isabel's understanding of such limitation – recognising that Mrs
Touchett's 'passive extent, in other words, was about that of a
knife-edge' and, in a wonderful simile of rigidity, that 'she was as
honest as a pair of compasses' (p. 204) – reflects Osmond's
aesthetic comparison: 'Her face is very much like some faces in
the early pictures; little, dry, definite faces, that must have had a
good deal of expression, but almost always the same one'
(p. 239). We do not have to rely solely on these judgements, since
Mrs Touchett clearly displays the schismatic bluntness of her
pragmatism: 'One either did the thing or one didn't, and what
one would have done belonged to the sphere of the irrelevant,
like the idea of a future life or of the origin of things' (p. 298).

In Mrs Touchett's paucity of surface we see once more the
formulaic response, the inflexible perspective that surface, played
upon by someone like Madame Merle or Eugenia, otherwise
ameliorates. Isabel's use of the idea of surface in her diagnoses of
Madame Merle, Countess Gemini and Mrs Touchett indicates her
progress on the road to performativeness. Through the social

representations she learns to assume, Isabel enters the processes of objectification that are necessary for the new (consumer) self as subject. She acknowledges that, 'The best way to profit by Madame Merle – this indeed Isabel had always thought – was to imitate her; to be as firm and bright as she' (p. 371), and imitating Madame Merle (or representing her, to use another of the novel's key terms) means above all the plenitude of variousness. As Osmond says to Madame Merle directly, 'yourself includes so many other selves – so much of everything. I never knew a person whose life touched so many other lives' (p. 220), and even the more limited range of Mrs Touchett manages to recognise that 'I knew she could play any part; but I understood that she played them one by one. I didn't understand that she could play two at the same time' (p. 310). The prime example of Isabel's imitation is that cultivated representativeness caught in the first image we are given of her after her marriage, 'framed in the gilded doorway' which strikes Ned Rosier as 'the picture of a gracious lady' (p. 339). In one sense, that image fixes her; it suspends her textual activity for a considerable time as the narrative attention focuses on the tale of Rosier and Pansy. But in another sense, and one that is much more important for the novel's preoccupatiôns with the issues of the 'representative', such a fixing effect displays how a woman moves to a sense of self as subject by a consciousness of self as object, a consciousness of the images cast upon her as a woman conceived as a vehicle for the representations of others. To be aware of this process, as Eugenia and Madame Merle are aware, and as Isabel learns awareness, is to engineer a degree of control over it, to be performative. To be unaware of these representations is to be limited by them, which is Pansy's fate. Pansy presents a good example of the fashioning of the female in that her main feature, obedience, becomes 'submission' (p. 343) and is a synecdoche for her availability to be formed by the representations of others; not only by those of Ned Rosier (for example pp. 340–1) and Osmond's general project whereby she remains in exquisite childhood, but by Isabel to whom 'She was like a sheet of blank paper – the ideal *jeune fille* of foreign fiction. Isabel hoped that so fair and smooth a page would be covered with an edifying text' (p. 257).[31]

Isabel's developing alertness to the necessities of the performative self, of the world as representation, inevitably reconstructs her early commitment to the essentialist, integral self. That development is traced against Casper Goodwood's apprehension of it which, naïve in matters of manners, finds her to be 'impenetrable' (p. 468) and 'so still, so smooth' (p. 471). Isabel is certainly capable of the dismantling effect of masks, as in the conversation with Madame Merle on the possibility of Lord Warburton marrying Pansy where we read, 'Isabel listened to this with a face which persisted in not reflecting the bright expressiveness of Madame Merle's' (p. 381), but Goodwood fails to understand the performative (and hence controlling and liberating) project of such masking because of his reliance on the integral self. Isabel has already recognised this reliance and its limitations:

> Oh, he was intrinsic enough; she never thought of his even looking for artificial aids . . . This gave his figure a kind of bareness and bleakness which made the accident of meeting it in one's meditations always a sort of shock; it was deficient in the social drapery which muffles the sharpness of human contact.
>
> (pp. 447–8)

The directness of social intercourse which would have been applauded, and was, indeed, necessary prior to the development of consumer culture and the modifications of manners, is now seen to be bare and bleak; and to be as anachronistic (and Goodwood is, surely, anachronistic) as is the supposition of the intrinsic self. Isabel might not want to emulate Madame Merle and, by conjunction, Osmond to the extent that they 'approached each other obliquely, as it were, and they addressed each by implication' (p. 226), but she certainly is able to appreciate the social and imaginative paucity of Goodwood who, strategically placed at the very end of the novel, still wants to maintain that 'It's too late to play a part' (p. 542), that 'we look at things as they are' (p. 543). The 'very straight path' revealed to Isabel by the liberation of Goodwood's kiss (p. 544) is in large part the direction away from essentialism towards the necessities of performance, and the directness and singularity in the path's straightness suggests the painful nature of her paradoxical freedom.

II

Representation, then, with its shifts in meaning, its reconstructions of the self, its questioning within received notions of sincerity and authenticity, is crucial to James's historicity in these novels of the late 1870s and early 1880s. It is the prevailing strategy for his most achieved performers, Baroness Munster and Madame Merle; it is the main lesson that has to be learned by Isabel Archer; and it provides the problematical arena in which Verena Tarrant focuses the activities of those who wish to possess her. By the end of the 1880s, James chose to write a novel which had everything to do with the aesthetic and political resonances of masks and performances. This was *The Tragic Muse* which negotiated the central, punning anxiety of represent/representation. *The Tragic Muse* is also a novel which continues the preoccupation of *The Bostonians* where the public and the private, the created and the uncreated self, are fraught with the instability of their struggle with each other.

The Tragic Muse calculatedly gives the first statement on representation, as it will give him the last, to Peter Sherringham: 'I am fond of representation – the representation of life: I like it better, I think, than the real thing.'[32] Sherringham is a diplomat and hence a social floater, a professional liver-away-from-home. He is thus in keeping with the displaced identities of most of the major figures in *The Europeans*, *The Portrait of a Lady* and *The Bostonians*. Such itinerancy seems to find the issue of representation particularly urgent, and it matches the dispersive world of consumption itself where the opposition between 'representation' and 'the real thing' is especially fragile and renders security of place, perception and solidity especially tenuous.

Sherringham at this stage in the novel, is alert to the simplifications of that opposition, but is simultaneously forced to confront the difficulties of questioning it in his first sustained response to Miriam Rooth, the artistic version of Baroness Munster and Madame Merle:

> It came over him suddenly that so far from there being any question of her having the histrionic nature, she simply had it in such perfection that she was always acting; that her existence was a series of parts assumed for the moment, each changed for the next, before the perpetual mirror of some curiosity or admiration or wonder – some spectatorship that she perceived or imagined in the people about her.
>
> (pp. 147–8).

Sherringham's response evinces the spectacle of spectatorship, the self imagined in the imagination of others. Experientially, this is not a comfortable concept to live with ('this idea startled him by its novelty and even lent, on the spot, a formidable, a really appalling character to Miriam Rooth'), and he continues by struggling to form an understanding of her figuration:

> It struck him abruptly that a woman whose only being was to 'make believe,' to make believe that she had any and every being that you liked, that would serve a purpose, produce a certain effect, and whose identity resided in the continuity of her personations, so that she had no moral privacy, as he phrased it to himself, but lived in a high wind of exhibition, of figuration – such a woman was a kind of monster, in whom of necessity there would be nothing to like, because there would be nothing to take hold of.

He comes close to recognising that, within spectacle, all that is solid does indeed melt into air ('there would be nothing to take hold of'). Nevertheless, the monstrosity of an identity which resides only in 'the continuity of her personations' has become by now the real character of social intercourse, as Sherringham perhaps begins to acknowledge in his choice of 'personations' over 'impersonations', which suggests graphically a more powerful retention of 'person'.

What Sherringham's response shows is, again, the problematical emergence of the new self, and 'monster' is certainly too prescriptive a term for the difficulties in articulating that emergence. So he switches the course of his account by seeking as a source for explanation something which he can 'take hold of', Miriam's face:

> The girl's very face made it vivid to him now – the discovery that she positively had no countenance of her own, but only the countenance of the occasion, a sequence, a variety (capable possibly of becoming immense), of representative movements. She was always trying them, practising them for her amusement or profit, jumping from one to the other and extending her range.

Sherringham has advanced little upon his earlier argument, but he does need to re-word the 'monster', that public shorthand for the obliteration of her 'moral privacy', and the closest he can manage is a suggested figure for absence: 'The expression that came nearest to belonging to her, as it were, was the one that came nearest to being a blank – an air of inanity when she forgot herself, watching something.' The approximative language here in fact refuses to yield that figure. Its effect is to propose the inadequacy of social vocabulary for the shift in manners that the novel witnesses; and so, finally, Sherringham is forced, in his search for expression, to rely upon a vaudevillian metaphor for Miriam's face, the same deliberately colourful metaphor employed earlier by Basil Ransom for what he regarded as the false publicity of Verena Tarrant: 'It was an elastic substance, an element of gutta-percha, like the flexibility of the gymnast, the lady who, at a music-hall, is shot from the mouth of a cannon' (p. 148).

Sherringham's additional choice of gutta-percha is striking. It is technically accurate, bearing a resemblance to india rubber, and defined by the 1890 edition of *Webster's* as a 'concrete juice', produced by various trees in the Malayan archipelago, which 'becomes soft and impressible at the temperature of boiling water, and, on cooling, retains its new shape'. Nevertheless, it is a calculatedly ugly-sounding word which draws attention to its ugliness and thus, despite its technical accuracy, to its inappropriateness to a face that is otherwise described here as 'fresh and strong, with a future in it' (p. 149). In part, its ugliness and inappropriateness hark back to his attempt to see Miriam as 'a kind of monster', but above all it is an uncomfortable word for Sherringham's efforts, and 'He coloured a little at this quickened view of the actress; he had always looked more poetically, somehow, at that priestess of art' (pp. 148–9). He needs, of course, to deconstruct the 'priestess' and the settled air of poetic perception, to question his imaginings, but for the moment he can only return to a less violent version of his vaudevillean image:

> But what was she, the priestess, when one came to think of it, but a female gymnast, a mountebank at higher wages? She didn't literally hang by her heels from a trapeze, holding a fat man in her teeth, but she made the same use of her tongue, of her eyes, of the imitative trick, that her muscular sister made of leg and jaw.
>
> (p. 149).

The discomfort Sherringham experiences here produces the awkwardness of the description he attempts of Miriam's representations, an awkwardness which illustrates the uncertainties involved in her modernity. It is Gabriel Nash who is concerned to stress Miriam's modernity, claiming 'The Tragic Muse is the great modern personage' (p. 298), and expressing delight at the prospect of her 'drawing forth the modernness of the age' (p. 410). The word 'modern' has a complex provenance in the 1880s, a provenance partly invoked by the Paterian and Wildean features of Nash himself. Its complexities are not germane to the present strain of this argument, but what is directly relevant is Nash's 'brilliant, amused, amusing vision' of ' that modernness' which sees it as 'something huge and ornamentally vulgar'. As such, it is associated with 'publicity', and the account we are given of Nash's vision bears a strikingly close resemblance to Ransom's view of the publicity which threatens Verena. Ransom's Carlylean distaste is supplanted by Nash's more sophisticated and knowing pleasure:

> Its vulgarity would rise to the grand style, like that of a railway station, and Miriam's publicity would be as big as the globe itself. All the machinery was ready, the platform laid; the facilities, the wires and bells and trumpets, the colossal, deafening newspaperism of the period – its most distinctive sign – were waiting for her, their predestined mistress, to press her foot on the spring and set them all in motion. Gabriel brushed in a large bright picture of her progress through the time and round the world, round it and round it again, from continent to continent and clime to clime; with populations and deputations, reporters and photographers, placards and interviews and banquets, steamers, railways, dollars, diamonds, speeches and artistic ruin all jumbled into her train. Regardless of expense the spectacle would be and thrilling, though somewhat monotonous, the drama – a drama more bustling than any she would put on the stage and a spectacle that would beat everything for scenery.
>
> (pp. 410–11).

While *The Bostonians* had conjoined the images of the vaudeville artist and the publicity machine in Ransom's anxieties about the spectacle of the female, *The Tragic Muse* shares these images between Sherringham and Nash where they are wielded to different effect. In the main, this is because Sherringham, unlike the 'reactionary' Ransom, is required to grow towards new knowledge and to recognise the new possibilities of spectacle rather than dismiss them as mere publicity. He is right to be distrustful and awkward in his use of the vaudevillean metaphor. Like Isabel Archer, he has to learn the more sophisticated lessons of representation, performance and surface, and the requirements of the new self. And he is right also to feel uncertain in the articulation of these changing shapes and mores.

Miriam's 'blank', the inadequate figure for absence which Sherringham's uncertainty struggles around, has, in another sense, a proper reality: that absence of production which is characteristic of any imaginary art-object, just as it is characteristic of commodities themselves. In this context, Nick Dormer's painting of Miriam, for example, is, in the most limited terms, nothing more than a representation of a representation. But at the more sophisticated level at which James suggests that 'blank' as part of his concern with his own representational efforts, his own art of writing, it becomes revealed within the general paradoxical arena where it is simultaneously imprisoning (in its abstraction and deception, the features of commodities and masks) and liberating (in its release from a knowable and codified world). James recognises the prison but, more urgently, holds to the promise of liberation through his commitment both to a relational ontology, denying closure, and to the representational, performative self of surfaces released by the new forms of commercial practices during the latter half of the nineteenth century. Fredric Jameson, writing of Ernst Bloch, reads the problem of the 'artist-novel' in a way that is helpful for these preoccupations. He argues that imaginary art-objects 'fail to ring true', that this failure is 'not accidental but inevitable', a work of art 'not being an object (which could be represented or used artistically) but a system of relationships', and concludes usefully:

> this emptiness of the work within a work, this blank canvas at the center, is the very locus of the not-yet-existent itself; and it is precisely this essentially fragmentary and aesthetically unsatisfying structure of the novel of the artist which gives it its ontological value as a form and figure of the movement of the future incomplete before us.[33]

James operates within a similar project; his loyalty to the possibilities of textual openness and its attendant freedoms for character and writer become most sharply focused on the issue of representation, particularly in a novel which, unusually for James, fails to register a remembrance of its origins. This failure is a productive failure in its release from the mystification of beginnings, its consequent distrust of closure, and hence its participation in the 'not-yet-existent', its relational dispersal of the formulae encoding both social and artistic life.[34] We witness here, again, the double nature of James's response to consumption; his resistance to formulae, to definition, is a means of resisting encoding and appropriation by others, but the tactics of that resistance (surface, performance, representation, the refusal of the essentialist self in favour of the relational self) themselves belong to the structures of commodities, to their publicity and exchangeability in the marketplace. Sherringham invokes artistic practice by employing its language to repeat the 'blank' of Miriam as a further stage in attempting some definition of her: 'What's rare in you is that you have – as I suspect, at least – no nature of your own . . . You are always playing something; there are no intervals. It's the absence of intervals, of a *fond* or background, that I don't comprehend. You're an embroidery without a canvas' (p. 163). His repetition repeats also the playfulness with Balzacian novelistic method in *The Bostonians* where James solemnly announces 'a figure is nothing without a setting' precisely in order to disrupt that relation.[35] Sherringham extends this earlier playfulness into the issues of performance and sincerity by claiming 'Your feigning may be honest, in the sense that your only feeling *is* your feigned. . . That's what I mean by the absence of a ground or of intervals. It's a kind of thing that's a labyrinth.' An embroidery without a canvas and a labyrinth are attractive because they present all the possibilities of form without the encoding intrusion of 'ground' and, as applied to the acting arts, they enable the 'personal' in the special sense that it leaves little room for what Sherringham terms 'character' (p. 164). He means this literally: earlier in the conversation, he announced his preference for acting as 'a personal art' which is threatened contemporaneously by the intrusion of 'ground' in the form of scenery. In London, 'the drama is already smothered in scenery; the interpretation scrambles off as it can', and the 'old personal impression' is now possible only in the 'poor countries', notably Italy, where the 'personal' is enabled precisely by the diminution of 'ground', of scenery:

You've seen the nudity of the stage, the poor painted, tattered screen behind, and in the empty space the histrionic figure, doing everything it knows how, in complete possession. The personality isn't our English personality, and it may not always carry us with it; but the direction is right, and it has the superiority that it's a human condition, not a mechanical one.

(pp. 158–9)

For Sherringham, then, there is a direct equation between the representative, the personal, the honest and the bareness of ground. And the equation depends above all on the plasticity of performativeness. At the end of the conversation Miriam chooses to understand his use of 'character' in its conventional association with an essential self. In response to his claim that the other arts, music and painting, are 'not personal, like yours' because they leave room for 'character', she asks 'And do you think I've got no character?' Sherringham replies: 'Delightful being, you've got a hundred!' By this, he grows towards the recognition that what Miriam represents is representation itself, a 'creature who is *all* an artist' (p. 164), and as such is an ideal image for representation disengaged from 'ground'. Later, after seeing Miriam perform for the first time, he reflects on how 'the uplifted stage and the listening house transformed her', and the transformation is such that all other forms of ground are dispensed with:

That idea of her having no character of her own came back to him with a force that made him laugh in the empty street: this was a disadvantage she was so exempt from that he appeared to himself not to have known her till tonight. Her character was simply to hold you by the particular spell; any other – the good-nature of home, the relation to her mother, her friends, her lovers, her debts, the practice of virtues or industries or vices – was not worth speaking of. These things were the fictions and shadows; the representation was the deep substance.

(p. 356)

From this point onwards, Sherringham develops a social sense of Miriam's representations, and this sense acknowledges a 'constructive' sensibility which is directly akin to the creative performativeness of Eugenia and Madame Merle: Miriam observes to Nick Dormer, late in the novel, 'You see amid what delightful alternatives one moves' (p. 545). Appreciating Miriam's 'infinite variety', he relies again upon the technical vocabulary of artistry to reinforce the proximity to James's house of fiction:

> To say she was always acting suggests too much that she was often fatiguing; for her changing face affected this particular admirer at least not as a series of masks, but as a response to perceived differences, an intensity of sensibility, or still more as something cleverly constructive, like the shifting of the scene in a play or a room with many windows. Her incarnations were incalculable, but if her present denied her past and declined responsibility for her future, it made a good thing of the hour and kept the actual very actual.
>
> (p. 419)

The place of Miriam's representations in the 'actual' of the 'present' incorporates not only the dispersal of temporal design, the 'ground' of past and future, but also the honesty of her 'feigning' which Sherringham had intended earlier in his figures of the 'embroidery without a canvas' and the 'labyrinth' as part of his attempt to explain her effect as a 'blank'. That honesty is revealed as a sincerity of technique, Sherringham's sense 'that if she was sincere it was the sincerity of execution, if she was genuine it was the genuineness of doing it well' (p. 448). It is the sincerity of performance, and Miriam herself here 'began to listen to herself, to speak dramatically, to represent' (p. 449). In an axiomatic utterance later, she claims that 'I represent, but I represent truly' (p. 493), and the truth of her representation is the truth of its machinery, not any pre-imagined objective relation.

While Sherringham appreciates Miriam's representation at a conceptual level, experientially it causes difficulties for him. He comes close again to the feelings about publicity of Basil Ransom when he worries about the image of himself as a man who 'should live on the money earned by an exhibition of the person of his still more accomplished and still more determined wife' (pp. 515–6). Miriam responds by insisting upon an entirely different notion of 'person', not the essentialist being whose potential abuse through exhibition worries Sherringham, but the performer:

> *Je vous attendais*, with the famous 'person'; of course that's the great stick they beat us with. Yes, we show it for money, those

of us who have anything to show, and some no doubt who haven't, which is the real scandal. What will you have? It's only the envelope of the idea, it's only our machinery, which ought to be conceded to us; and in proportion as the idea takes hold of us do we become unconscious of the clumsy body. Poor old 'person' – if you know what *we* think of it! If you don't forget it, that's your own affair: it shows that you're dense before the idea.

(p. 516)

Sherringham may be 'dense' experientially, but James ends the novel's debate about representation, and the novel itself, as he began it, with Sherringham; and it is at the point where Miriam's portrayal of Juliet begins to release his experiential denseness (or, in other terms, frees the embroidery from the canvas) by the machinery of her representation: 'The great trouble of his infatuation subsided, leaving behind it something tolerably deep and pure . . . he felt somehow recalled to reality by the very perfection of the representation' (p. 573).

Representation, then, is, above all, constructive. As such, it is in keeping with the 'picturesque' light in which James envisaged *The Europeans*, anticipating Oscar Wilde's aphorism in a note of 1885 that 'the true artist does not wait for life to be made picturesque for him, but sees life under picturesque conditions always'.[36] Wilde is not chosen idly for this account of sincerity, surface, performance and representation. Any reading of the three novels under present discussion cannot help but discover Wildean echoes. Madame Merle's position in that central conversation with Isabel Archer, for example, or the general project of Eugenia Munster both incorporate the 'barrier of beautiful style' announced in 1889,[37] and Miriam Rooth's notion of representation occurs immediately prior to Wilde's ironic posture for the 'pose' in 1890 as 'a formal recognition of the importance of treating life from a definite and reasoned standpoint'.[38] On the male side, Wilde's shadow over Gilbert Osmond and Gabriel Nash is hardly tacit. We shall not enter here into a case for the arena shared by Wilde and James, but merely suggest that James's handling of the complex of sincerity and representation belongs to a line of thought which achieves its richest expression in Wilde's doctrine of masks, what Lionel Trilling in writing about a version of this complex has called 'the intellectual value of the ironic posture'.[39]

When Wilde claims, for example, in his 'philosophy of clothes', 'The Truth of Masks' of 1885, that 'Costume is a growth, an evolution, and a most important, perhaps the most important, sign of the manners, customs, and mode of life of each century', and that 'Whoever understands the costume of an age understands of necessity its architecture and its surroundings also',[40] those clothes which are so expressive for Madame Merle and those decorations which are so characteristic of Eugenia do not lurk far behind.

The Wildean pose is a posture for dealing with the world, in particular with matters of art; he claims 'The Truth of Masks' is a similar posture when he talks of it as an essay which 'simply represents an artistic standpoint, and in aesthetic criticism attitude is everything'. And that 'standpoint' and 'attitude' is not fixed, not confining; it is calculatedly various: 'Not that I agree with everything that I said in this essay. There is much with which I entirely disagree.'[41] The freedom Wilde secures here is that of the contemplative spectator who provides the main figure for 'The Critic as Artist' and the cultivation of a disconnective, creative distance from the confining immediacy of experience: a necessary fictionalising of experience which refuses both singleness of being and singleness of perception where, as Trilling puts it, the human relation 'need not be fixed and categorical; it can be mercurial and improvisational'.[42] Wilde continues the argument of 'The Truth of Masks' for the improvisational pose by a concluding invocation of Hegel: 'For in art there is no such thing as a universal truth. A Truth in art is that whose contradictory is also true . . . it is only in art-criticism, and through it, that we can realize Hegel's system of contraries.'[43] It is because masks incorporate this creative distance and this improvisational variousness that they are truly 'expressive', to return to a key word in *The Portrait of a Lady*. Writing of Thomas Wainewright in 'Pen Pencil and Poison' of 1889, Wilde asserted: 'A mask tells us more than a face. These disguises intensified his personality',[44] and in 'The Critic as Artist' he maintained: 'Man is least himself when he talks in his own person. Give him a mask, and he will tell you the truth', to sustain a view that 'the objective form is the most subjective in matter'.[45] It is here that Wilde gives clearest expression to his earlier instruction to 'realize Hegel's system of contraries' by claiming: 'To arrive at what one really believes, one must speak through lips different from one's own. To know the truth one must imagine myriads of falsehoods' and here, consequently, that he provides his fullest statement on the self within the issue of sincerity and variousness:

> A little sincerity is a dangerous thing, and a great deal of it is absolutely fatal. The true critic will, indeed, always be sincere in his devotion to the principle of beauty, but he will seek for beauty in every age and in each school, and will never suffer himself to be limited to any settled custom of thought, or stereotyped mode of looking at things. He will realize himself in many forms, and by a thousand different ways, and will ever be curious of new sensations and fresh points of view. Through constant change, and constant change alone, he will find his true unity. He will not consent to be the slave of his own opinions. For what is mind but motion in the intellectual sphere? The essence of thought, as the essence of life, is growth . . . What people call insincerity is simply a method by which we can multiply our personalities.[46]

The multiplication of personalities and the realising of the self in many forms are shorthand for what Wilde had previously argued as the basis for the modernity of the 'critical spirit': the imagination of heredity which enables a release from the limits of immediate experience and action by realising 'the collective life of the race', enabling us to live 'countless lives'.[47] His position deliberately echoes Pater's case for Leonardo's 'La Gioconda' as 'the symbol of the modern idea' in its 'fancy of a perpetual life, sweeping together ten thousand experiences . . . the idea of humanity as wrought upon by, and summing up in itself, all modes of thought and life'.[48] James, in his turn, offers a more domestic version in presenting Madame Merle as 'a dweller in many lands' with 'social ties in a dozen different countries' (p. 179). All three are allied within consumption's effects by their acknowledgement of modernity's dispersal of the self understood in essentialist terms and, through that dispersal, other settled positions inevitably become available for questioning; the codes of presentation and representation, for example, which in James are always so closely entwined with notions of the self. On these matters, Wilde employs an assertive, unyielding rhetoric to make his case, but the effect of that rhetoric, by its very extravagance, is not in fact to seal the positions it advances; rather, it is to persuade us that those positions should be made available for interrogation. We may see this persuasion in his views on 'form' and 'feeling', for example, a topic which varies the general complex of sincerity and representation:

> For the real artist is he who proceeds, not from feeling to form, but from form to thought and passion . . . if he had something to say, he would probably say it, and the result would be tedious. It is just because he has no new message, that he can do beautiful work. He gains his inspiration from form, and from form purely, as an artist should. A real passion would ruin him. Whatever actually occurs is spoiled for art. All bad poetry springs from genuine feeling. To be natural is to be obvious, and to be obvious is to be inartistic.[49]

These unsettlements of self, feeling, form, sincerity and nature, dialogical in structure as in argument, are directly pertinent to the Jamesian design for liberation in both the self and the function of writing. That design belongs to what Richard Poirier has designated the 'comic sense' of James with its commitment to fiction as entertainment in order to release the reader from formulaic ethical judgements. Hawthorne's 'latitude' shared the same formal ambition, but James's advance is to rely upon the historically resonant features of manners and surfaces to make us 'expatriates of the ordinary'. The later phrase is Poirier's,[50] and it is wonderfully expressive, catching precisely that double element of alienation and inclusion which is characteristic of the self under consumption. Poirier is not interested in the effects of consumption, but his excellent account of how the play of performance and surface can be both deadening and enriching, self-centred and self-expressive, provides a good ground for tracking consumption's general re-fabrication of manners and identity. He shows well, for example, how Isabel Archer's ideal of being 'what she appeared' and appearing 'what she was'[51] is, at best, naïve in its exposure of a world consisting entirely in surfaces, but his case errs in regarding the cultivation of surface as a choice; it is not solely a matter of selection for the purposes of enriching contact with others and extending one's own possibilities, it is a matter of new social and historical realities of manners as epistemologies of self undergo radical changes. These changes are from the essentialist to the relational,[52] and they exhibit succinctly the awkwardness of commodities in the marketplace where goods are appropriated and understood not by use but by suppression of their productive history in order to maintain their magical style. That is, we purchase essentially (the acquiring of the unique object), but at the same time we perceive and behave relationally following the decline in social reputability of the direct, integral self. The conversation between Isabel and Madame Merle lays the ground for opening up this awkwardness. For James, it is not simply a question of one version of the self being historically superseded by another, but of the extent to which the fiction of the essential self may be tested for survival in circumstances which are antagonistic towards it. And the problem is not only that of survival, but of the way in which that self, sealed off from relation, in fact becomes vulnerable to purchase. Isabel's faith in the essential self renders her a cultural fetish which, as Robert Clark has noticed, is 'a sign that she has passed into a world where all things appear priceless because they have no system outside themselves in which to measure their cost', seeking an environment 'whose chief requirement is that it should give the impression that an absence of labour and history makes for beauty and art'.[53]

The question of the self in James has to do with questions of shifts in manners, of the marketplace within a consumer society, and of the practice of writing. It has to do also with the question of the female, not least because James chooses invariably to focus these issues, as he focuses so many of his major concerns, through female figures. In the world of signs whereby consumption inevitably and increasingly perpetuates itself, the woman is especially at risk by being simultaneously the interpreter and the interpreted which translates all too swiftly into the appropriator and the appropriated; inhabiting the world of signs is a relational activity, an exhibiting of the self for others. While such exhibition may hold generally true for both sexes, it is particularly characteristic of the female since a woman's identity, in male-orientated social terms, resides to such a large extent in her appearance: as Elizabeth Allen puts it, echoing John Berger, 'Men look at women, women watch themselves being looked at . . . How a woman appears can determine how she will be treated', and so to gain any degree of control over this process, women need to 'contain it, and interiorise it'.[54] The woman is an extreme and visible case of the ways in which the self under consumption is composed by the structures of representation it inhabits. Allen is partly helpful for our understanding of this composition in arguing that a woman's interiorisation of her situation involves a 'growing consciousness of her existence as object for the world, and her construction as subject out of this knowledge', learning to become the subject of existence as female by 'a conscious employment of signification, so that the woman controls how she is seen and what she represents'. But this argument is only partly true for James's fiction because it relies at root on an implied opposition between the employment of signification and a proposed essentialist self to carry out the activity: the success of the female as subject is thus seen as being 'at the cost of unadorned, unmystified communication, which the man is shown as being unable to take'.[55]

Allen's case is limited because it fails to take account of the historical shifts in manners and in notions of the self in its social relations. As a result, her sense of James's concerns with female identity – and indeed with identity in general – is wholly innocent of the re-fabrications engineered by consumption where the world of signs is not merely a display of some other, more essentialist, reality, but is the totality of the reality we apprehend. And what Allen misses out is the fact that the process of gaining control over the determining representations by others (and for others), of moving to a sense of self as subject through recognising the self as object, is above all performative. She thus misses also the real complexity of the conscious employment of signification, performance; in James's work, performance maintains the double role of reflecting the signification of the consumer world and offering a means of understanding the manufacture of that signification. The integral self may be an illusion, but it remains a necessary one, an indispensable fiction for the assumption of any relationship. It takes the shapes of performativeness partly out of a sense of its own repression (the extent to which it is not allowed the further illusion of free individual expansion), and the greater that repression (by others or by societal forces), that diminishing of the necessary illusion of the integral self, then the greater becomes its urge and need to articulate itself by other means, such as masks or performances. By these, new roles are tested out not only to seek the self's solidity but, paradoxically, to compensate for the original repression: performativeness is taken to be the opposite of sincerity for the imagined lost self in order to create the fiction of not needing that lost self in a further act of exclusion. Performance secures control over the self as object for others, as socially understandable. At the same time, by its multiplicity, it places others at a distance; it is both exploratory and self-protective.

Judith Fryer, posing the question of James's choice to write about women, asks 'What more logical way for an artist, alienated by the commercial "masculine" values of his society, to probe his own identity?' and claims that James, like Hawthorne, 'would probe the concept of self-reliance most profoundly through a heroine'.[56] James's probing has two major interests in the female envisaged within the structures of consumption. The first analyses the fate of those women, Isabel Archer and Verena Tarrant, for example, who fall prey to the appropriations of representation and publicity; who become fetishised by those appropriations and thus emptied of content and history. The notion of fetishisation, particularly in the contexts of the female and of works of art (visibly combined in the cases of Isabel and Verena), is especially useful for illuminating the central contradiction in James's concern with surface and performance which, while attempting to liberate the self from the categories of others and to liberate writing from convention, leads back into those very conditions he mistrusts. To put it another way: James's attempts to escape the abstractions and repressions of the commodity form find themselves inextricably caught up within the structure and features of that form. But, by a further contradiction, those attempts have the effect of returning us to a reminder of the manufacture that is repressed in the first place.

Theodor Adorno, in his meditation on Wagner, has provided a good instance of the ways in which these contradictions work. He notes the repressive nature of the art-object and its necessary deception:

> Works of art owe their existence to the division of labour in society, the separation of physical and mental labour. At the same time, they have their own roots in existence; their medium is not pure mind, but the mind that enters into reality and, by virtue of such movement, is able to maintain the unity of what is divided. It is this contradiction that forces works of art to make us forget that they have been made. The claim implicit in their existence and hence, too, the claim that

existence has a meaning, is the more convincing, the less they contain to remind us that they have been made, and that they owe their being to something external to themselves, namely to a mental process. Art that is no longer able to perpetrate this deception with good conscience has implicitly destroyed the only element in which it can thrive.

In this respect, the art-object is closely comparable to the character of consumer goods, but Adorno continues by suggesting that in high capitalism, under the complete hegemony of exchange-value, the art-object becomes not only problematic but programmatic, so that what is exposed is the paradoxical truth of its own artifice, its structure of manufacture:

> The social isolation of the work of art from its own production is also the measure of its immanent progress, that of its mastery of its own artistic material. All the paradoxes of art in high capitalism . . . culminate in the single paradox that it speaks of the human by virtue of its reification, and that it is only through the perfection of its character as illusion that it partakes of truth.[57]

The word 'fetish' itself bespeaks the process of this paradox. Jean Baudrillard reminds us that its customary meaning, whereby supernatural or magical properties are ascribed, involves a 'curious semantic distortion' in that its etymology signifies the opposing meaning of 'a *fabrication* an artifact, a labor of appearances and signs', revealing an 'aspect of faking, of artificial registering'.[58] Faking is making, is performing the signs that place the body, especially the female body, in its relation of fascination to desire, and the submission of the body to the system of signs is what marks the most intimate effects of the consumer world:

> The signs are there to make the body into a perfect object, a feat that has been accomplished through a long and specific labor of sophistication. Signs perfect the body into an object in which none of its real work (the work of the unconscious or psychic and social labor) can show through.[59]

Faking is making in this double sense of the sign which reveals one form of labour by repressing another: the work of 'sophistication' and the work of the 'real'. James recognises, in his portrayals of Eugenia, Madame Merle and Miriam Rooth, for example, the illusion of privileging either form over the other; and he expresses this by acknowledging the creative work of performance, representation and surface through the female as the site of change and alterability where consciousness of the self as subject is made available through an awareness of the self as object. Inevitably, James remains caught up within the structures of consumption and the commodity form which his texts attempt to subvert, but in the process of questioning that paradox he becomes alert to the possibilities inherent in those structures for revealing the making of their faking.

If, on behalf of the woman, we pursue the argument whereby under consumption the 'natural' is displaced by 'naturalness' and 'person' by 'personality', then we might conclude that the 'female' is displaced by the 'feminine'. That seems to be a problem only if we enter into the kind of privileging which is disputed by the historicity of James's texts where the 'feminine' is not to be understood as a disparaging displacement of an imagined totality of being, but as a female performative strategy, a conscious and calculated signification that is thoroughly bound up with the deceptions of consumptive forms ('real' history) while at the same time revelatory of their manufacture. Consequently the female site of alterability offers, above all, a possibility for transformation precisely through the tactics of performance and the surfaces of the masks which constitute social intercourse.

The theatre, metaphorically and literally so central to the Jamesian aesthetic, provides the most accurate image for such tactics, and recent work by Helene Keyssar on contemporary feminist theatre suggests the major categories in which they can be considered. Keyssar finds the distinctively female key to be role-playing and its capacity for dispersing essentialist performance and presentation where 'the impetus is not towards self-recognition and revelation of a "true" self but towards recognition of others and a concomitant transformation of the self and the world'.[60] The shift is from the conservative stability of recognition to the risks of transformation which guarantees the authenticity of experience through alterability: 'Drama that embraces transformations inspires and asserts the possibility for change; roles and role-playing, not hidden essences, merit attention . . . no one, neither woman nor man, is restricted from becoming other.'[61] Comparable is the general project within contemporary feminist poetry, best exemplified in the work of Adrienne Rich, to reject the intolerance of power-as-force by the variousness of power-to-transform.

If faking is making in a transformative sense, as it appears to be in James's insistence on its female characteristic, then performance accommodates the rich paradox of the trope 'as if' which, in Hans Vaihinger's formulation, posits the real and the temporary simultaneously.[62] That is, a performance is recognised at once as temporary in terms of its periodicity and yet as real and concrete for its immediate occasion. It suggests the world as provisional, perpetually looking to the site of the future: it is prospective, exhibiting a choice for an imagined projective role. At the level of writing, we have here again the Hawthornesque 'latitude' for character and for reader. At the level of James's enquiries into the issues of the self, we have the occasion for alterability. But at the same time James is alert to the social glamour of performance, a glamour which partakes of the design of objects for the desire of others within the commodity relation. James's raising of the notions of sincerity, authenticity, the natural and the integrated self against the notions of artifice, performance, representation and surface, does not privilege either side. Its effect is to recognise the historicity of the urge to read those terms as competing, to recognise the extent to which each produces and relies upon the other. What distinguishes Eugenia from her successors, Madame Merle and Miriam Rooth, is the very excess of her performances where later performances are more easily accommodated (by the social acceptability of style in a more recent period, or by the role itself of actress). By going extravagantly beyond the norm of the existing manners and mores of New England life, her play ends up by enabling them to reinforce themselves (as we see in her final exclusion, and in the limited possibilities witnessed in the alliance between Felix and Gertrude).

Eugenia's play and its reinforcements extend beyond the localism of the 1840s. The possibilities for transformation within her play are a feature of the late 1870s, and her style (her main characteristic) is, through its glamour and novelty, closely allied to that of the commodity in its artfulness. We can see the specificity of James's project here by reminding ourselves briefly of the model of a different form of artfulness he presents in *The American*, the companion-piece to *The Europeans* where his main concern is with the way in which the language of commerce becomes translated into that of art. There the artful figure is Noemie Nioche, and we encounter her first when she is engaged in her version of representation, copying the old masters in the Salon Carré of the Louvre:

> The cultivation of the fine arts appeared to necessitate, to her mind, a great deal of by-play, a great standing off with folded arms and head drooping from side to side, stroking of a dimpled chin with a dimpled hand, sighing and frowning and patting of the foot, fumbling in disordered tresses for wandering hairpins.[63]

This is extravagance of a different order, coquettish, crudely dramatic and confined to display only. Its comedy, however, has a serious point in comparison to Eugenia in that it trivialises the issue of performance and acts as a warning of how not to read it. The description is genuinely frivolous, genuinely superficial, and its distance from the performativeness of Eugenia precludes any attribution of those features to the Baroness where James's project is to test out the glamour itself of the commodity form.

Through Eugenia, James attempts an imaginative and romantic (in Hawthorne's sense) re-writing of the commodity form by stressing its glamour, uniqueness and resistance to confinement. He aestheticises the commercial object in the late 1870s within the earlier history of the 1840s in order to display the extent to which an unconscious valorisation of the terms used to describe commodities (surface, performance and representation) perpetuates those terms in an apparently innocent manner. Eugenia's artfulness provides grounds for questioning the bourgeois respectability of the Wentworths, and thus also the nascence of American commercial expansion which commences its more visible phase in the 1870s. But at the same time her artfulness is obliged to assume the features whereby that respectability will achieve commercial success in the age of consumption. Eugenia's relation to New England is not far removed from the relation of the 'romance' to the 'novel', where the extravagantly literary seeks to establish itself as an arena for interrogating and interpreting the seemingly given of factuality, realism and history. James's achievement is to display how the tactics of that interpretation, the tactics of 'latitude', not only comment upon but reproduce history.

Notes and References

Introduction: The Jamesian Balloon

1. H.G. Wells, *Boon* (London: T. Fisher Unwin, 1915), pp.102–3, 106.
2. Stuart Hutchinson, *Henry James: An American as Modernist* (London and Totowa, NJ: Vision Press and Barnes & Noble, 1982), p.15
3. Robert Louis Stevenson, 'A Humble Remonstrance', *Longman's Magazine* (1884): reprinted in Janet Adam Smith (ed.), *Henry James and Robert Louis Stevenson. A Record of Friendship and Criticism* (London: Rupert Hart-Davis, 1948), p.92. James wrote to Stevenson after reading his 'Remonstrance', and Stevenson replied (a letter dated 8 December 1884) with an elaboration of his position:

   > People suppose it is 'the stuff' that interests them; they think, for instance, that the prodigious fine thoughts and sentiments in Shakespeare impress by their own weight, not understanding that the upolished diamond is but a stone. They think that striking situations, or good dialogue, are got by studying life; they will not rise to understand that they are prepared by deliberate artifice and set off by painful suppressions.
   > (reprinted in Smith, *Henry James and RLS*, p.103)

   Stevenson gives here a clear version of one of James's major imperatives: his constant stricture against the confusions between the satisfactions of art and those of experience, which so beset the realist claims for fiction.
4. James, Preface to *The Aspern Papers*, in Leon Edel (ed.), *Henry James: Literary Criticism. French Writers, Other European Writers, The Prefaces to the New York Edition* (New York: The Library of America, 1984), p.1176.
5. James, Preface to *The American*, in Edel, *Literary Criticism, French Writers*, pp.1059, 1060.
6. Ibid., pp.1063, 1064, 1068.
7. Ibid., p.1064.
8. Ibid., pp.1057–8. Michael T. Gilmore has rightly asserted of the years from 1832 to 1860 that 'The American romantic period was the era of the marketplace' (*American Romanticism and the Marketplace*, Chicago and London: University of Chicago Press, 1985, p.1).
9. James McNeill Whistler, 'The Ten O'Clock', in *The Gentle Art of Making Enemies* (London: Heineman, 1890), p.15. I find it interesting that a large part of James's critical reception has been beset by a

version of this same misconception in its reliance upon what are assumed to be his experiential limitations. Wayne W. Westbrook exemplifies this when he writes: 'Henry James's understanding of finance is blocked by a reserve that allows him to present it only in abstractions, never portraying the marketplace or the business-financiers as they really are' (*Wall Street in the American Novel*, New York and London: New York Univesity Press, 1980, p.43). There is nothing to be achieved in reading James as a failed Dreiser, and Westbrook misses the entire point of the 'witness' James's fiction properly bears. Jamesian abstractions are precisely the most intimate effects of the marketplace upon human relations: it is precisely those abstractions which reveal the real history of the fiscal changes during the late nineteenth century, particularly in their display of the process whereby the advent of paper money engenders new practices of speculation and transaction: the new arts of power which are a permanent concern for the novels. In any case, and from another angle, it is simply wrong to see James in terms of such removal: as Mark Seltzer, Michael Anesko and Stuart Culver have shown, James's project for the 'art of fiction' in his essays and prefaces (unparalleled by any of his contemporaries) and his detailed involvement with the publishing world belong closely to the general social movement of professionalisation during the late nineteenth century (see Mark Seltzer, *Henry James and the Art of Power*, Ithaca, NY, and London: Cornell University Press, 1984; Michael Anesko, *'Friction with the Market': Henry James and the Profession of Authorship*, New York and Oxford: Oxford University Press, 1986; and Stuart Culver, 'Representing the Author: Henry James, Intellectual Property and the Work of Writing', in Ian F.A. Bell (ed.), *Henry James: Fiction as History*, London and Totowa, NJ: Vision Press and Barnes & Noble, 1984).

10.   Jean-Christophe Agnew, 'The Consuming Vision of Henry James', in R.W. Fox and T.J. Jackson Lears (eds) *The Culture of Consumption, Critical Essays in American History 1880–1980* (New York: Pantheon Books, 1983), pp.75, 73. Whilst agreeing substantially with Agnew's historical-materialist position, I want to interject a note of caution since we might be in danger of leaving the special 'witness' to consumption which James's fiction affords as in itself too unproblematically mimetic. James would find it too comfortable to read the competing claims of realism and romance as being 'in the balance'. Their competition is above all unsettling for him. A more formalist a-historical critic like Stuart Hutchinson, unwittingly perhaps, engenders a sense of what is at stake here in his rephrasing of the debate. Writing of *The Bostonians* (arguably, along with *The Princess Casamassima*, James's closest exploitations of the realist mode), he asks: 'When the bonds of a recently invented country are as indistinguishable as they are in *The Blithedale Romance, The Confidence Man, Adventures of Huckleberry Finn* and *The Bostonians* itself, how can any artist be sure his own invention is the real thing?', and in pursuing his question, Hutchinson employs a revealing financial metaphor: 'Nothing comes pre-packed in a

sustaining historical and social shape to an American writer. Like
Verena, the nation may take *any* shape. This blank cheque which is
offered to American writers "partly" explains their almost inevitable problems with form, structure and perspective' (Hutchinson,
Henry James, pp.45, 59). The issue here is that of counterfeit: the
alarming fiscal instability that resulted from the bank wars of the
1830s, the concomitant debate over coined and paper money that
continued through to the end of the century and the epidemic of
speculation and accelerated commercial development, all of which
receive 'witness' in *Washington Square*. Counterfeit comes close to
performance: both rely on invention, variousness and the dispersal
of the unified self which are the great Jamesian subjects. The
matter of trust in all its forms (financial, social and aesthetic) is
deeply embroiled in the general issues of representation which
James's reworking of the Romance negotiates, and confidence, the
antidote to counterfeit, becomes the one thing that is increasingly
impossible in the world of display and gesture that is the marketplace. John Vernon runs the risk of exaggerating the issue in
arguing that 'As long as paper money has existed, it has been
tempting to suggest that all fiction (like all art) is counterfeit'
(*Money and Fiction. Literary Realism in the Nineteenth and Early
Twentieth Centuries*, Ithaca, NY and London: Cornell University
Press, 1984, p.97), but his argument underlines the materially
destabilised world James confronted. Faking and making are
closely allied here and, such are the distortions involved, we
recognise that the issue is not that simple and a-historical matter of
testing the 'real' against the 'counterfeit', but of the criteria
whereby we have more confidence in some counterfeits, or representations, than in others. Mr. Wentworth in *The Europeans*, for
example, makes his money by conducting 'a large amount of highly
confidential trust-business' (note how the commercial vocabulary of
the 1870s invests these key moral terms of the 1840s with a
powerful ambiguity) and he exhibits a notorious distrust for that
other form of counterfeit, Felix Young's offer to paint his portrait.
How do we respond to that distrust? Do we haughtily dismiss
Wentworth as a philistine, or sympathise with the limitations of his
New England orthodoxies perhaps? That distrust surely belongs to
the profession James outlines for Wentworth, to the uncertainties
of counterfeit which are common to the affairs of both art and
business. And those uncertainties point towards a world that is
becoming alien, where characters are obliged to operate within a
more public arena, to *perform* at the behest of the changing social
demands of a consumptive culture in the way that Eugenia,
Madame Merle, Verena Tarrant and Miriam Rooth perform. Vernon summarises the general issue of the new reality well:

> 'Realism' does not refer to a phenomenon by which the novel
> suddenly opened its eyes and discovered reality. Rather, the
> novel in the nineteenth century was part of a general cultural
> shift that was creating the reality we see in fiction – creating a

world in which individuals were forced more than ever to act publicly and conspicuously to fulfil their private ambitions and desires.
(p.103)

This performativeness is itself the paradoxical authenticity of the history witnessed by James's novels in that it is engendered by uncertainties which are read most productively in terms of economics. Where *The Europeans* and *Washington Square* are concerned, for example, we have two novels written during a space of two years, both of which choose their settings in the speculative 1830s and 1840s, a period whose fiscal disorder is recapitulated during the period of the novels' composition. That disorder is decisive for the counterfeit of art, as Neil Schmitz has noted: 'When bullion is scarce and paper money plentiful, when the right ratio is disregarded, there is a subsequent disconnection of language from reality. A pathological condition appears in discourse, the need to inflate meaning and value' ('Mark Twain, Henry James, and Jacksonian Dreaming', *Criticism*, 27, Winter 1985, p.158). Inflation underwrites performativeness, and the progress of my present argument from *Washington Square* through *The Bostonians* to *The Europeans* is designed to show exactly this movement from the material disorder of financial speculation to its inevitable consequences in the displays of consumption. It is within this movement that the Jamesian concerns with representation and the self may most productively be understood.

11. William Leiss, *The Limits to Satisfaction: An Essay on the Problems of Needs and Commodities* (Toronto and Buffalo: University of Toronto Press, 1976), pp.88–9. Daniel Horowitz, similarly, has noted the agitation of consumption: 'In a world where appearances and symbolism took on more weight than goods and experiences themselves, consumers became restless, anxious, and frenetic' (*The Morality of Spending: Attitudes toward the Consumer Society in America, 1875–1940* (Baltimore and London: The Johns Hopkins University Press, 1985), p.xxvii.

12. James, 'Alphonse Daudet', in Edel, *Literary Criticism. French Writers*, pp.239, 242.

13. Leo Bersani, *A Future for Astyanax: Character and Desire in Literature* (New York: Columbia University Press, 1984), p.148.

14. 'James's fiction is notoriously dense in . . . psychological detail, but it is remarkably resistant to an interest in psychological depth . . . the grounds for what we might think of as a "vertical" motive (plunging down "into" personality), eventually disappear from James's fiction' (Bersani, *A Future for Astyanax*, pp.130–1). Broadly, I am in agreement with Bersani's position, but in stressing 'surface' *at the expense* of 'depth,' he runs the risk of privileging the former over the latter in a way that might distort what actually does go on in a James novel. We need to recognise also the more tensile procedure noted by Evan Carton:

James demands of art and of personal life both surface (formal definition and control) and depth (moral and emotional susceptibility). He also fears the dominion of each, and his effort to hold the two in a state of tension accounts for his distinctive critical tendency to cast matters of literary mechanics in intimate human terms and to depict the most affecting human situations as technical challenges.
('Henry James the Critic', *Raritan*, 1986, p.130).

Carton's formalism lacks the historical density we may persuade out of Bersani's argument. Nevertheless, we should remember that James's permanent hostility to schismatic perception (while maintaining the reconstructed accuracy of surface), would secure the realignment of the relationship between the two terms only within their new history, that of consumption's displays.

15. Bersani, *A Future for Astyanax*, p.132.
16. Ibid, p.138.
17. Bersani has extended this point to underline the psychology of the dispersed self that I take to be one of James's most decisive interventions in the aesthetics of fiction:

An imagination of the deconstructed, perhaps even demolished, self is the necessary point of departure for an authentically civilizing skepticism about the nature of our desires and the nature of our being . . . in the literary universe of partial selves . . . there is a greater likelihood of movements *among* different forms of desire and of being than in a world of fixed character structures. For what we call character is also a partial self. Its appearance of completeness, of wholeness, may be nothing more than the illusion created by the *centralizing* of a partial self. Such centralization involves both the organization of our desires into psychic structures and the expulsion of nonstructurable desires. Character, in short, is also a piece of a person; it has the factitious coherence of all obsessions. Only the mobility of desublimated desires preserves the mobility of being itself. An exuberant indefiniteness about our own identity can both preserve the heterogeneity of our desires and rescue us from the totalitarian insistence natural to all desire. (Bersani, *A Future for Astyanax*, pp.313–14).

It is not difficult to see the relevance of Bersani's argument for the psychology and presentation of Jamesian character: what is equally important is to see this dispersed and mobile self as the product also of designs for selling: of the advertisements which effect consumption by their literal dismantling of the body and their playing upon the variousness of desire disengaged from any totalising notion of the self.

18. Seltzer, *Henry James and the Art of Power*, p.24.
19. Ibid, pp.169, 144. Cf. William Greenslade, 'The Power of Advertising: Chad Newsome and the Meaning of Paris in *The Ambassadors*', *English Literary History*, 49 (1982), pp.99–122.

20. Guy Debord, *Society of the Spectacle* (Detroit: Black & Red, 1973), paragraph 10.
21. James, 'Alphonse Daudet', p.230. Robert Clark, in seeking a different kind of historical reading for James, understands his art of surface as his 'characteristic elegance of suggestion' which resists the Eliotic 'realistic' truth of fiction. Clark finds parallels in the 'retinal effect' of the Impressionists and the Cubists' representation of 'temporally discrete perspectives' in the 'same plane' in order to place James within the 'late nineteenth century shifts from realism to relativism' where there is a movement from a 'transparent mimesis' to a 'foregrounding of the techniques that mark out the aesthetic object as a distinct commodity'. But, he argues, these parallels also 'mask an important peculiarity of James's work: what he represents is not the perception of an object-in-itself but the perception of a fiction' ('The Transatlantic Romance of Henry James' in Richard Gray (ed.), *American Fiction: New Readings*, London and Totowa, NJ: Vision Press and Barnes & Noble, 1983, p.108). The point is that this representation is not a 'peculiarity' unless it is intended as a 'singularity'; this perception is the very feature of James's most alert historicism since, within the images whereby consumption reconstructs the experiental world, the 'object-in-itself' can never retain such innocence. Nevertheless, Clark is right in his implication that James's fiction is very much a spatial affair because consumption itself relies upon space at the expense of time (the display and spectacle of commodities suppress always the history of their production). Georges Poulet's brief but dense pages on James recognise his spatial art as an act of suppression in its fear for the loss of the self amongst an 'inexhaustible reservoir of memories', a fear which occasions a specific tactic: 'Instead of allowing memory constantly to enlarge and deepen the field of consciousness, James acts to restrain it, to give it limits. These limits are those of the present. Life is a surface affair'. Poulet thus argues:

> The Jamesian novel, therefore, will most often be divested of the past. Its characters undergo an infinity of experiences and incessantly discover themselves in new relationships with each other, but these experiences and relationships are oftenest the direct effect of present junctures; they are a new disposition of beings that corresponds to their displacement. An affair of the surface, and not one of depth; a movement in space, and not one in time. Ordinarily the Jamesian character has little duration; or rather his duration is not composed, like that of the Flaubertian or Tolstoian character, of a temporal density; between his immediate existence and the depths of his mind stretch no thick layers of memories. *Studies in Human Time* (New York: Harper, 1959, pp.350–1).

But history is not only an affair of memory, of the past, particularly in an American context which is distinctly spatial. Frederick J.

Hoffman touches on this when he claims that the 'American self' has always been 'a man in motion, a man occupying a space so long as it served him, and always aware that there were other spaces to inhabit'. Implicit here is the great Jamesian lesson of variousness, of the alternatives available for design and re-design in the sense that 'historical progress is most satisfactorily described as a succession of events in which the self *experiences* space, knows it in the act of occupying it, and alters its form to adjust to the experience of knowing it' ('Freedom and Conscious Form: Henry James and the American Self', *Virginia Quarterly Review*, 37, 1961, pp.269, 270–1). James in general, then, belongs to the singularly American tradition of history as space rather than as time, and within which resides the key notion of alterability. And to sketch broadly, this tradition is one of the reasons why the consumer society developed its origins and its practices so stridently and so rapidly in America rather than anywhere else.

22. The post-modernist notion that the unity of subject is wholly dependent upon a suppression of those others against whose difference it locates itself is a reworking of that decentring project so characteristic of American thought during the nineteenth century and achieving its apotheosis in Henry Adams's claim that 'The object of study is the garment, not the figure' (*The Education of Henry Adams*, ed. Ernest Samuels, Boston, MA: Houghton Mifflin, 1973, p.xxx). An excellent recent discussion of this project (although, oddly, it neglects any analysis of James) is Joseph G. Kronick, *American Poetics of History: From Emerson to the Moderns* (Baton Rouge and London: Louisiana State University Press, 1984).

23. James's earliest lesson in literary variousness came from the 'latitude' proclaimed by Hawthorne's account of the Romance, and it was sharpened considerably by his acquaintance with Robert Louis Stevenson. His 1887 essay on Stevenson sets the Scotsman's 'liberty' against the potentially 'meagre' realism of the French:

> The breath of the novelist's being is his liberty; and the incomparable virtue of the form he uses is that it lends itself to views innumerable and diverse, to every variety of illustration. There is certainly no other mould of so large a capacity. The doctrine of M. Zola himself, so meagre if literally taken, is fruitful, inasmuch as in practice he romantically departs from it. ('Robert Louis Stevenson' in Janet Adam Smith (ed.), *Henry James and RLS*, p.149).

24. Mikhail Bakhtin, *The Dialogic Imagination*, ed. Michael Holquist, trans. Caryl Emerson and Michael Holquist (Austin, TX: University of Texas Press, 1981), p.276.

25. James, Preface to *Roderick Hudson*, in Edel, *Literary Criticism, French Writers*, p.1041.

26. Bakhtin, *The Dialogic Imagination*, pp.276–7.

27. Ross Posnock, 'Henry James, Veblen and Adorno: The Crisis of the Modern Self', *Journal of American Studies*, 21 (1987), pp.37–8. Consequently, Posnock claims, 'What is natural for James is the act of

representation, which made him from childhood onwards conceive life as a canvas to be embroidered, and human interaction a social text to be read and interpreted' (pp.45–6). Posnock's careful deployment of domestic vocabulary here enables us to see that such textuality is not a choice for James, not a symptom of that removed artistry to which he has been so long condemned by commentators, but the very history through which he lived, the history of consumption's turning the world into the images, signs and codes of spectacle. What James's art 'represents' above all is a representation of this history.

28. Eric J. Sundquist, 'The Country of the Blue', in Eric J. Sundquist (ed.), *American Realism: New Essays* (Baltimore, MD, and London: The Johns Hopkins University Press, 1982), pp.11, 12, 14.

29. Peggy McCormack has provided a good commentary on this production of display, of characteristics: 'Society immediately sets prices upon merchandizable assets such as physical attractiveness, mental acuity, culture, title, or money itself. Hence, despite their frequent lack of real jobs, James's characters *do* work, but the products of their labor are their social personae' ('The Semiotics of Economic Language in James's Fiction', *American Literature*, 58, 1986, p.541). McCormack's list omits manners which arguably present the most expressive arena for consumption's reconstructions of the self: an invaluable foray into this question is Richard Godden 'Some Slight Shifts in the Manner of the Novel of Manners', in Bell, *Henry James: Fiction as History*, pp.156–83.

30. Although it is concerned principally with the 1920s, some pertinent propositions on this issue are raised in Mike Featherstone, 'The Body in Consumer Culture', *Theory Culture and Society*, 1 (1982), pp.18–32. It is a mistake to assume that an analysis of consumer culture's effects upon literary techniques may only properly take the turn of the century as its starting-point. Karen Halttunen's excellent *Confidence Men and Painted Women: A Study of Middle-Class Culture in America, 1830–1870* (New Haven, CT and London: Yale University Press, 1982) provides abundant evidence that the issues of self, authenticity and performativeness foregrounded by consumption are urgent for a consideration of social and commercial manners from the 1850s onwards. My present exercise, which examines the Jamesian enterprise of the 1870s and 1880s, intends to elaborate on Halttunen's work by reading James's fiction as a registration of the period when consumption and the economic shifts from accumulation to production re-inscribed those issues for the marketplace.

1 Commodity and Style

1. The opening three chapters of the novel, prior to the beginning of the story's action in Chapter 4, stress the period in which the novel is set to a degree that is unusual for James. Chapter 1 contains nine

references to specific dates and to the ages of the characters, and Chapters 2 and 3 each contain eight such references. The time-scale in general of the novel has a distorting office, to which I shall return later.

2. Sloper's first 'edifice of red brick', within five minutes' walk of City Hall just north of Wall Street, 'saw its best days' about 1820, after which 'the tide of fashion began to set steadily northward, as, indeed, in New York, thanks to the narrow channel in which it flows, it is obliged to do, and the great hum of traffic rolled farther to the right and left of Broadway'. He moves north to Washington Square in 1835 when 'the murmur of trade had become a mighty uproar' and when the neighbouring houses became converted into 'offices, warehouses, and shipping agencies, and otherwise applied to the base uses of commerce' (pp.16–17). Page references are to the first book edition of *Washington Square*, along with two shorter tales, *The Pension Beaurepas* and *A Bundle of Letters*, reprinted from the *Cornhill Magazine* by Macmillan, London, 1881. All subsequent references will be included parenthetically in the main text.

3. Douglas T. Miller tells us:

> The city was compact, extending from the southernmost point at the Battery north along the Hudson for about two miles and along the East River for approximately two and a half miles. Canal Street marked the northern limit in the late 1820s; beyond that were several separate villages – Greenwich, Chelsea, Bloomingdale, Manhattanville, and Harlem – and scattered farms and elegant county seats.

At this time, 'all was hustle and bustle in the metropolis; everything was given over to business and speculation' as New York became 'the indisputed commercial centre of the New World' (*Jacksonian Aristocracy, Class and Democracy in New York 1830–1860*, New York: Oxford University Press, 1967, pp.70–71).

4. Ibid, p.113.
5. Douglas C. North, *The Economic Growth of the United States 1790–1860*, 1961 (New York: Prentice Hall, 1966), p.205.
6. See Miller, *Jacksonian Aristocracy*, pp.114–5.
7. Ibid, pp.116, 118.
8. Edward Pessen *Jacksonian America: Society, Personality and Politics*, 1969, rev. ed. (Homewood, II: The Dorsey Press, 1978), pp.102–3.
9. Ibid, p.114.
10. Miller, *Jacksonian Aristocracy*, p.107.
11. Ibid, p.120.
12. Ibid, p.80.
13. Peter Conrad's recent reading of the novel's geography unproblematically views James's tactic as an 'occlusion of the city and the sanctification of an interior to shelter the private life' (*The Art of the City. Views and Versions of New York*, Oxford and New York: Oxford University Press, 1984, p.26). Such a reading is clearly accurate insofar as it goes, but it makes no attempt to discern the

imperatives for James's 'occlusion'. Grievances against indus-
trialisation, the shifts to the factory system, the diminished value of
labour and the exploitative tactics of the corporate structure sought
their inevitable expressions in the form of social disorder. (See the
accurately entitled Michael Feldberg, *The Turbulent Era: Riot and
Disorder in Jacksonian America*, New York: Oxford University Press,
1980, and Leonard L. Richards, '*Gentlemen of Property and Standing*'.
Anti-Abolition Mobs in Jacksonian America, New York: Oxford University Press, 1970. Two years prior to James's departure for Europe,
and six years prior to the composition of *Washington Square*, Joel
Tyler Headley attempted an historical explanation of the Draft Riots
of 1863 and the Orange Riots of 1870 and 1871 which included
substantial discussions of the unrest during the 1830s and 1840s in
The Great Riots of New York 1712–1873, (1873), New York: Dover
1971). The prevailing fear of disorder was summarised by the
Commercial Advertiser in August 1840: 'Destructive rascality stalks at
large in our streets and public places, at all times of the day and
night, with none to make it afraid; mobs assemble deliberately . . .
in a word, lawless violence and fury have full dominion over us
whenever it pleases them to rage.' (Quoted in James F. Richardson,
The New York Police. Colonial Times to 1901, New York: Oxford
University Press, 1970, p.26.) In 1834, the year before Sloper's
move to Washington Square, civil disturbances were so frequent
that the year 'was long remembered in New York history as the
year of the riots' (Richardson, *The New York Police*, p.27).

14. It is a view strongly informed by a fascination with domestic
versions of the technology which creates the ground whereby
economic and social transformations are effected:

> So you see we'll always have a new house; it's a great advantage
> to have a new house; you get all the latest improvements. They
> invent everything all over again about every five years, and it's a
> great thing to keep up with the new things. I always try and
> keep up with the new things of every kind (p.32).

Townsend's abbreviated syntax and limited vocabulary are a telling
Jamesian indictment. The reiteration of 'things' suggests both an
abstractive imagination and a reliance upon the static world of
reification.

15. It embodies 'the last results of architectural science' (p.17) and is
built in 1835 at the very time when Washington Square became a
fashionable address with its new neo-classic houses.

16. This part of New York 'appears to many persons the most
delectable' because of its 'established repose' and its 'riper, richer,
more honourable look then any of the upper ramifications of the
great longitudinal thoroughfare' (pp.17–18).

17. Washington Square is familiarised as the place where 'your grand-
mother lived, in venerable solitude', dispensing hospitality to 'the
infant imagination and the infant palate', where 'you took your
first walks abroad' and 'your first school' was kept by 'a broad-

bosomed, broad-based old lady with a ferule, who was always having tea in a blue cup, with a saucer that didn't match' (p.18).

18. Mrs Almond's house is, loosely, 'much farther up town, in an embryonic street, with a high number', in a region where 'the city began to assume a theoretic air' and which is characterised by a long vanished 'rural picturesqueness' (pp.18–19). Mrs Montgomery's 'little red house', out on the eastern edge of Manhattan, at least has the limited specificity of being somewhere on Second Avenue, but it 'looked like a magnified baby-house' which 'might have been taken down from a shelf in a toy-shop' (p.94).

19. *The American Scene* (London: Chapman & Hall, 1907), pp.100–1.

20. Thorstein Veblen, *The Theory of the Leisure Class*, 1899 (London: Unwin Books, 1970), p.75.

21. Roland Barthes, 'Myth Today', *Mythologies* (1957), trans. Annette Lavers (St Albans: Paladin, 1973), pp.152–3.

   It is entirely appropriate that Sloper's feelings for his wife were determined above all by his sense that she was a 'reasonable' woman (p.8).

22. See, for example, pp.43, 50, 53, 54, 63, 64, 85, 91, 101, 102, 237.

23. Two familiar examples make the point to cover the span of James's career: in a letter of 1883, he urged Grace Norton to 'content yourself with the terrible algebra of your own [life]' (*Henry James Letters*, ed. Leon Edel, Cambridge, MA: Harvard University Press, 1975, Vol. II, p.424), and in the Preface to *Roderick Hudson*, he stressed the importance for the artist to have a 'geometry of his own' (*The Art of the Novel*, ed. R.P. Blackmur, 1934, New York, Charles Scribner's Sons, 1962, p.5).

   'Surface' has a crucial role in both *The Europeans* (published two years prior to *Washington Square* and the only other of James's major works to be set in the 1840s) and *The Portrait of a Lady* (which so preoccupied James during his composition of *Washington Square*).

24. Barthes, 'Myth Today', pp.155, 141–2.

25. Alfred Sohn-Rethel, *Intellectual and Manual Labour. A Critique of Epistemology*, 1970, trans. Martin Sohn-Rethel, (London: Macmillan, 1978), pp.132–3, 112–13, 125.

26. Ibid, p.132.

27. Ibid, p.25.

28. Ibid, pp.48–9. The defeat of history and difference by assumptions of timelessness and universality involves, of course, a denial of possibilities for human intervention, for materially altering the world conceived in terms of fixed objects which are authorised by custom, organisation or institution. The abstraction of commodities is part of their fixed status, visibly refusing their potential for use in the interests of exchange.

29. Ibid, p.49. Hence Sohn-Rethel finds the emergence of mathematical reasoning at 'the historical stage at which commodity exchange becomes the agent of social synthesis, a point in time marked by the introduction and circulation of coined money' (p.47).

30.   'Their classical form is the maxim. Here the statement is no longer
       directed towards a world to be made; it must overlay one which is
       already made, bury the traces of this production under a self-
       evident appearance of eternity' (Barthes, 'Myth Today', pp.154–5).
31.   It is a characteristic of the maxim, even in clever hands, that it
       refuses to acknowledge its own form. In Sloper's case, this refusal
       is often expressed by his irony: Catherine, for all her simplicity,
       recognises an 'exchange of epigrams' between Sloper and Mrs
       Penniman (p.39), and Sloper himself is certainly prepared to read
       epigrammatic form into Catherine's pressurised prose of that
       dreadful evening in the library when she tells him of her wish to
       see Townsend again. Against Sloper's 'logical axiom' and 'scientific
       truth' during this conversation, Catherine can only repeat herself
       as her words are forced into frozen blocks. Her moment of logical
       triumph, 'inspiration' as she terms it to herself, 'If I don't marry
       before your death, I will not after', is easily defused by Sloper's
       alertness for epigrammatic expression: 'To her father, it must be
       admitted, this seemed only another epigram; and as obstinacy, in
       unaccomplished minds, does not usually select such a mode of
       expression, he was the more surprised at this wanton play of a
       fixed idea' (pp.133–4).
         Such is the subtlety of James's critique of balance that commenta-
       tors of a liberal persuasion read the novel as 'written in a clear
       classical novelistic prose, an English unchanged since the time of
       Jane Austen, a prose in which wit and precision are simply two
       names for one and the same endeavour' (Mark Le Fanu, 'Introduc-
       tion' to *Washington Square* published in 'The World's Classics'
       series, Oxford: Oxford University Press, 1982, p.viii). Le Fanu thus
       admires its 'elegance', 'deftness of epigram' and 'balance or equi-
       librium of tone' (p.ix). Nothing could be further from the truth: not
       only do we have here a misunderstanding of James's entire
       enterprise (which is exactly to liberate fiction from such conven-
       tions), but also, I suspect, of Jane Austen's own irony.
32.   See, for example, his deployment of her words 'kindness', 'gently'
       and 'position' (pp.58–60).
33.   A good example occurs in chapter 11 when Catherine informs
       Sloper of Townsend's proposal (pp.78–9).
34.   See, for example, the conversations with Catherine (pp.80–1) and
       with Morris (pp.88–90).
35.   He claims of Mrs Montgomery, prior to meeting her: 'If she stands
       up for him [Townsend] on account of the money, she will be a
       humbug. If she is a humbug, I shall see it. If I see it, I won't waste
       time with her' (p.92). Needless to say, the dominance of Sloper's
       style is effected with its greatest nastiness during his interview
       with Mrs Montgomery in Chapter 14. Here even the ironic veneer
       of that style is dispensed with. His presence alone seems to inflict a
       state of hypnosis on Townsend's sister as she is virtually mes-
       merised into acquiescing to his power.
36.   The field has been well defined by V.N. Volosinov as 'abstract
       objectism':

What interests the mathematically minded rationalists is not the relationship of the sign to the actual reality it reflects nor to the individual who is its originator, but the *relationship of sign to sign within a closed system* already accepted and authorized. In other words, they are interested only in the *inner logic of the system of signs itself*, taken, as in algebra, completely independently of the ideological meanings that give the signs their content. (*Marxism and the Philosophy of Language*, 1930, trans. Ladislav Matejka and I.R. Titunik, New York and London: Seminar Press, 1973, pp.57–8).

The particular incapacity suggested by 'abstract objectism' is given a more complex reading in the paradox (distinctly germane to the Jamesian exercise) noted by Theodor Adorno and Max Horkheimer:

> As a system of signs, language is required to resign itself to calculation in order to know nature, and must discard the claim to be like her. As image, it is required to resign itself to mirror imagery in order to be nature entire, and must discard the claim to know her. (*Dialectic of Enlightenment* (1947), trans. John Cumming, London: New Left Books, 1979, p.18).

37. L.C. Knights, 'Henry James and Human Liberty', *Sewanee Review*, 83 (1975), p.17.

38. See, for example, pp.27, 29, 45, 151, 156, 158. Inevitably, Catherine herself is not free from such vocabulary: she has a sense of breaking a 'contract' with her father (p.160), and she views Townsend as 'her own exclusive property' (p.190).

39. John Lucas, '*Washington Square*', in *The Air of Reality*, ed. John Goode (London: Methuen, 1972), p.58.

40. Millicent Bell, 'Style as Subject. *Washington Square*', *Sewanee Review*, 83 (1975), p.19.

41. Against the 'philological type of passive understanding which excludes response in advance', Volosinov argues:

> Any genuine kind of understanding will be active and will constitute the germ of a response. . . . To understand another person's utterance means to orient oneself with respect to it, to find the proper place for it in the corresponding context. . . . *Any true understanding is dialogic in nature.* . . . Therefore, there is no reason for saying that meaning belongs to a word as such. In essence, meaning belongs to a word in its position between speakers; that is, meaning is realized only in the process of active, responsive understanding.(*Marxism and the Philosophy of Language*, pp.101–2).

Catherine certainly attempts such orientation, but (because of her father's interlocution and her own immobolised referentiality that issues from the breach between exchange and use) she cannot effect its office since Sloper permits no dialogical context to which it may correspond. I should say that, in general, Volosinov's concern with this issue seems to me to be extremely useful in any consideration of a writer whose main interest is always in the ways in which his characters talk to each other.

42. Lucas, 'Washington Square', p.58.

43. The nexus of society is established by the network of exchange and by nothing else. It is my buying my coat, not my wearing it, which forms part of the social nexus, just as it is the selling, not the making of it. . . . In enforcing the separation from use, or more precisely, from the actions of use, the activities of exchange presuppose the market as a time-and-space-bound vacuum devoid of all interchange of man with nature. (Sohn-Rethel, *Intellectual and Manual Labour*, p.29).

44. Money, of course, presents the dominating cipher of the exchange network, and as an equalising factor, it belongs to the quantitative differentiation of balance, type and geometry whereby the opening of *Washington Square* is organised. Both money and trade rely upon a uniformity which elides the differences of people, locality and date (see Sohn-Rethel, *Intellectual and Manual Labour*, p.30). Such uniformity may be matched with Volosinov's notion of non-dialogical intercourse and with Barthes's 'figure of the scales' in its reliance on a ready-made world which discourages difference and the grounds for human intervention. Commodities are equated in this view solely by virtue of being exchanged and not because of any intrinsic equality they may possess. The equating effect of exchange is thus, for Sohn-Rethel, of a 'non-dimensional quantity' which is directly comparable to the abstractions of mathematics (*Intellectual and Manual Labour*, pp.46–7).

45. Ibid, pp.49, 56.

46. This conflict has been ably documented in J.L. Winter, 'The Chronology of James's *Washington Square*', Notes and Queries, NS, 28,5 (1981), pp.426–8. More recently, Brian Lee's 'Introduction' to the Penguin English Library edition of the novel is content merely to set the time of the action in the 1850s (Harmondsworth: Penguin, 1984, p.16).

47. Additionally, the novel provides a domestic version of its wider chronological conflict in those two scenes where, oddly, Catherine lies (p.78) and Townsend is evasive (p.84) about the time of their first meeting. Their obfuscation of so trivial a detail can only be read as symptomatic of the purposiveness of James's strategic diffusing of temporal specificity.

48. With the fall of men like Fisk came the rise of figures such as E.H. Harriman and the elder J.P. Morgan, initiating a period of unbridled expansion, even larger fortunes and battles for personal financial dictatorship. It was a period in which the older Republican ideal of freedom (tainted at its inception, perhaps, by its close relation to Lockean notions of property) became transformed into a freedom to make money in the form of *laissez-faire* capitalism. (One of the most intelligent accounts remains Robert Green McCloskey, *American Conservatism in the Age of Enterprise 1865–1910*, 1951, New York: Harvard University Press, 1964).

49. Quoted in Robert C. Le Clair, *Young Henry James: 1843–1870* (New York: Bookman Associates, 1955), p.66.

50. *Letters*, Vol.II, p.145.

51. Ibid, Vol.II, p.209. A year later, as part of his increasing disillusionment with the vacuousness of the social circuit, he notes: 'the country is in a very dismal state – everyone poor' (Vol.II, p.261).

52. Terry Eagleton, *Criticism and Ideology* (London: New Left Books, 1976), p.103.

53. Both Democrat and transcendentalist agreed in asserting the rights of the free mind against the pretentions of precedents or institutions. Both shared a living faith in the integrity and perfectibility of man. Both proclaimed self-reliance. Both detested special groups claiming authority to mediate between the common man and the truth. Both aimed to plant the individual squarely on his instincts, responsible only to himself and to God. (Arthur M. Schlesinger Jr, *The Age of Jackson*, 1945, Boston MA,: Little, Brown & Co., 1950, p.381).

This conjunction was clearly part of the intellectual furniture in the household of Henry James, Sr, with its weighty respect for the conditions of individual rights. In itself, the conjunction enabled a curious paradox in the viewing of the most radical of individual expressions, rioting. The period's most concentrated years of social disorder (see note 13 above) between 1834 and 1837 occurred at the moment of Sloper's move to Washington Square and became authorised by the prevailing political rhetoric. Dissent in America (always sanctioned by the wider traditions of European thought articulated in the Declaration of Independence) was freshly approved in the Jacksonian position. David Grimsted expresses the paradox well:

> The psychological appeal of riot in democratic society is that the situation gives a sense of acting by a higher code, of pursuing justice and possessing power free from any structural restraint, and at the same time allowing a complete absorption in the mass so that the individual will and the social will appear to be one . . . this is a kind of apotheosis for democratic man, fulfilling the official doctrine that power belongs to him and allowing him to escape the real system that attempts to share influence by making everyone powerless. ('Rioting in its Jacksonian Setting', *American Historical Review*, 77, 1972, p.393).

It is tempting to suggest that this paradox might provide part of the ground whereby James ignores the riotous aspect of commercial lower Manhattan which Washington Square is designed to resist: in the fictional and historical spheres, the potential of dissent as an expression of social divisiveness is defused as a liberty of disagreement.

54. See Eagleton, *Criticism and Ideology*, pp.141–5.

55. Ibid, p.142.

2 Money, History and Writing

1. Henry James, *Washington Square* (London: Macmillan, 1881), p.17. All subsequent references will be included parenthetically in the body of the text. In the short story, 'An International Episode', published shortly before *Washington Square* (in the *Cornhill Magazine*, December 1878–January 1879), James presents a clear picture of the pressures within New York's commercial world.

2. Mrs Penniman's travesties of what is usually a prime value in James, the imaginative faculty, suggests accurately her social place. Mary Doyle Springer notes:

   > Aunt Penniman exists to reveal by her acts the real heart of darkness: that in such a milieu women ('the imperfect sex') not only co-operate passively with what the ethics of a paternalistic society makes necessary, but also co-operate actively in exploiting each other because that is what the whole social system gives them to do, and gives them little else to do if they are unmarried. (*A Rhetoric of Literary Character: Some Women of Henry James*, Chicago, IL: University of Chicago Press, 1978, p.81).

3. Millicent Bell, 'Style as Subject: *Washington Square*', *Sewanee Review*, 83 (1975), p.23.

4. Millicent Bell suggests: 'If *Washington Square* derives from *Eugenie Grandet* it may also be said to come out of "Rappaccini's Daughter" ' ('Style as Subject' p.24). We might note, on behalf of James's choice of profession for Sloper, that Hawthorne's fictions are well staffed by scientific figures who are not only felt to be cruel with respect to human affections but arrogant in their distortions of nature: to Rappaccini we may add Aylmer, Ethan Brand, Dr Heidegger and Roger Chillingworth.

   For bibliographical information on the relationship between *Washington Square* and Hawthorne's works, see Thaddeo K. Babiiha, *The James–Hawthorne Relation* (Boston, MA: G. K. Hall, 1980), pp.264–6).

5. This issue has recently been investigated, albeit rather one-sidedly, by William W. Stowe, *Balzac, James and the Realistic Novel* (Princeton, NJ: Princeton University Press, 1983).

6. Alfred Sohn-Rethel, *Intellectual and Manual Labour: A Critique of Epistemology*, 1970, trans. Martin Sohn-Rethel (London: Macmillan, 1978), pp.56 and 49.

7. James's worries about novelistic conventions are summarised early in his writing life when he concludes his anonymous review of *Middlemarch* with a well-known question: 'It sets a limit, we think, to the development of the old-fashioned English novel. Its diffuseness, on which we have touched, makes it too copious a dose of pure fiction. If we write novels so, how shall we write History?' (The review was first published in the *Galaxy*, March 1873; my quotation is taken from the reprint in *Nineteenth-Century Fiction*, 8, 1953, p.170.) Towards the end of that life, such worries are to an extent allayed by a faith in the dramatic 'objectivity' he defines in his Preface to *The Awkward Age*:

> The divine distinction of the act of a play – and a greater than any other it easily succeeds in arriving at – was, I reasoned, in its special, its guarded objectivity. This objectivity, in turn, when achieving its ideal, came from the imposed absence of that 'going behind,' to compass explanations and amplifications, to drag out odds and ends from the 'mere' storyteller's great property shop of aids to illusion. (*The Art of the Novel*, ed. R.P.Blackmur, 1934; New York: Charles Scribner's Sons, 1962, pp.110–11).

8. The tensions constituting this complex are, indeed, apparent in Hawthorne's own investigations into the notions of power and authority concomitant upon his craft, particularly in the tales and in the Prefaces. Recently, Brook Thomas has provided an acute analysis of Hawthorne's deployment of the Romance form in 'The *House of the Seven Gables*. Reading the Romance of America', Publications of the Modern Language Association, 97 (1982), pp.195–211.

9. Leo Bersani, 'The Jamesian Lie', *Partisan Review*, 36 (1969), p.54.

10. Ibid, pp.57–8. More recently, Bersani has extended his account of James's efforts to deconstruct the novelistic pretensions of fiction to suggest their political effect:

> Because of James's remarkable indifference to that diversification of behaviour by which other novelists seek to convince us that their characters have more than verbal authority, his novels demystify literature's claim to be a reflector of nonliterary life and they diagram the specific mechanisms of power when its exercise is limited to verbal exchanges.

These literary diagrams, by virtue of their very removal from novelistic furniture, thus have 'the exemplary value of demonstrating that transactions of power always involve communications, and that these communications frequently take the form of equivocal donations of knowledge'. And here lies the core of James's political function: 'literature, exactly because it is power enacted uniquely as a form of organized knowledge, can serve the politically useful role of dramatizing the nothingness of all epistemological fictions' ('The Subject of Power', *Diacritics*, Fall 1977, pp.10–12). I am not absolutely clear what Bersani intends by 'nothingness' here but, as applied to James, it would make sense to read it as an implication of James's stress on imaginative variousness: an effect of interruption whereby the world is revealed as constructed, and, beyond the field of its historical production, no one fiction has any more privileged access to a transcendental authenticity than any other – no more than a purely private guarantee of the 'real'.

11. Tzvetan Todorov, *The Poetics of Prose*, 1971, trans. Richard Howard (Oxford: Basil Blackwell, 1977), p.150. Todorov's account of what he terms 'the quest for an absolute and absent cause' (p.145) in Jamesian narrative (an account which is little recognised by the commentators) is extremely perceptive about this important topic,

but ultimately relies on a primacy of the 'unreal' (or psychic reality) over the 'real' which marks a distortive and potentially reductive reading of the complex which my present concern attempts to maintain as a more tensile construct.

12. My quotations are taken from *The Centenary Edition of the Works of Nathaniel Hawthorne*, ed. William Charvat, Roy Harvey Pearce, Claude M. Simpson (Columbus, OH: Ohio University Press, 1965), pp.1–3.

13. The reverse is true of James, but the effect is the same, as Taylor Stoehr notes:

> The notebooks in which James stored his materials are filled with plots and the making of plots – relationships, encounters, sketches of action. There is little interest in facts or truths observed from life, and the stories he hears at dinner-parties are chiefly regarded as 'germs' for his imagination to work with, the less of the actuality known the better. ('Words and Deeds in *The Princess Casamassima*', *English Literary History*, 37, March 1970, p.132).

By the time of the New York edition, James was capable of being coy about even his 'germs' (of which he makes great play at the beginning of his Preface to *The Awkward Age*), but, nevertheless, the notebooks, more so than his published essays, provide good evidence of James's interest in the *pattern* of things prior to the more familiar statements in the Prefaces.

14. Henry James, *Hawthorne* (1879), ed. Tony Tanner (London: Macmillan, 1967), p.119.
15. Ibid, p.127.
16. Ibid, p.126.
17. Ibid, p.129.
18. Ibid, p.88.
19. Leon Edel, *The Life of Henry James*, 2 vols (Harmondsworth: Penguin, 1977), Vol.I, p.595.
20. *Henry James Letters*, ed. Leon Edel (Cambridge, MA: Harvard University Press, 1975), Vol.II, p.268.
21. James, *Hawthorne*, p.55.
22. Edel, *Letters*, Vol.II, p.268.
23. James, *Hawthorne*, p.54.
24. Idem.
25. My quotations are taken from the *Centenary Edition* version (see note 12) of *The Marble Faun*, 1968, p.3.
26. James, *Hawthorne*, p.24.
27. W.D. Howells, 'James's *Hawthorne*', *Atlantic Monthly* (February 1880); reprinted in *W.D. Howells as Critic*, ed. Edwin H. Cady (London & Boston: Routledge & Kegan Paul, 1973), p.54.
28. James, *Hawthorne*, p.23.
29. Idem.
30. Ibid, pp.123–4.
31. Hawthorne, *The House of the Seven Gables*, p.2.

32. Thomas, 'The House of the Seven Gables', p.199.
33. I have principally in mind here the models for balance within
     bourgeois behaviour offered by Roland Barthes, 'Myth Today',
     Mythologies 1957, trans. Annette Lavers (St Albans: Paladin, 1973),
     and Theodor Adorno and Max Horkheimer, *Dialectic of Enlighten-*
     ment, 1947, trans. John Cumming (London: New Left Books, 1979).
     Barthes writes of an 'intellectual equilibrium based on recognised
     places' whereby 'reality is first reduced to analogues; then it is
     weighed; finally, equality having been ascertained, it is got rid of'.
     It is here that 'one flees from an intolerable reality, reducing it to
     two opposites which balance each other only inasmuch as they are
     purely formal, relieved of all their specific weight'. Material process
     is erased in favour of a 'final equilibrium' which 'immobilizes
     values, life, destiny, etc.' so that 'one no longer needs to choose,
     but only to endorse' (pp.152–3). For Adorno and Horkheimer,
     'Bourgeois society is ruled by equivalance. It makes the dissimilar
     comparable by reducing it to abstract quantities'. Such 'equiv-
     alence' is seen to 'dominate bourgeois justice and commodity
     exchange' (p.7) as a form of abstraction which characterises not
     only the exchange relation of commodities, the determining objects
     of the bourgeois world, but also the distortive function of the main
     feature whereby the bourgeois advertises itself, so that 'the bour-
     geois ideal of naturalness intends not amorphous nature, but the
     virtuous mean' (p.31). It is not accidental that one of the more
     problematical of the novel's terms is 'natural' itself as applied,
     predominantly, to Morris Townsend.
34. Marc Shell, 'The Gold Bug', *Genre*, 13 (1980), p.18.
35. Ibid, p.15.
36. James Roger Sharp, *The Jacksonians versus the Banks* (New York:
     Columbia University Press, 1970), pp.5 and 6. For further discus-
     sions of the Jacksonian bank debate, see Bray Hammond, *Banks and*
     Politics in America: From the Revolution to the Civil War (Princeton, NJ:
     Princeton University Press, 1957); Marvin Meyers, *The Jacksonian*
     Persuasion (Stanford, CA: Stanford University Press, 1957); Robert
     V. Remini, *Andrew Jackson and the Bank War* (New York: W.W.
     Norton, 1967); Peter Temin, *The Jacksonian Economy* (New York: W.
     W. Norton, 1969).
37. The Jacksonian attack on the banks was but a single episode in an
     extended debate over banking, credit, and currency that lasted
     throughout the nineteenth century. The rhetoric of the Jacksonians
     and their fears were similar in tone and content to those expressed
     earlier by John Taylor of Caroline [the clearest and most persuasive
     exponent of Jeffersonian principles, always the ground for the
     century's agrarian argument] in the early nineteenth century and
     nearly a century later by Populist leaders. All were representatives
     of an agrarian society who felt that their moral values were being
     eroded away by the commercialization of society and the quicken-
     ing tempo of industry.   (Sharp, *The Jacksonians*, p.6)
38.   Throughout the century there was a fervently held belief that
     privately issued paper money was an exploitative device by

which capitalists and bankers could control prices and the money supply. This, in turn, it was argued, gave these special citizens enormous political and economic power and made a mockery of a society that emphasized equal rights for all and special privileges for none.   (Sharp, *The Jacksonians*, p.8)

39.   Ibid, pp.9–18.
40.   William Leggett, 'Equality', *Evening Post*, 6 December 1834; reprinted in *Builders of American Institutions. Readings in United States History*, ed. Frank Freidel and Norman Pollack (Chicago, IL: Rand McNally, 1966), pp.157–8.
41.   Andrew Jackson, 'Farewell Address', 1837; reprinted in *Builders of American Institutions*, p.156.
42.   At the very beginning of his Bank Veto in 1832, Jackson expresses 'the belief that some of the powers and privileges possessed by the existing bank are unauthorised by the constitution, subversive of the rights of the States, and dangerous to the liberties of the people' (reprinted in *Select Documents Illustrative of the History of the United States 1776–1861*, ed. William Macdonald New York and London: Macmillan, 1898, p.262). His Fifth Annual Message of 1833 reiterates the warning of constitutional infringement by offering what he terms 'unquestionable proof' that the Bank of the United States had been converted into a 'permanent electioneering machine' as a justification for his removal of the Bank's deposits:

> In this point of the case, the question is distinctly presented, whether the people of the United States are to govern through representatives chosen by their unbiased suffrages, or whether the money and power of a great corporation are to be secretly exerted to influence their judgement, and control their decisions.   (Reprinted in *Select Documents*, pp.301–2).

The point is repeated in his Sixth Annual Message of 1834 where, condemning the Bank as 'the scourge of the people', Jackson urges that 'measures be taken to separate the Government entirely from an institution so mischievous to the public prosperity, and so regardless of the Constitution and laws' (reprinted in *Select Documents*, p.320).

43.   'Specie Circular', 1836; reprinted in *Select Documents*, pp.328–39.
44.   Jackson, 'Farewell Address', pp.154–5.
45.   Some of the evils which arise from this system of paper press with peculiar hardship upon the class of society least able to bear it. A portion of this currency frequently becomes depreciated or worthless, and all of it is easily counterfeited in such a manner as to require peculiar skill and much experience to distinguish the counterfeit from the genuine note. These frauds are most generally perpetrated in the smaller notes, which are used in the daily transactions of ordinary business, and the losses occasioned by them are commonly thrown upon the laboring classes of society, whose situation and pursuits put it out of their power to guard themselves from these impositions, and whose daily wages are necessary for their subsistence.
                                              (Ibid, p.155)

46. Ibid, p.157.
47. Walter T.K. Nugent, *The Money Question During Reconstruction* (New York: W.W. Norton, 1967), pp.16–17.
48. Nugent notes: 'No one realized in 1865, but money was destined to become the chief perennial issue in national politics for over thirty years. . . . Its peculiar dimensions were established in almost all important ways during the Reconstruction years, from 1867 to 1879' (*The Money Question*, pp.21–2). Richard Hofstadter similarly claims:

> A whole generation of Americans were embroiled from the 1870s to the 1890s in the argument over silver. To the combatants of that era, silver and gold were not merely precious metals but precious symbols, the very substance of creeds and faiths which continued long afterward to have meaning for men living on the echoes of nineteenth-century orthodoxies.
>
> ('Free Silver and the Mind of "Coin" Harvey', reprinted in Hofstadter's *The Paranoid Style in American Politics*, 1964, New York: Alfred A. Knopf, 1967, pp.238–9)

Hofstadter's essay deals mainly with the 'Free Silver' campaigns of the 1890s, but offers a brief and readable account of monetary events during the 1870s (pp.250–7). Irwin Unger, in one of the best discussions of the subject, has argued: 'In the decade and a half following Appomattox, national finance absorbed more of the country's intellectual and political energy than any other public question except Reconstruction' (*The Greenback Era: A Social and Political History of American Finance 1865–1879*, 1964, Princeton, NJ: Princeton University Press, 1967, p.3). Unger may be paired with Robert P. Sharkey (*Money, Class, and Party: An Economic Study of Civil War and Reconstruction*, 1959, Baltimore MD: Johns Hopkins University Press, 1967) as providing the most detailed and reliable guide to the history of money during the period. Both also offer excellent bibliographies of the massive literature concerned with the subject.

49. Quoted in Nugent, *The Money Question*, pp.96–7. In addition to Bland's catalogue of dominating moneyed interests, we might note the expansion of the corporate device during Reconstruction. Jan W. Dietrichson has claimed:

> In use before the Civil War mainly as a means to accumulate capital for turnpikes, railroads, and banks, the corporation rapidly became the dominant force of business organization in the post-war years, making easier the raising of large amounts of capital. It gave continuity of control, easy expansion of capital, concentration of administrative authority, diffusion of responsibility, and the privileges and immunities of a 'person' in law and in interstate activities.
>
> (*The Image of Money in the American Novel of the Gilded Age*, New York: Publication of the American Institute, University of Ohio, 1969, p.11).

Such abstractive 'diffusion of responsibility' and 'immunities' would have been anathema to James, who always hated institutional or organised intrusions into private liberties. It is instructive that the only other novels he wrote which explicitly advertise a social history, *The Bostonians* (usefully, from the point of view of *Washington Square*, set in the 1870s) and *The Princess Casamassima*, are both concerned with the impositions by organisations (of feminists and of anarchists respectively) upon personal freedom. His concern extends to language; Taylor Stoehr, on behalf of *The Princess Casamassima*, paraphases an argument from *The Theories of Anarchy and Law* by James's friend, Henry B. Brewster: 'Man must learn to enjoy this freedom from settled formulations. He must accept the responsibility for creating reality through speech, and must refrain from the fetishism of names that embalms life with words' ('Words and Deeds in *The Princess Casamassima*', *English Literary History*, 37, 1970, p.130). Diagrammatically here we have the debate of Hawthorne versus Balzac, albeit in somewhat reductive form since the issue was never so clearly presentable to James. In a paradoxical way, we might want to consider Verena Tarrant's 'natural' and 'spontaneous' oratory in *The Bostonians* as belonging to the same field of enquiry as Catherine Sloper's silence, since Verena's voice, too, is made subject to the pressures of abstract organisation; her voice is offered as a form of pure utterance whose contents are rendered vacuous by the rhetoric of Olive Chancellor's privileged ideals. Catherine's silence and Verena's utterance are equally emptied of material process and paralysed by domestic versions of institutions.

50. Sohn-Rethel, *Intellectual and Manual Labour*, p.59.
51. Ibid, p.60.
52. B.J. Williams has offered a good argument for seeing Sloper as a 'hard' money figure (associated with the solidity of the earlier Republican values evinced by Jefferson and Adams who recognised the 'cheat' of any discrepancy between a bank bill and the quantity of gold and silver which sanctioned it) and Townsend as belonging to the world of 'soft' money, the paper world of extended credit: see '*Washington Square*: Fiction as History', unpublished, BA Dissertation, University of Keele, 1983.
53. Irwin Unger, on a more technical model, has seen this instability in terms of specific confusions, claiming an absence of consensus for the very definition of money:

> Some writers held that only gold and silver coin, bank notes, and government paper that performed exchanges and passed from hand to hand functioned as money; others said bank credits and deposits also qualified. They disagreed, too, over the significance of the interest bearing debt, much of which circulated as money between interest paying periods. From the point of view of a modern economist the whole financial discussion has an air of unreality.

(*The Greenback Era: A Social and Political History of American Finance 1865–1879*, 1964; Princeton, NJ: Princeton University Press, 1968, p.36)

54. Gerald T. Dunne, *Justice Story and the Rise of the Supreme Court* (New York: Simon & Schuster, 1970), pp.142–3.
55. Brook Thomas, 'The House of the Seven Gables: Hawthorne's Legal Story'. I am grateful to Professor Thomas for permission to quote from the typescript of his as yet unpublished essay.
56. Marc Shell has noted how 'paper counted for nothing as a commodity and was thus "insensible" in the economic system of exchange' ('The Gold Bug', p.15). This suggests the inadequacy of its symbolism, and we may add that its danger, beyond local effects such as counterfeiting, lies in its partaking of the equalising world of cardinal numbers and their attendant abstractions.
57. Ibid, p.18.
58. My quotation is taken from the Riverside Edition of Emerson's *Works; Nature, Addresses, and Lectures*, Cambridge, MA: Belknap Press of Harvard University Press, 1894, pp.35–6.
59. Ibid, pp.36–8.
60. James, 'Emerson', reprinted in *Henry James, Selected Literary Criticism*, ed. Morris Shapira (Harmondsworth: Penguin, 1968), p.114.
61. Henry James, *The Notebooks of Henry James*, ed. F.O. Matthiessen and Kenneth Murdock (New York: Oxford University Press, 1955), pp.12–13.
62. A random sample suggests that the most common epithets are, of course, 'fortune-hunter' and 'adventurer' (see, for example, Richard Poirier, *The Comic Sense of Henry James*, London: Chatto & Windus, 1960, p.178), usually in contexts, such as Poirier's, which include no substantial discussion of Townsend at all. The closer analyses are more specifically condemnatory. John Lucas refers to Townsend's 'coarseness' and finds him to be a 'coward' ('Washington Square', in *The Air of Reality: New Essays on Henry James*, ed. John Goode, London: Methuen, 1972, pp.42, 55 and 56); for F.W. Dupee, he 'crudely deserts' Catherine (*Henry James*, New York: William Sloane, 1951, p.64); Springer locates an 'insufficiency of moral character' (*A Rhetoric of Literary Character*, p.78); Stuart Hutchinson, who is generally more sympathetic towards Townsend than most of the commentators, finds that he treats Catherine 'abominably' (*Henry James: An American as Modernist*, London and Totowa, NJ: Vision Press & Barnes & Noble, 1982, p.19); J.A. Ward sees him as 'a conniver and a scoundrel' ('Henry James's America: Versions of Oppression', *Mississippi Quarterly*, 13, 1959–60, p.40); Robert R. Johannsen writes of his 'devilish charms' ('Two Sides of Washington Square', *South Carolina Review*, 7, 1974, p.63); William Kenney regards him as 'devious and calculating' ('Dr. Sloper's Double in *Washington Square*', *The University Review – Kansas City*, 36, 1970, p.301); and Bell summarises Townsend's character as 'unnatural, unspontaneous, insincere' with 'a well-developed sense . . . of the uses of things' ('Style as Subject', p.25).
63. He had forgotten that in any event Catherine had her own ten thousand a year; he had devoted an abundance of meditation to this circumstance. But with his fine parts he rated himself high, and he had a perfectly definite appreciation of his value, which

seemed to him inadequately represented by the sum I have
mentioned.   (p.159)

64. 'Doctor Sloper's opposition was the unknown quantity in the
problem he had to work out. The natural way to work it out was by
marrying Catherine; but in mathematics there are many short cuts,
and Morris was not without a hope that he should yet discover
one' (p.159).

65. The idea of paralysis here refers to the ways in which both science
and commerce empty their objects of process understood historically, freeze them, as it were, from the ravages of nature. Such
paralysis is shared by scientific law and commodities in the market.

66. Lucas, 'Washington Square', p.39. Cf. Poirier, *The Comic Sense*,
p.166.

67. Mrs Penniman, the most explicitly theatrically inclined character in
the novel, marks its extreme disablement; as an unmarried woman,
she simply has no function other than to co-operate within
society's determinant nexus by means of her melodramatic machinations. (This is a point usefully touched upon in Springer, *A
Rhetoric of Literary Character*, p.81–5).

68. James, *Hawthorne*, p.45.

69. There is, of course, considerable doubt as to whether he is telling
the truth about his job; his evasiveness suggests that he may well
be lying.

70. Norman Sidney Buck, *The Development of the Organisation of Anglo-
American Trade 1800–1850*, 1925 (Newton Abbot: David & Charles,
1969), p.16.

71. We should note in addition, however, that in his protrayal of
Townsend, James is probably also making a point about the
presentation of character to realign an imbalance he notes on behalf
of Hawthorne's presentation in *The House of the Seven Gables*.
Holgrave, in James's reading, is given as 'a kind of national type',
'that of the young citizen of the United States whose fortune is
simply in his lively intelligence, and who stands naked, as it were,
unbiased and unencumbered alike, in the centre of the far-stretch-
ing level of American life'. James regrets the potency of
Hawthorne's typology in this instance because it is simply too
strong for the battle with Judge Pyncheon; a more 'lusty conservative' is needed to match the 'strenuous radical' and so, 'As it is, the
mustiness and mouldiness of the tenants of the House of the Seven
Gables crumble away rather too easily' (James, *Hawthorne*, p.123).
I am not inviting a view of Sloper and Townsend as James's
version of a similar clash between the old and the new which
would correct the imbalance he notes in Hawthorne, but suggesting that his concern with Townsend's shadowiness might be
further considered in the wider terms of the disposition of character. At the least, James's reading of Holgrave suggests possibilities
for some sympathy on behalf of Townsend.

72. Barthes, 'Myth Today', p.155.

73. Ibid, p.138.

3 Publicity and Emptiness

1. I would strongly echo the argument by Jean-Christophe Agnew for seeing James as 'one of American consumer culture's earliest critics' ('The Consuming Vision of Henry James', *The Culture of Consumption: Critical Essays in American History 1880–1980*, ed. R.W. Fox and T.J. Jackson Lears, New York: Pantheon Books, 1983, p.67). The history of that culture is the most important history of the period in terms of its intimate restructuring of human perceptions. Its general schema has been summarised most recently by Rachel Bowlby:

> The second half of the nineteenth century witnessed a radical shift in the concerns of industry: from production to selling and from the satisfaction of stable needs to the invention of new desires. . . . Stores, Posters, brand-name goods, and ads in the daily and magazine press laid the groundwork of an economy in which selling and consumption, by the continual creation of new needs and new desires, became open to infinite expansion, along with the profits and productivity which lay behind them. (*Just Looking: Consumer Culture in Dreiser, Gissing and Zola*, London: Methuen, 1985, pp.2–3)

In stressing the centrality of the novel's negotiations of 'public' and 'private', I am aware of the attention paid to them by several of its most serious commentators, but I would argue that they have yet to receive the detailed analysis within a specific history that I hope to provide in the following pages. The customary feature of that attention has been to use these terms as a shorthand for describing the familiar issue of the relationship between the individual and the community.

2. Richard Godden, in one of the most pertinent essays we have on the novel, presents a powerful case for a reading in which '*The Bostonians*, in detail and in structure, derives its shape from a singular shift in the history of accumulation' ('Some Slight Shifts in the Manner of the Novel of Manners', *Henry James: Fiction as History*, ed. Ian F.A. Bell, London and Totowa, NJ: Vision Press and Barnes & Noble, 1984, p.181).

3. *The Notebooks of Henry James*, ed. F.O. Matthiessen and Kenneth B. Murdock (New York: Oxford University Press, 1961), p.47.

4. I take John Goode and David Howard as examples of the best of such critics. Goode, with other preoccupations in mind, leaves the novel at the level of generalisation: '*The Bostonians* develops out of the historical commitment. It is an attempt to render the historical forces at work in the society of the United States in the period of reconstruction. ('The Art of Fiction: Walter Besant and Henry James', *Tradition and Tolerance in Nineteenth Century Fiction*, ed. David Howard, John Lucas and John Goode, London: Routledge & Kegan Paul, 1966, p.268). David Howard's essay, '*The Bostonians*' (*The Air of Reality: New Essays on Henry James*, ed. John Goode,

London: Methuen, 1972, pp.60–80), persuasively claims that '*The Bostonians* is a novel about union, even "The Union" ' (p.60), and although he has some excellent things to say about the issues of 'private' and 'public' (pp.70–1), they are allowed to maintain a stability which the economic resonances of the novel, as I hope to show, refuse to permit.

5. Agnew, 'The Consuming Vision', p.76.
6. Godden, 'Some Slight Shifts', p.171.
7. Matthiessen and Murdock, *Notebooks*, p.47.
8. Alan Trachtenberg, *The Incorporation of America: Culture and Society in the Gilded Age* (New York: Hill & Wang, 1982), p.136.
9. Ibid, pp.122–4, 114, 136; cf. T.J. Jackson Lears, 'From Salvation to Self-Realization: Advertizing and the Therapeutic Roots of the Consumer Culture, 1880–1930', *The Culture of Consumption*, p.18.
10. Matthiessen and Murdock, *Notebooks*, p.47.
11. *The Bostonians* (Harmondsworth: Penguin, 1966), pp.107–8. Subsequent references to this edition appear parenthetically in the text.
12. Matthiessen and Murdock, *Notebooks*, p.67.
13. Trachtenberg, *The Incorporation of America*, p.125.
14. Idem.
15. Guy Debord, *Society of the Spectacle* (Detroit: Black & Red, 1973), paragraph 18.
16. Debord has claimed, succinctly and accurately, that 'The spectacle is the moment when the commodity has attained the *total occupation* of social life'(*Society of the Spectacle*, paragraph 42).
17. Trachtenberg, *The Incorporation of America*, p.125.
18. *The American* (New York: The New American Library, 1963), pp.183, 170–1.
19. Henry James, *Literary Criticism. Essays on Literature, American Writers, English Writers*, ed. Leon Edel (New York: The Library of America, 1984), p.211. James remembered his diagnosis in *The Portrait of a Lady* where the 'inscrutable' abbreviations of Mrs Touchett's telegram occasion considerable difficulties of interpretation: 'Changed hotel, very bad, impudent clerk, address here. Taken sister's girl, died last year, go to Europe, two sisters, quite independent' (my quotation is taken from the reprinting of the first edition of the novel; New York: The New American Library, 1964, p.13).
20. Ibid, pp.211–12.
21. Ibid, p.212. In the same year, James reviewed Charles Nordhoff's *The Communistic Societies of the United States* where, in thinking of the Oneida community, he found occasion to berate the intrusion of privacy in the stronger terms that he is to use in his *Notebook* preparations for *The Bostonians*: 'The whole scene, and all that it rested on, is an attempt to organise and glorify the detestable tendency toward the complete effacement of privacy in life and thought everywhere so rampant with us nowadays' (*Literary Criticism. Essays on Literature*, p.567). Again, his non-fiction provides too bald a model for the complexities of the novel where the notion

of privacy is neither so stable nor so innocent as this passage suggests.

22. George M. Beard, *American Nervousness: Its Causes and Consequences* (New York: G.P. Putnam's Sons, 1881), pp.96, 105.
23. Bowlby, *Just Looking*, pp.8–9.
24. Alfred Habegger, *Gender, Fantasy, and Realism in American Literature* (New York: Columbia University Press, 1982), pp.108–9.
25. Theodor Adorno, 'Gold assay', *Minima Moralia*, trans. E.F.N. Jephcott (London: New Left Books, 1974), pp.155, 152.
26. For a recent discussion of this issue that is particularly apposite to the present argument, see Godden, 'Some Slight Shifts', pp.160–2.
27. Lears, 'From Salvation to Self-Realization', p.25.
28. Trachtenberg, *The Incorporation of America*, pp.129–30.
29. Matthiessen and Murdock, *Notebooks*, p.47.
30. Peter Buitenhuis, *The Grasping Imagination. The American Writings of Henry James* (Toronto: University of Toronto Press, 1970), p.142.
31. 'Alphonse Daudet', *Literary Criticism. French Writers, Other European Writers, The Prefaces to the New York Edition*, ed. Leon Edel (New York: The Library of America, 1984), p.236.
32. Marx, *Grundrisse*, trans. Martin Nicolaus (Harmondsworth: Penguin, 1973), p.141. For an excellent modern discussion of this issue, see Agnew, 'The Consuming Vision,' pp.70–3.
33. I take it for granted that this instability, what Marx called 'the separation between the value of things and their substance' (*Grundrisse*, p.149), applies also to language and to epistemology; or, as Agnew puts it: 'The "fluid medium" of the mass market dissolves the social and cultural sediment in which symbolic forms are embedded; it continually and systematically dislodges the meanings that humans have always expressed through and attached to their own artifacts' ('The Consuming Vision', p.72).
34. It is left to Mrs Luna, for whom Verena 'looks like a walking advertisement' (p.225) anyway, to point the comical extreme of this rhetoric: 'She will run off with some lion-tamer; she will marry a circus-man!' (p.177).
35. Ruth Evelyn Quebe sees Verena's origins in a 'new and amorphous' culture that exemplifies the general 'readjustment of values' during the period following the Civil War ('*The Bostonians*: Some Historical Sources and Their Implications', *The Centennial Review*, 25, 1981, p.87); while Susan L. Mizruchi claims that 'of all the novel's characters, she manifests the greatest capacity for an awareness of historical change' ('The Politics of Temporality in *The Bostonians, Nineteenth-Century Fiction*, 40, 1985, p.208). Mizruchi, rightly, presents this awareness mainly in terms of the access Verena provides to the contemporary circumstances of the women's movement, but that access seems to me to tell only a part, albeit an important one, of the story. What needs stressing also is the presentation of Verena as a member of a new, emergent social class characterised by flexibility and motion: in an instructive, although paradoxical, sense, she is the novel's most free character as the object for everyone's desire, and that freedom is precisely

one of the illusory effects of consumption itself. Furthermore, on behalf of the gender issue which the novel engages specifically, and of the more general question of Jamesian historicism, it is crucial that the location of change is articulated through the female. Change is pictured primarily through the idea of her difficult uniqueness, a quality competed over by Olive and Ransom not only for the purposes of control, but to disguise the threat of change to their own position and to shore up the fragility of their own desire.

4 Language, Setting and Self

1. *The Bostonians* (Harmondsworth: Penguin, 1966), pp.52–3. Subsequent references to this edition appear parenthetically in the text.
2. The implication of vampiric possession is strengthened by the grotesque figuration of her father's smile 'which made his mouth enormous, developed two wrinkles, as long as the wings of a bat, on either side of it, and showed a set of big, even, carnivorous teeth' (p.41). Selah Tarrant's capacity for draining Verena is as extensive as Basil Ransom's and Olive Chancellor's, and his smile (in conjunction with his hands, a literalisation of that draining) is, I shall show, further associated with the inflation of the self which so concerns James in the novel.
3. David Howard, 'The Bostonians', in *The Air of Reality: New Essays on Henry James*, ed. John Goode (London: Methuen, 1972), p.64–5. While pursuing this moment in the novel as an important item of James's formal concern with setting, I neglect a further aspect of his historicism. Richard Godden has suggested to me that the site of Ransom's lodging provokes an image of small merchandising (linked to the small farmer, who now produces for the market) which reaches back towards the pre-Civil War Republican alliance of free soil and free labour. Such a reading belongs to an account of Ransom as Southerner which lies beyond the confines of the present exercise, but is explored in the opening chapters of Godden's forthcoming monograph, *Fictions of Capital: The American Novel from James to Mailer* (Cambridge: Cambridge University Press).
4. 'Honoré de Balzac', *Literary Criticism. French Writers, Other European Writers, The Prefaces to the New York Edition*, ed. Leon Edel (New York: The Library of America, 1984), pp.49–50. In his description of Ransom and Verena leaving Central Park, James displays his awareness of the dangers whereby a novelistic sense of place may veer towards the factitiousness of the 'picturesque' (*The Bostonians*, p.295).
5. Jean-Christophe Agnew has a perceptive account of James's later view of the hotel in 'The Consuming Vision of Henry James', *The Culture of Consumption*, ed. R.W. Fox and T.J. Jackson Lears (New York: Pantheon Books, 1983), pp.76–9.

6. Alan Trachtenberg, *The Incorporation of America: Culture and Society in the Gilded Age* (New York: Hill & Wang, 1982), pp.130–3.
7. Rachel Bowlby, *Just Looking: Consumer Culture in Dreiser, Gissing and Zola* (London: Methuen, 1985), pp.34, 29.
8. *The Notebooks of Henry James*, ed. F.O. Matthiessen and Kenneth B. Murdock (New York: Oxford University Press, 1961), p.47.
9. Our first view of this characteristic is of 'a slow, deliberate smile, which made his mouth enormous, developed two wrinkles, as long as the wings of a bat, on either side of it, and showed a set of big, even, carnivorous teeth' (p.41). Its next occurrence is during the negotiations with Olive for the sale of Verena when his 'large joyless smile' becomes transposed into 'the strange and silent lateral movement of his jaws' (p.144) and, finally, at the Music Hall itself, Tarrant's Mecca of publicity, we have 'a smile so comprehensive that the corners of his mouth seemed almost to meet behind' (p.381).

    Another smile which approximates to Tarrant's is, as Marius Bewley has pointed out, that of the sinister Westervelt in Hawthorne's *The Blithedale Romance* (see *The Complex Fate*, London: Chatto & Windus, 1952, p.15), but here the smile is signally less fantastic and serves only to detail its owner as a 'sham'.
10. *Literary Criticism. Essays on Literature, American Writers, English Writers*, ed. Leon Edel (New York: The Library of America, 1984), pp.854, 856.
11. 'Alphonse Daudet', *Literary Criticism. French Writers*, p.237.
12. Walt Whitman, *The Complete Poems*, ed. Francis Murphy (Harmondsworth: Penguin, 1975), p.463.
13. The potency of the garment is such that it infects his wife whom we see in 'a flowing mantle, which resembled her husband's waterproof – a garment which, when she turned to her daughter or talked about her, might have passed for the robe of a sort of priestess of maternity' (p.98).
14. At Miss Birdseye's funeral, 'Selah still sported (on a hot day in August), his immemorial waterproof; but his wife rustled . . . in garments of which . . . Olive could see that the cost had been large' (p.354). The permanence of the waterproof resists not only the heat, but the new wealth resulting from the sale of his daughter.
15. See Peter Buitenhuis, *The Grasping Imagination: The American Writings of Henry James* (Toronto: Univesity of Toronto Press, 1970), p.144.
16. Whitman, *The Complete Poems*, p.118.
17. Pound shared to a significant degree James's ambivalence towards Whitman but, again in tune with James's earlier thoughts, he was always troubled by the Whitmanian self which he compared revealingly with that of François Villon in his first volume of criticism. He had in mind a particularly banal example of Whitman's assertion of authority ('When I eat water-melons the world eats water-melons through me') where, as in 'A Noiseless Patient Spider', the extent of the self is imaged through an inconsequential natural object, and he observed:

Villon never forgets his fascinating revolting self. If, however, he sings the song of himself he is, thank God, free from that horrible air of rectitude with which Whitman rejoices in being Whitman. Villon's song is selfish through self-absorption; he does not, as Whitman, pretend to be conferring a philanthropic benefit on the race by recording his own self-complacency. Human misery is more stable than human dignity; there is more intensity in the passion of cold, remorse, hunger, and the fetid damp of the mediaeval dungeon than in eating water melons.

(*The Spirit of Romance*, 1910, London: Peter Owen, 1970, p.168)

That 'self-complacency' is an affront to art as to ethics; shortly afterwards, continuing to think of Whitman in his 'Patria Mia' of 1911–12, Pound commented: 'you cannot call a man an artist, until he shows himself capable of reticence and restraint' (*Patria Mia and The Treatise on Harmony*, London: Peter Owen, 1962, p.31). This double affront was precisely that which had proved troublesome for James.

18. *Literary Criticism. Essays on Literature*, p.630.
19. Whitman, *The Complete Poems*, p.85.
20. For a succinct and accurate account of these interests, see chapter 9 of Floyd Stoval, *The Foreground of* Leaves of Grass (Charlottesville: The University Press of Virginia, 1974).
21. See Alfred Habegger, *Gender, Fantasy and Realism in American Literature* (New York: Columbia University Press, 1982), p.58.
22. *Literary Criticism. Essays on Literature*, pp.672, 662, 671. The very humility which James responds to here is precisely that which he found lacking when he reviewed *Drum-Taps* in 1865, and Whitman himself in his later years was eager to deflate his earlier exaggerations. Revealingly in his 1876 Preface to *Leaves of Grass*, he stressed the 'political significance' of 'Calamus' in such a way as to return his previous metaphysical proclamations of the 'Union' to the modesty of a world that was ordinary and available:

In my opinion, it is by a fervent, accepted development of comradeship, the beautiful and sane affection of man for man, latent in all the young fellows, north and south, east and west – it is by this, I say, and by what goes directly and indirectly along with it, that the United States of the future, (I cannot too often repeat) are to be most effectually welded together, intercalated, anneal'd into a living union.

(*Prose Works 1892*, ed. Floyd Stoval, New York: New York University Press, 1964, 2 vols, Vol.II, p.471)

23. *Literary Criticism. Essays on Literature*, p.630.
24. Ibid, pp.632–4.
25. Ibid, p.252.
26. James takes his quotation from Vol.II, pp.41–2 of James Elliot Cabot, *A Memoir of Ralph Waldo Emerson*, 2 vols, (London and New York: Macmillan, 1887). What the quotation selects from the full text is interesting on behalf of the sexual promise offered by

Ransom. James includes the analogy to the Indian and his bride, but he omits the second analogy which Emerson provides: 'as a monk should go privily to another monk and say, Lo, we two are of one opinion; a new light has shined in our hearts; let us dare to obey it' (p.42).

27. *Literary Criticism. Essays on Literature*, p.267.
28. Cabot, *A Memoir*, Vol.II, p.226. Emerson himself included this stanza amongst those he chose as the epigraph for 'The Emancipation Proclamation' of 1862, one of his rare excursions into a public pronouncement upon a contemporary political issue.

To read Ransom in this particular Emersonian context is to recognise an important strategy of James's novelistic procedure in a text which, unusually, explicitly advertises itself as aiming to be 'very national, very typical' and 'very characteristic of our social conditions'. The strategy has to do with his handling of source itself; a handling which extends beyond the mere location of an informing base or idea. *The Bostonians* occasioned one of James's most strident commentaries on the nature of source in his lengthy disavowal of 1885 to William James that the novel's Miss Birdseye was modelled on Elizabeth Peabody (*Henry James Letters*, ed. Leon Edel, Cambridge, MA: Harvard University Press, 1980, Vol.III, pp.68–70). I want to draw attention not so much to James's unwillingness to reveal his 'source', even under pressure, but to the selectivity of his memory in what he *is* prepared to admit. He claims not to have seen Miss Peabody for twenty years (exactly the gap between hearing Emerson reading the 'Boston Hymn' and composing the novel), but he does confess to remembering the details of her displaced spectacles (ibid, p.69) which becomes one of Miss Birdseye's defining features. In his essay on Daudet (of 1883, the year in which James reviewed the Carlyle/Emerson correspondence and began composing *The Bostonians*), the author whose *L'Evangéliste* James did acknowledge as a source for *The Bostonians* (Matthiessen and Murdock, *Notebooks*, p.47) in a 'very rare confession of this sort' (Buitenhuis, *The Grasping Imagination*, p.142), James regarded it as 'not only legitimate but inevitable' that a writer should 'put people into a book', and argued also that 'the question in the matter is the question of delicacy, for according to that delicacy the painter conjures away recognition or insists upon it' ('Alpohnse Daudet', p.235). It is James's practice generally to conjure away sources rather than insist upon them: this practice is in the interest, as he expressed it in his study of Hawthorne some four years earlier, of divergence from an imprisoning verisimilitude in presenting character, of 'following what may be called new scents' (*Hawthorne*, ed. Tony Tanner, London: Macmillan, 1967, p.127). The obliquity of the 'source' for Ransom's surname may stand as a synecdoche for James's habitual conjuring away of the overt relations between his fiction and a community of experience or history.

29. For James, 'The great Scotchman thought *all* talk a jabbering of apes' (*Literary Criticism. Essays on Literature*, p.245), and he provides a pertinent quotation from Carlyle:

> Man, all men, seem radically dumb, jabbering mere jargons
> and noises from the teeth outward; the inner meaning of them
> . . . remaining shut, buried forever . . . Certainly could one
> generation of men be forced to live without rhetoric, bubble-
> ment, hearsay, in short with the tongue well cut out of them
> altogether, their fortunate successors would find a most
> improved world to start upon! (ibid, p.244)

But James also builds into his Carlylean Ransom connections which
are forced into disconnections by Ransom's usage. Here, the key
passage in the novel concerns Ransom's genealogy:

> I know not exactly how these queer heresies had planted
> themselves, but he had a longish pedigree (it had flowered at
> one time with English royalists and cavaliers), and he seemed at
> moments to be inhabited by some transmitted spirit of a robust
> but narrow ancestor, some broad-faced wig-bearer or sword-
> bearer, with a more primitive conception of manhood than our
> modern temperament appears to require, a programme of
> human felicity much less varied. He liked his pedigree, he
> revered his forefathers, and he rather pitied those who might
> come after him. (*The Bostonians*, p.164)

Ransom's romance of 'royalists and cavaliers' directly opposes
Carlyle's Cromwell. James's review quotes Carlyle's general complaint: 'my heart is sick and sore on behalf of my own generation
. . . I feel withal as if the one hope of help for it consisted in the
possibility of new Cromwells and new Puritans', and quotes his
specific difficulties in writing his book on Cromwell: 'No history of
it *can* be written to this wretched, fleering, sneering, canting,
twaddling, God-forgetting generation. How can I explain men to
Apes by the Dead Sea?' (*Literary Criticism: Essays on Literature*,
pp.243, 248). And Ransom's liking for his 'pedigree' is revealed as
merely parochial by comparison with Carlyle's sense of his 'stock',
a sense which James expresses in terms that are strikingly similar to
those he has used to describe the 'local' qualities of Hawthorne in
his study of 1879. Carlyle is presented as 'a signal instance of the
force of local influences, of the qualities of race and soil', a man
who

> was intensely of the stock of which he sprang, and he remained
> so to the end . . Readers . . . will remember how the peasant-
> group in which he was born . . . appeared to constitute one of
> the great facts of the universe for him; and we mean not as a son
> and a brother simply, but as a student of human affairs. He was
> impressed, as it were, with the historical importance of his
> kinsfolk. (Ibid, p.249; compare *Hawthorne*, pp.23–5)

30. In his essay on 'Anthony Trollope' of 1883, James regarded as a
'blemish' the parody of Carlyle in the figure of Dr Pessimist
Anticant in *The Warden* from the pen of one who had 'absolutely no

gift' for satire (*Literary Criticism. Essays on Literature*, p.1342). In 1877, Swinburne's pamphlet, *Note of an English Republican on the Muscovite Crusade*, presented an occasion of 'thunderous' exaggeration where James, in reviewing the pamphlet, displayed his alertness to the dangers of over-dramatising the savagery and utter opposition to 'the human race' which Carlyle seemingly evinced (ibid, pp.1283–5).

31.   Leon Edel has noted that James wrote the word 'Reformers' on the flyleaf of the *Correspondence* and attached a page number referring to a letter of Emerson's in which he commented: 'We are all a little wild here with numberless projects of social reform' (*The Life of Henry James*, 2 vols, Harmondsworth: Penguin, 1977, Vol.I. p.738).

32.   *Literary Criticism. Essays on Literature*, p.233.

33.   Ibid, p.240–1.

34.   Ibid, p.242.

35.   Ibid, pp.252, 264, 260.

5 The Peculiarity of Social Life: Reform and Gender

1.   Emerson, 'Man the Reformer', *Nature, Addressess, and Lectures* (Cambridge, MA: The Riverside Press, 1894), pp.218, 220. In the same year his 'Lecture on the Times' claims in similar vein that, 'The present age will be marked by its harvests of projects for the reform of domestic, civil, literary, and ecclesiastical institutions' (ibid, p.256), and his lecture on 'The Conservative' recognises: 'Now that a vicious system of trade has existed so long, it has stereotyped itself in the human generation, and misers are born', to conclude that 'amidst a planet peopled with conservatives, one Reformer may yet be born' (ibid, pp.301, 307).

2.   Emerson, 'Man the Reformer', pp.222, 223.

3.   Ibid, pp.224–31. For an analysis of Emerson's relationship to commercial practices during the 1830s and 1840s, see Ian F.A. Bell, 'The Hard Currency of Words: Emerson's Fiscal Metaphor in *Nature*', *English Literary History*, 52 (1985), p.733–53.

4.   Ibid, p.236. The pun is repeated in Emerson's 'Lecture on the Times' (p.267).

5.   Emerson, 'New England Reformers,' *Essays: Second Series* (Cambridge, MA: The Riverside Press, 1892), p.242.

6.   Although Emerson maintained his faith in the genuineness of originality throughout his work, regretting, as late as 1878 in his lecture on 'The Fortune of the Republic', the general 'secondariness and aping of foreign and English life' besetting America where 'We lose our invention and descend into imitation. A man no longer conducts his own life. It is manufactured for him' (*Miscellanies*, Cambridge, MA: The Riverside Press, 1883, pp.415, 416), his faith undergoes some modification. In 'Quotation and Originality', for example, he argues that 'in a large sense, one would say there is no pure originality. All minds quote. Old and new make the warp and

woof of every moment' and that 'The originals are not original. There is imitation, model, and suggestion, to the very archangels, if we knew their history'. Nevertheless, if originality is a fiction, it is a useful, indeed indispensable, fiction whose purpose is to persuade us in considerable measure of our own capacity for invention. In asking 'And what is Originality?' Emerson replies that 'It is being, being one's self, and reporting accurately what we see and are', for 'Only an inventor knows how to borrow, and every man is or should be an inventor' within the general 'omnipotency' with which 'Nature decomposes all her harvest for recomposition' (*Letters and Social Aims*, Cambridge, MA: The Riverside Press, 1883, pp.170, 172, 191, 194). Invoked again in this reply is the earlier pun on the 'Reformer' as 'Re-maker'.

7.   Emerson, 'New England Reformers', pp.243–4.
8.   Ibid, pp.239, 245, 241, 247.
9.   Ibid, p.241.
10.   Ibid, pp.248, 248–50.
11.   Emerson, 'Lecture on the Times', pp.263–7.
12.   Emerson, 'New England Reformers', pp.250–4.
13.   Added weight is given to Emerson's dissociations by their being experiental as well as theoretical. His disquisition on 'The Fugitive Slave Law' in 1854, for example, marks a rare excursion into a 'public' pronouncement upon a contemporary political topic; in fact it opens by proclaiming 'I do not often speak to public questions' on the grounds that they are 'odious and hurtful' and such speaking 'seems like meddling or leaving your work' which produces intellectual 'havoc' and a 'dissipated philanthropy' (*Miscellanies*, Cambridge, MA: The Riverside Press, 1883, p.205). For Emerson, the 'public' has always been rather too broad a category for comfort, for a philosophy of self-reliance, and here contemporaneity produces an important shift in range. He asks 'who are the readers and thinkers of 1854?' and concludes that owing to the 'silent revolution' wrought by the 'newspaper' (the decisive organ of publicity in *The Bostonians*), 'this class has come in this country to take in all classes' (ibid, p.206). This shift constitutes a large part of the ground for his attack on Webster whom he sees as responsible for the passing of the Fugitive Slave Law 'by his personal influence' (ibid, p.207). The implication is that the 'personal' nature of that influence would not have been so effective without the organ which begins to register the transformation of private responsibility into personal opinion. And Emerson is keen to stress his own distance from the 'personal' at this point: 'I have lived all my life without suffering any known inconvenience from American Slavery' (a distance he reiterates at ibid, p.215). Webster's enabling of the Law's passage 'by his personal and official authority' (ibid, p.211) is particularly disquieting for Emerson in its marking of a disproportion between his 'moral sensibility' and 'the force of his understanding', where the latter is admirable mainly because the element of the 'personal' has, hitherto, been subordinated: 'Though he knew very well how to present his own personal

claims, yet in his argument he was intellectual, – stated his fact pure of all personality, so that his splendid wrath . . . was the wrath of the fact and the cause he stood for'. That subordination accounts for the 'propriety' of his argumentation and enables him to take 'very naturally a leading part in large private and in public affairs' (ibid, p.210). The 'private' may often be a subterfuge for the 'personal', just as the 'public' may often be a subterfuge for the 'private', but these are necessary discourses, and Emerson's dissociations at the moment when the 'public' is being established by the 'newspaper' indicate the beginnings of the difficulties James is to confront in *The Bostonians*. It is worth noting that the idea of 'union', one of the governing precepts in the novel, is here viewed by Emerson as nothing more than a spurious rhetoric of a nation whose 'principles of culture and progress' had been bastardised by acceptance of the Law (ibid, p.216; compare pp.217, 220).

14. *Literary Criticism. Essays on Literature, American Writers, English Writers*, ed. Leon Edel (New York: The Library of America, 1984), pp.244–5.
15. Ibid, p.245; compare p.242.
16. Idem.
17. In associating the Southerner with 'aristocratic premises', James, in one sense, is echoing a familiar cultural image (1883 saw the publication of Twain's *Life on the Mississippi* with its famous diatribe against the South's assimilation of the aristocratic landscape in Scott's novels, and Emerson himself, in 'The Emancipation Proclamation' of 1862, declared simply: 'in the Southern States, the tenure of land and the local laws, with slavery, give the social system not a democratic but an aristocratic complexion'; *Miscellanies*, p.302), but my point is that Ransom's patrician language not only belongs to that image and to his reading of Carlyle, but it shares the office of his other characteristic languages (theatrical and arcadian) to sustain his own publicity of Verena.
18. For a brilliant commentary on this aspect of the play, see D.J. Gordon, 'Name and Fame: Shakespeare's Coriolanus', *The Renaissance Imagination. Essays and Lectures by D.J. Gordon*, ed. Stephen Orgel (Berkeley: University of California Press, 1975), pp.203–19, 313–5.
19. *The Bostonians* (Harmondsworth: Penguin, 1966), p.83. Subsequent references to this edition appear parenthetically in the text.
20. Verena's imminent lecture at the Music Hall involves the fullest display of this world. Mrs Luna notes how 'all the walls and fences of Boston' are 'flaming today with her name', that her 'portrait' is in 'half the shop-fronts' and her 'advertisement' on 'all the fences', and that Olive is emerging into full entrepreneurship: 'She can't sit still for three minutes, she goes out fifteen times a day, and there has been enough arranging and interviewing, and discussing and telegraphing and advertising, enough wire-pulling and rushing about, to put an army in the field' (pp.362–4). It is at this point, appropriately, that Matthias Pardon reappears, wanting to 'work up these last hours for her' and seeking 'any little personal items',

all in the expectations of the 'Boston public' (pp.366–9). Privacy is not so much invaded here as exploited for the purposes of publicity and spectacle.

21.   Shortly after *The Bostonians*, in 'Frances Anne Kemble', an appreciation to mark the actress's death in 1893, James returns to the new commercial conditions of public and private in the specific context of the theatre. He admires her as a 'moralist' who 'if she read Shakespeare in public it was very much because she loved him, loved him in a way that made it odious to her to treat him so commercially'. She offered the plays 'in a succession from which no consideration of profit or loss ever induced her to depart', recognising that some plays 'drew' more than others (James names *Coriolanus* in the latter category), and when pressed to concentrate on the crowd-pullers, 'her answer was always her immutable order, and her first service was to her master'. Thus, 'If on a given evening the play didn't fit the occasion, so much the worse for the occasion: she had spoken for her poet, and if he had more variety than the "public taste," this was only to his honor'. Here, 'public' is debased by the age of commerce as misguided in its determining 'taste', but Kemble's stance is admired revealingly by James in the particular instance of her American visits before the war. She would never read in the Southern States for two reasons: she 'disapproved of sources of payment proceeding from the "peculiar institution" ', and it was 'insupportable' to her that 'people should come not for Shakespeare but for Fanny Kemble' (*Literary Criticism. Essays on Literature*, pp.1084–5).

22.   James speculates that Carlyle was 'probably not a little irritated,' by Emerson's 'enumeration of characters so vaguely constituted'. He quotes Carlyle's wish for 'some *concretion* of these beautiful *abstracta*' and his comment on *The Dial*: 'it is all spirit-like, aeriform, aurora-borealis-like. Will no *Angel* body himself out of that; no stalwart Yankee *man*, with color in the cheeks of him and a coat on his back?' James finds himself in agreement here, noting how 'Emerson speaks of his friends too much as if they were disembodied spirits. One doesn't see the color in the cheeks of them and the coats on their back', and making his final comparison:

> The fine touch in his letters, as in his other writings, is always the spiritual touch. For the rest, felicitous as they are, for the most part they suffer a little by comparison with Carlyle's; they are less natural, more composed, have too studied a quaintness . . . The violent color, the large, avalanche-movement of Carlyle's style . . . make the effort of his correspondent appear a little pale and stiff. (*Literary Criticism. Essays on Literature*, p.246)

James notes later that 'If the merit of a style lies in complete correspondence with the feeling of the writer, Carlyle's is one of the best', but his cautionary note here is revealing as he goes on to invoke one of the dangers of the authoritarian self as he had detected in Whitman. He finds Carlyle's style to be 'victorious' if 'not defensible' on this merit, and comments:

> It is true, nevertheless, that he had invented a manner, and that his manner had swallowed him up. To look at realities and not at imitations is what he constantly and sternly enjoins; but all the while he gives us the sense that it is not at things themselves, but straight into this abysmal manner of his own that he is looking. (Ibid, p.249)

His cautionary invocation further problematises the use we may make of the review for reading the novel: colour is admirable and necessary, but, simultaneously, as its capacity to allow feeling and specification to become 'swallowed' by its own manner (again, Whitman would provide an apposite example), so it emerges as authoritarian inflexibility.

23. Emerson, 'Woman', *Miscellanies*, p.340. For an account of *The Bostonians* which reads it as James's acknowledgement (in his presentation of Olive and Verena) of the final decline in the principles of self-culture, friendship and renunciation associated not only with Emerson but with Margaret Fuller, see Paul John Eakin, *The New England Girl. Cultural Ideals in Hawthorne, Stowe, Howells and James* (Athens: University of Georgia Press, 1976), pp.195–217).

24. Ibid, p.355.

25. Ibid, pp.347, 349.

26. Ibid, pp.341–2.

27. Alfred Habegger, 'The Disunity of *The Bostonians*', *Nineteenth-Century Fiction*, 24 (1969), pp.198–9.

28. Susan L. Mizruchi has written well of the narrative's evasions and expressions of self-doubt about its capacities for description and concludes that they reveal James's 'equivocal will to power over the reader's perceptions and opinions. Like many of the democratic characters he describes, the narrator is decidedly ambivalent about authority' ('The Politics of Temporality in *The Bostonians*', *Nineteenth-Century Fiction*, 40, 1985, p.214).

29. It is significant that the only clear statement of 'union' is given early in the novel, almost as if it is a premise which is to be put out of the way, and that it is presented in the empty political rhetoric of Olive, whose view of North and South is of 'a single, indivisible political organism' (p.13). The emptiness of that view is displayed by history itself: even before the war, Emerson had dismissed what he called 'the miserable cry of Union' that had been used to support the passing of the Fugitive Slave Law ('The Fugitive Slave Law', p.216; compare pp.217, 220).

30. As Mizruchi notes, 'Verena is compelled to face her predicament as a set of binomial oppositions' ('The Politics of Temporality in *The Bostonians*', p.210), and the result is a kind of paralysis in which the meaningfulness of alternatives becomes frozen. During the traumatic final scenes of the novel Verena confronts an absolute immobilising of choice where choice itself is impossible; Ransom's 'muscular force' literally wrenches her decision from her. This frozen condition where, again literally, her 'face and her identity'

are concealed (p.389), is exactly the feature of the commodity in general.

31. Letter to Grace Norton, dated 4 March 1885, *Henry James Letters*, ed. Leon Edel (Cambridge, MA: Harvard University Press, 1980), Vol.III, p.76. James's reference invokes his own newly 'public' enterprise in *The Bostonians* and *The Princess Casamassima:* that is, the foray into his fresh style of literary realism.

32. The narrative again collaborates with Ransom at Marmion in referring to 'the sex to which she in a manner belonged' (p.348).

33. The only gender distinction Dr Prance offers is at Marmion, in a satirical observation on the women's movement which has a 'lucidity' that is, again, pleasing to Ransom: 'They think women the equals of men; but they are a great deal more pleased when a man joins than when a woman does' (p.306).

34. Guy Debord, *Society of the Spectacle* (Detroit: Black & Red, 1973), paragraph 49.

35. Richard Godden, 'Some Slight Shifts in the Manner of the Novel of Manners', *Henry James: Fiction as History*, ed. Ian F.A. Bell (London and Totowa, NJ: Vision Press and Barnes & Noble, 1984), p.161.

36. Debord, *Society of the Spectacle*, paragraph 17.

37. Thorstein Veblen, *The Theory of the Leisure Class*, 1899 (London: Unwin Books, 1970), p.75.

38. The point is made more neutrally by Theodore C. Miller who argues 'Basil himself wants the attention of the world as much as any Yankee reformer or Boston journalist. Indeed it is his publishing success at the climax of the novel that gives his life meaning, that impels him to propose marriage to Verena' ('The Muddled Politics of Henry James's *The Bostonians*', *The Georgia Review*, 26, 1972, p.342), and by David Howard, who is virtually alone amongst the major commentators on the novel in noting how Ransom's tactics are so closely entwined with what Verena finds plausible: 'it is Ransom's dedication to a cause, his forlorn but powerful hope of public success, that is part of his persuasion of her' ('*The Bostonians*', in *The Air of Reality: New Essays on Henry James*, ed. John Goode, London: Methuen, 1972, p.72). In the most recent tracing of James's debt to Hawthorne, Richard H. Brodhead notes how, in *The Blithedale Romance*, one of the clearest antecedents for *The Bostonians*, speech (he is thinking specifically of 'Eliot's Pulpit') is made powerful 'not by the truth or falsity of its contentions but rather by the emotional and sexual energy that is invested in it'. This provides a key feature in Ransom's persuasion of Verena, and I would suggest that we can transpose directly Brodhead's summary of what happens between Hollingsworth and Zenobia to Ransom's oratory and its effects in Central Park:

> What public speaking produces in its audience, then, is not so much enlightenment as attraction. Zenobia is converted into that loving and dependent thing Hollingsworth says woman rightly is not because she sees the truth of his position but because she feels the force of his masculine presence, enacted in his ideological language.

(*The School of Hawthorne*, New York: Oxford University Press, 1986, p.149)

Brodhead's recognition is important because it shows how power over others, perhaps James's greatest single theme, is always a matter of style rather than the overt articulation of ideas; a matter of desire rather than a codified platform. The effective forces in *The Bostonians* are the sound of Verena's voice rather than what it utters, the attractiveness of Ransom's masculinity rather than its reactionary ideas; and in a consumer culture it is precisely style which overlays content, which, indeed, offers itself *as* content.

39. T.J. Jackson Lears, 'From Salvation to Self-Realization: Advertizing and the Therapeutic Roots of the Consumer Culture, 1880–1930', *The Culture of Consumption*, ed. R.W. Fox and T.J. Jackson Lears (New York: Pantheon Books, 1983), and Rachel Bowlby, *Just Looking: Consumer Culture in Dreiser, Gissing and Zola* (London: Methuen, 1985).

40. Lears, 'From Salvation', p.27. For James and the profession of authorship, we need to remember also that the objects of women's consumption included those of fiction; and that this proved problematical for the male writer. Rachel Bowlby gives general expression to the difficulty:

> If culture, as a space marked off from business or working concerns, was also associated with femininity, that meant that being an artist might not sit well with a male identity. In the case of novels . . . women were the main consumers, the main readers. The male novelist, then, might be in something of an ideological bind: neither pure artist nor fully masculine, and unable to alter one side of the pairing without damaging the other. Practicality in relation to the market meant catering to feeble feminine taste, while ignoring it meant withdrawing altogether from the normal conditions of masculine achievement. (Bowlby, *Just Looking*, p.11)

More specifically, Alfred Habegger points out that it was during the 1850s that James and Howells first sought literary mouldings, the 'one decade in American history in which women wrote practically *all* the popular books', and argues persuasively that they 'were born to, and then established themselves against, the maternal tradition of Anglo-American women's fiction'. Habegger cleverly presents the two as 'sissies' to claim for their realism of the 1870s and 1880s: 'Essentially, Howells and James seized a popular women's literary genre, entered deeply into the feminine aspirations it articulated, yet brought to bear on them the critical sense of reality that was at that time basically masculine' (*Gender, Fantasy, and Realism in American Literature*, New York: Columbia University Press, 1982, pp.ix, 56). In a novel that is so deeply concerned with issues of masculinity and femininity, the gender orientations of James's own profession are not insignificant elements. They pro-

vide a further lens whereby we are returned forcefully to the
questions of self and authority which the novel poses.
41.   Howard, *'The Bostonians'*, p.69.
42.   Habegger, *Gender, Fantasy, and Realism*, p.64.
43.   'The Art of Fiction,' *Literary Criticism. Essays on Literature*, pp.52, 54,
      55.

6   The Personal, the Private and The Public

1.   I wish to trace the effects of publicity's disarrangements rather than
     their mechanisms, and acknowledge a general indebtedness to the
     proposals in Irving Howe's 1956 Introduction to the Modern
     Library edition of the novel. Howe schematises the novel's main
     issue thus:

> *The Bostonians* charts the parallel disarrangement, sometimes
> verging on a derangement, of public and private, political and
> sexual life. James was bold enough to see that the two spheres
> of experience could not be kept apart, and that it would be a
> fatal error for a novelist if he tried to. He was even bolder in
> supposing that the ideological obsessions which form so con-
> stant a peril for public life will leave their mark, not merely on
> social behaviour, but also on the most intimate areas of private
> experience. (Reprinted in *Politics and the Novel*, London: New
> Left Books, 1961, p.186)

     My present intention is to attempt a reading of this 'disarrange-
     ment' within James's historicism. I take it that Howe's 'ideological
     obsessions' refer to Olive Chancellor's strategic feminism and Basil
     Ransom's 'reactionary' masculinity, both of which encode the
     novel's varying dispositions of 'private' and 'public'. Whereas
     Howe wants, generally, to see these dispositions as a response to
     the 'sapping of individuality' within the emergence of the 'mass
     industrial society' towards the end of the nineteenth century
     (p.190), my concern is to examine them as part of a more specific
     history of social behaviour by considering their relation to the
     'personal' within a world where consumerism and publicity begin
     their sway.
2.   This is not to deny that Verena herself is somehow innocent of
     active participation in publicity's manipulations (see Alfred Habeg-
     ger, 'The Disunity of *The Bostonians*', *Nineteenth-Century Fiction*, 24,
     1969, p.207; David Howard, *'The Bostonians'*, in *The Air of Reality:
     New Essays on Henry James*, ed. John Goode, London: Methuen,
     1972, p.72; Susan L. Mizruchi, 'The Politics of Temporality in *The
     Bostonians*', *Nineteenth-Century Fiction*, 40, 1985, p.209), but it is to
     argue for her vacuousness as spectacle and as character in the
     sense of novelistic realism.
3.   Walter Benn Michaels, *'Sister Carrie's* Popular Economy', *Critical
     Inquiry*, 7 (1980), p.381. Interestingly, Michaels, at this point in his
     argument, is drawing a distinction between Howells and Dreiser in

which he sees the former as associating character with autonomy and the latter as conceiving character impelled by desire. I would not want to maintain quite this division between the two, but I would want to place James in the arena of desire. The distinction is useful for the extent to which the narrative in *The Bostonians* so insists on Ransom as 'reactionary'. His imposition of the will implies an anachronistic notion of character (Ransom is, after all, a writer of sorts) where fixed autonomy recalls an earlier conception of the self (as integral, as separable from its various performances) which, under publicity, is undergoing radical reconstruction.

4. Rachel Bowlby, *Just Looking: Consumer Culture in Dreiser, Gissing and Zola* (London: Methuen, 1985), p.34.

5. 'The Art of Fiction', *Literary Criticism. Essays on Literature, American Writers, English Writers*, ed. Leon Edel (New York: The Library of America, 1984), pp.50, 52. In the essay on Daudet, the one 'defect' James finds in *L'Evangéliste* is directly concerned with the same issue but refuses the use of 'personal' as a defining term:

> Daudet's weakness has been simply a want of acquaintance with his subject. Proposing to himself to describe a particular phase of French Protestantism, he has 'got up' certain of his facts with commendable zeal; but he has not felt or understood the matter, has looked at it solely from the outside, sought to make it above all things grotesque and extravagant.
> ('Alphonse Daudet', *Literary Criticism. French Writers, Other European Writers, The Prefaces to the New York Edition*, ed. Leon Edel, New York: The Library of America, 1984, pp.247–8)

6. 'Alphonse Daudet', pp.228-9. I have found it impossible to trace what James means by finding the epithet 'personal' so 'valuable' in 'the vocabulary of French literary criticism', but David Gervais, with the aid of Geoffrey Strickland, has speculated that Sainte-Beuve and his emphasis on biography in criticism might provide a useful starting point (letter to the author, dated 30 January 1987). My colleague David Walker points out (again in a note to the author of December 1986) that '*personnel*' carries the connotations of 'original' and 'eccentric', both of which would apply to James's appreciation of Daudet.

7. He acknowledges of Daudet that he 'expresses many things; but he most frequently expresses himself – his own temper in the presence of life, his own feeling on a thousand occasions. This personal note is especially to be observed in his earlier productions.' ('Alphonse Daudet', p.231), and he noted that Ernest Daudet's memoir, *Mon Frère et Moi*, is 'one of those productions which it is difficult for an English reader to judge in fairness: it is so much more confidential than we, in public, ever venture to be. The French have, on all occasions, the courage of their emotion' (ibid, p.232).

8. Ibid, p.233. Central to James's appreciation of the 'personal' in Daudet is the Frenchman's southern origin, born in Provence of 'an expressive, confidential race', possessing a style that is 'impreg-

nated with southern sunshine' and a talent characterised by 'the sweetness of a fruit that has grown in the warm open air' (ibid, p.232). Given James's acknowledgement of the importance of Daudet for *The Bostonians*, it is impossible not to see this origin as casting an ironic slant upon Ransom's Southernness, particularly since the novel's opening description extravagantly and satirically tells us that 'his discourse was pervaded by something sultry and vast, something almost African in its rich basking tone, something that suggested the teeming expanse of the cotton field' (*The Bostonians*, Harmondsworth: Penguin, 1966, p.6: subsequent references to this edition will appear parenthetically in the text). James even employs military imagery to describe Daudet's experience of Paris as 'artistically, a mine of wealth to him, and of all the anxious and eager young spirits who, on the battlefield of uncarpeted *cinquièmes*, have laid siege to the indifferent city, none can have felt more deeply conscious of the mission to take possession of it' ('Alphonse Daudet', pp.233–4). His portrayal of Paris itself is signally informative for a reliance on the vocabulary of theatre and spectacle through which Ransom will express his response to the North:

> The French have a great advantage in the fact that they admire their capital very much as if it were a foreign city. Most of their artists, their men of letters, have come up from the provinces, and well as they may learn to know the metropolis, it never ceases to be a spectacle, a wonder, a fascination for them.
>
> (Ibid, p.234)

Here, the language of consumption is shorn of its commercial resonance to indicate a 'faculty of appreciation' which is at an utter remove from Ransom's literary activities: instead of expansion, we witness in him a contraction, a hardening of all his prejudices where 'spectacle' constitutes the vocabulary not of 'wonder' and 'fascination', but of a limited and fearful response to the new, obliged to assume the terminology of that which it opposes.

9.   James's aesthetic and social worries about the size of Whitman's hyperbolical presentation of the self are clearly stated in his review of *Drum-Taps* in 1865 (*Literary Criticism. Essays on Literature*, pp.629–34).

10.   James began his review of Sainte-Beuve's *Premiers Lundis* in 1875 by calling him 'The acutest critic the world has seen' (*Literary Criticism. French Writers*, p.669).

11.   *Literary Criticism. French Writers*, pp.679–80; compare p.689. Given *The Bostonians'* engagement with the issues of gender, we should note that, immediately following the discrimination of the 'personal' in Sainte-Beuve, James demarcates further evidence for the homogeneity of his temperament in its combining of feminine and masculine qualities:

> there is something feminine in his tact, his penetration, his subtlety and pliability, his rapidity of transition, his magical

divinations, his sympathies and antipathies, his marvellous art of insinuation, of expressing himself by fine touches and of adding touch to touch. But all this side of the feminine genius was re-enforced by faculties of quite another order – faculties of the masculine stamp; the completeness, the solid sense, the constant reason, the moderation, the copious knowledge, the passion for exactitude and for general considerations.

(Ibid, p.681)

The great irony in reading *The Bostonians* through the lens of this model is that, despite James's insistence on the consanguinity of these faculties ('they melt into each other like the elements of the atmosphere'), he clearly finds the feminine side more appealing than the masculine; and it is striking that none of the features he lists on either side is displayed by any of the characters of the novel.

12. *Literary Criticism. Essays on Literature*, p.242.
13. Ransom effects a similar overlaying later. Mrs Luna may be misguided in imagining that 'her views of public matters, the questions of the age, the vulgar character of modern life' would elicit a 'perfect response' in Ransom's mind (p.168), but she does not warrant the dismissal whereby Ransom diagnoses her in finding her furnishings 'delightfully private and personal' (p.170). It is a disparagement that is particularly offensive given the large divide between public and private in Ransom's own habits; 'He had always had a desire for public life; to cause one's ideas to be embodied in national conduct appeared to him to be the highest form of human enjoyment. But there was little enough that was public in his solitary studies' (p.163); a judgement which precedes immediately his early efforts at writing and being told that his doctrines 'were about three hundred years behind the age.'
14. James's joke about his own enterprise resounds through to the Music Hall scene where a policeman, in effect the guardian of publicity, is given similar phrasing in his dry response to Ransom's request for a 'private' talk with Verena: 'Yes – it's always intensely private' (p.375).
15. Howard, '*The Bostonians*', p.70.
16. According to Alfred Habegger, composition took place between mid-August 1884 and mid-April 1885 (letter to the author, dated 25 February 1987).
17. *Henry James Letters*, ed. Leon Edel (Cambridge, MA: Harvard University Press, 1980), Vol.III, pp.59–60. Edel slips into the same error as Howard by remarking in his footnote to this letter that James 'was also at this moment writing "the private history of the public woman" in *The Bostonians*' (p.60). I would not want to isolate Howard as the sole perpetrator of such separations. Virtually every commentary on the novel finds itself assuming the divisions James engages, and the result, invariably, is a flattening-out of the novel's concerns with precisely the habit of mind which rests with those divisions in the first place. Most recently, for example, Ruth Evelyn

Quebe writes of James's view of feminism as 'the ultimate usurpation of private human needs by abstractions and conforming groups', contrasting 'personal satisfaction' with 'impersonal causes' (Ruth Evelyn Quebe, *'The Bostonians*: Some Historical Sources and Their Implications', *The Centennial Review*, 25, 1981, pp.82, 88). Of course such usurpations and separations are important for the novel, but the point is that they tell only part of the story which, in its most interrogative exercise, is to question how they came about.

18. Alfred Habegger has provided an excellent diagnosis, in a different context, of how feminism's display of selflessness disguises the most insidious urge for power. He argues that James 'sees feminism as an outgrowth of a deeper American failure that happened to be particularly in evidence in Boston', and he documents that failure in terms of its distortions of the self:

> The other-worldly zeal and 'ethicism' of the city have degenerated into the deadliest sort of selflessness – a selflessness that suspects all personal enjoyment and represses sexual and emotional demonstrations to the point that people end up dealing with one another in tragically stunted ways. But the self, denied its legitimate satisfactions and believing itself to be purged of selfishness, develops a monstrous need for power and personal domination. Olive Chancellor enslaves Verena instead of liberating her and what is worse, convinces her that slavery is liberation.
>
> (Habegger, 'Introduction' to *The Bostonians*, Indianapolis: Bobbs-Merrill, 1975, p.xx)

Nevertheless, Habegger remains too willing to see Ransom as a genuine alternative to such selflessness. He sees Ransom's secrect visit to Verena in Cambridge, for example, as bringing 'the private life into being' (ibid, p.xxxiii); but to restrict privacy as a matter of secrecy inevitably isolates it from a communality that would give it meaning (Habegger writes revealingly of this secret as the novel's 'intrigue plot' in 'The Disunity of *The Bostonians*', pp.205–9). Furthermore, as part of my argument that the novel's seeming alternatives are themselves products of the schisms induced by publicity, I would want to reiterate that it is impossible to find Ransom more attractive than Olive, that his promise of privacy is as restrictive as Olive's promise of the public platform.

19. Howard, *'The Bostonians'*, p.61. Howard gives a fine summary of the shared world inhabited by Ransom and Olive:

> Ransom and Olive are rivals but they both seek to rescue Verena from Pardon's world, which is in many ways her natural world. But then we come to James's major irony. Both Ransom and Olive have a partial discriminatory intelligence which enables them to see through the world of publicity. But like most other characters in the novel . . . they both seek a place in it, and in the end both have compromised with it. Olive plans to

'launch' Verena finally with Pardon's co-operation. Ransom has had his best article accepted. They both of course distinguish *their* public role from the world of publicity. They will offer the best article.

He concludes, however, that 'I don't think the book allows this kind of distinction final weight' (ibid, p.69). It is my argument that the novel *does* allow this distinction; not only through its display of the proximity between 'public' and 'publicity', but through the ways in which Ransom and Olive refuse one form of publicity, Pardon's, by replacing it with the respective forms of their own choosing.

20. T.J. Jackson Lears, 'From Salvation to Self-Realization: Advertizing and the Therapeutic Roots of the Consumer Culture, 1880–1930', *The Culture of Consumption*, ed. R.W. Fox and T.J. Jackson Lears (New York, Pantheon Books, 1983), p.8. Lears's analysis of the way in which the 'decline of autonomous selfhood lay at the heart of the modern sense of unreality' (pp.7–11) is the best succinct summary I know of amongst recent accounts of the subject.

21. Concise overviews of the deceit of advertisements are provided by Lears, 'From Salvation to Self-Realization', pp.21–2, and Alan Trachtenberg, *The Incorporation of America: Culture and Society in the Gilded Age* (New York: Hill & Wang), 1982, pp.138–9.

7 Sincerity and Performance

1. George Gissing, *A Life's Morning* (London: Eveleigh Nash & Grayson, 1914), p.31. The novel was written in 1885 and published in 1888. My attention was alerted to this moment in Gissing's work by Charles Swann, 'Sincerity and Authenticity: The Problem of Identity in *Born in Exile*', *Literature and History*, 10 (1984), pp.165–88.

2. Swann, 'Sincerity and Authenticity', p.170.

3. Gissing, *A Life's Morning*, pp.31–2.

4. Walter Benn Michaels, '*Sister Carrie*'s Popular Economy', *Critical Inquiry*, 7 (1980), p.381.

5. Karen Halttunen, *Confidence Men and Painted Women: A Study of Middle-Class Culture in America, 1830–1870* (New Haven, CT and London: Yale University Press, 1982).

6. See Tony Tanner's 'Introduction' to the Penguin edition of *The Europeans* (Harmondsworth, 1984), Richard Poirier's 'Afterword' to the Signet edition (New York, 1964) and the chapter on the novel in his *The Comic Sense of Henry James* (London: Chatto & Windus, 1960).

7. It is tempting to suggest that Eugénie de Guérin, or rather her Christian name, has echoes for James's Eugenia. If so, it is by contrast rather than by similarity, since James's account of her in his review stresses her simplicity and her charity, describing her at one point as 'a mediaeval saint' (*Literary Criticism. French Writers,*

Other European Writers, The Prefaces to the New York Edition, ed. Leon Edel, New York: The Library of America, 1984, p.433). The contrast works with restrained economy to graph the general shift from sincerity to theatricality in nineteenth-century perceptions of the self.

8. Ibid, pp.434–5.

9. It is in this sense that the titles of one of the major analyses of consumption, Guy Debord's, *Society of the Spectacle* (Detroit: Black & Red, 1973), and of a more recent study, Rachel Bowlby's, *Just Looking: Consumer Culture in Dreiser, Gissing and Zola* (London: Methuen, 1985), are not idly chosen. It is beyond the scope of the present exercise to enter into the debate about the historical course of consumption, but on behalf of James's choice in the late 1870s to set *The Europeans* in the 1840s we may acknowledge the time-scale proposed by David Horowitz. Horowitz approves the judgement of Faye E. Dudden's ' "Getting Started" in Commodity Consumption': 'The evidence of material culture demonstrates a great expansion of consumer goods aimed at a middle-class market in the decades after 1830 – ever more elaborate fashions, furniture, decorative arts, carpeting, china, glassware, even "collectibles," manufactured in the expectation of selling not one but many nonessentials', and claims himself that, 'From 1880 through 1920 the shift from a producer to a consumer culture gained new momentum' (*The Morality of Spending: Attitudes toward the Consumer Society in America, 1875–1940*, Baltimore, MD, and London: The Johns Hopkins University Press, 1985, pp.xxv, xxvi).

10. R.W. Emerson, 'Experience', *Essays: Second Series*, Vol.III in the Riverside edition of *Emerson's Complete Works* (London: George Routledge & Sons, 1898), pp.49, 51–52.

11. Ibid, p.77.

12. Ibid, p.61.

13. Repose and stasis, perennial anxieties for Emerson, were tantamount to mercantile paralysis, the abstractions of the commodity relation. In a journal entry for 10 December 1836, he asked a question of which James would have thoroughly approved: 'Do you not see that a man is a bundle of relations, that his entire strength consists not in his properties but in his innumerable relations?' (*The Journals and Miscellaneous Notebooks of Ralph Waldo Emerson*, ed. Merton Sealts, Cambridge, MA, Harvard University Press, 1965, Vol.V, p.266). James's notions of 'relations' are amongst his great discoveries as a novelist, and they owe much to Emerson. Here the fluidity and alterability of 'relations' are opposed to the frozen, immutable qualities of 'properties' as a shorthand for a presiding argument about the deadness of a world coming to be dominated by commercial models. A journal entry for 2 August 1837, the year of financial panic, stated Emerson's antipathy to the 'repose' of commercial immutability with unusual clarity, a clarity impelled by his recognition of the extent of contemporary paralysis:

I find it to be a mischievous notion of our times that men
think we are come late into nature, that the world is finished
and sealed, that the world is of a constitution unalterable, and
see not that in the hands of genius old things are passed away
and all things become new.   (Ibid, Vol.V, p.349).

The notion of alterability is central to the lecture on 'Politics' in 1840
as an antidote to a commercial culture that is 'monumental in its
repose' (*The Early Lectures of Ralph Waldo Emerson*, ed. R.E. Spiller
and W.E. Williams, Cambridge, MA, Harvard University Press,
1972, Vol.III, p.240) and 'Man the Reformer' of 1841 is essentially
man the 'Re-Maker'. For a fuller discussion of Emerson's transcendentalist ideas as structured by the new commerce, see my 'The
Hard Currency of Words: Emerson's Fiscal Metaphor in *Nature*',
English Literary History, 52 (1985), pp.733–53.

14. Emerson, 'Experience', p.80.
15. Ibid, p.66. A substantial part of James's innovativeness as a writer
lies in his appropriations of ideas about surface, about a world
which 'has no inside', and here, too, lies an important part of his
lesson for the modernist novelist. Wyndham Lewis's *Tarr* of 1918
will exemplify my point. In the crucial conversation between Tarr
and Anastasya which claims 'deadness' as the 'first condition for
art', the second condition is announced as 'absence of soul, in the
human and sentimental sense', a proposition which Tarr expands
by embellishing that of Emerson: 'With the statue its lines and
masses are its soul, no restless inflammable ego is imagined for its
interior: it has *no inside*: good art must have no inside: that is
capital' (my quotation is taken from the revised 1928 text, Harmondsworth: Penguin Books, 1982, p.312). James's version occurs
most famously in his Preface to *The Awkward Age* when he defines
the 'objectivity' of drama as an absence of any 'going behind'
(*Literary Criticism: French Writers*, p.1131).
16. Ibid, p.58.
17. Emerson, 'Politics', p.240.
18. Emerson, 'Experience', p.62.
19. These terms are too extensive and, I suspect, too familiar to
warrant a complete catalogue. The following passage from 'The
Story-Teller at Large: Mr. Henry Harland' of 1898 will exemplify
the function of 'surface' within Jamesian registration:

It is a very wonderful thing, this Europe of the American. . . . Mr. Harland tends, in a degree quite his own, to give
it the romantic and tender voice, the voice of fancy pure and
simple, without the disturbance of other elements, such as
comparison and reaction, either violent or merciful . . . It is a
complete surrender of that province of the mind with which
registration and subscription have to do. Thus is presented a
disencumbered, sensitive surface for the wonderful Europe to
play on. The question for the critic is that of the value of what
this surface, so liberally, so artfully prepared, may give back.

(*Literary Criticism. Essays on Literature, American Writers, English Writers*, ed. Leon Edel, New York: The Library of America, 1984, p.287)

Stressed here is a 'fancy' which is 'pure and simple', uncluttered by the 'disturbance of other elements'. It is this very freedom from a 'comparison and reaction' with anything else that ensures a 'surface' which is not only 'sensitive' but, crucially, 'disencumbered'. In other words, we recognise the important part played by 'surface' on behalf of the Jamesian project for liberated writing and liberated reading; liberations from the confusions arising out of the failure to discriminate accurately between the questions of execution and those of morality, between the satisfactions of art and those of experience, that had concerned James in 1884, in 'The Art of Fiction' (see *Literary Criticism. Essays on Literature*, pp.62–3).

20. *Literary Criticism. French Writers*, p.1301. James acknowledges the value of 'a firm iridescent surface' in his Preface to *The American* (ibid, p.1055).
21. *Washington Square* (Harmondsworth: Penguin, 1965), pp.101–2.
22. *The Ambassadors* (New York: The New American Library, 1960), p.57.
23. Ibid, p.128.
24. Ibid, pp.34–5.
25. Idem. The private James of his letters would seem to contradict the case I am trying to make for his distrust in art of the opposition between surface and depth. In 1879, for example, during one of his many early grumbles about the lightness of sociability he detects in the English, he complains to his mother:

> I confess I find people in general very vulgar-minded and superficial – and it is only by a pious fiction, to keep myself going, and keep on the social harness, that I succeed in postulating them as anything else or better. It is therefore a kind of rest and refreshment to see a woman who . . . gives one a sense of having a deep, rich, human nature and having cast off all vulgarities. The people of this world seem to me for the most part nothing but *surface* and sometimes . . . such desperately poor surface! Mrs. Kemble has no organized surface at all; she is like a straight deep cistern without a cover, or even, sometimes, a bucket, in which, as a mode of intercourse, one must tumble with a splash.
>
> (*Henry James Letters*, ed. Leon Edel, Cambridge, MA: Harvard University Press, 1975, Vol.II, p.212)

The point is, however, that James is writing here about lived experience and not aesthetic experience (hence the almost aggressively physical texture of his final images, the cistern and the bucket, and of the plunging therein): he never offers a similar instance without irony in his fiction or his criticism. And we may note additionally his acknowledgement of the artifice and performativeness encoding lived experience itself, the 'fiction' which enables social intercourse and which, as any reader of a James novel knows, constitutes in fact the main arena of such intercourse.

26. *Literary Criticism. French Writers*, pp.229–31.
27. Harry B. Henderson III, *Versions of the Past: The Historical Imagination in American Fiction* (New York and Oxford: Oxford University Press, 1974), p.212. Henderson is a good example of those commentators who find it difficult to recognise James's historical sense. He notes that 'For James an attitude towards historical "atmosphere" replaces attitudes towards history', and, in a monograph which takes the historical imagination as its subject, the paucity of space afforded to James is symptomatic of a general neglect which persists still. It is not surprising that Henderson neglects also what I understand as the main effect of Eugenia.
28. Richard Poirier, *The Performing Self: Compositions and Decompositions in the Languages of Contemporary Life* (London: Chatto & Windus, 1971), p.xiii. Here, Poirier perceptively applies this liberation to the practice of writing itself. We might add Hawthorne's model for liberation, announced most pertinently in his Preface to *The House of the Seven Gables*, a model to which James always responded positively.
29. Ibid, p.xiv.
30. Pierre Macherey, *A Theory of Literary Production*, trans. Geoffrey Wall (London: Routledge & Kegan Paul, 1978), p.96.
31. Idem.
32. Ibid, pp.98–101.
33. Richard Poirier, *The Comic Sense of Henry James* (London: Chatto & Windus, 1960), pp.100, 95.
34. Ibid, p.104.
35. Richard Poirier, 'Afterword' to the Signet edition of *The Europeans* (New York: The New American Library, 1964), p.186.
36. Tony Tanner, 'Introduction' to the Penguin edition of *The Europeans* (Harmondsworth: Penguin, 1984), p.18.
37. *The Europeans* (Harmondsworth: Penguin Books, 1984), p.128; compare p.184. All subsequent references to this edition will appear parenthetically in the text.
38. Tanner, 'Introduction', p.22.
39. For a good, recent discussion and application of Baudrillard's argument, see Rachel Bowlby, *Just Looking*, pp.25–6.
40. Tanner, 'Introduction', p.15.
41. *Henry James Letters*, ed. Leon Edel (Cambridge, MA: Harvard University Press, 1975), Vol.II, pp.105–6.
42. A journal entry for 15 April 1834, for example, maintained: 'The least change in our point of vision gives the whole world a pictorial air, shall I say, dramatizes it' (Sealts, *The Journals*, Vol.IV, p.277).
43. *Hawthorne*, ed. Tony Tanner (London: Macmillan, 1967), p.88–9.
44. *Letters*, Vol.II, p.106.
45. Idem.

46. Similar discriminations may be seen in their initial acts of visual appropriation. For Eugenia, an omnibus is seen as a 'life-boat' in a perfectly congruent context (p.34), while Felix likens the fire in their room to 'a fire in an alchemist's laboratory' (p.36) with no congruency whatsoever.

47. We need a firm sense of Felix's imaginative limitations. Gertrude herself recognises his blandness. Her request for his reactions to her family elicits the reply, 'You seem to me the best people in the world', to which she responds: 'You say that because it saves you the trouble of saying anything else' (p.90; compare pp.81 and 114 for further examples of his genial indiscriminateness towards, respectively, his female cousins and 'forms'). By comparison, when Eugenia offers a similar judgement to describe her cousins as 'very pretty . . . very handsome', Gertrude's response is instructively different. She is 'extremely pleased', but not by the 'compliment' since 'she did not believe it; she thought herself very plain'. Her 'satisfaction' is derived from 'something in the way the Baroness spoke' and it is not 'diminished' but rather 'deepened' by her 'disbelief' (p.64). The comparison shows clearly the paradoxical social value of Eugenia's white lies, her performativeness; a value displayed by the difference between Eugenia and Felix, a difference of style between 'a copious provision of the element of costume' (p.79) and a physiognomy that is 'at once benevolent and picturesque' (p.38). At one point, James relies upon a telling image of humdrum domesticity to convey that benevolence: 'Felix felt, at all times, much the same impulse to dissipate melancholy that a good housewife feels to brush away dust' (p.124). The distance between Felix's housewife and Eugenia's cook, between functionality and decoration, is precisely the distance between their respective styles. Their choice of metaphor establishes the point succinctly. Eugenia employs horticulture on a grand scale: 'the social soil on this big, vague continent was somehow not adapted for growing those plants whose fragrance she especially inclined to inhale, and by which she wished to see herself surrounded – a species of vegetation for which she carried a collection of seedlings, as we may say, in her pocket' (p.152). Felix has a more limitingly local use for the same metaphor on behalf of Gertrude: 'She's a folded flower. Let me pluck her from the parent tree and you will see her expand' (p.176). While Eugenia's usage incorporates creation and cultivation, Felix's connotes little more than an appropriation of the already given. The most benevolent reader is surely irritated by a smile whose perpetual occurrence erodes its initial charm and frankness into the semblance of little more than, to be charitable, an automatic grin, possessed of an indiscriminate generality that will serve all occasions. Even Gertrude's first sight which sees Felix as 'remarkably handsome', finds his smile 'almost a grimace' (p.52). I am sensitive to Tanner's warning that in some ways Eugenia is 'too rich, too ambiguous, too large a character' for the novel, and that her glamorous sophistication will make Felix seem 'merely trivial, vacuously good-natured and shallow' (Tanner,

'Introduction,' p.10), but these latter qualities do seem to me to present an accurate diagnosis of a convivial simpleton. The limitations of Felix's undeniable charm and sunny disposition are, for the purposes of my argument, important aspects of James's negotiations with the 1840s through the perspectives of the 1870s, and it is for this reason predominantly that I find arguments for the moral and social supremacy of Felix at the particular expense of Eugenia to be utterly misleading: see, for example, J.W. Tuttleton, 'Propriety and Fine Perception: James's *The Europeans*', *Modern Language Review*, 73 (1978), pp.488ff., and Gail Fincham, ' "The Alchemy of Art": Henry James's *The Europeans*', *English Studies in Africa*, 23 (1980), pp.84, 88–91.

48. *Literary Criticism. Essays on Literature*, p.854.
49. Ibid, p.853.
50. The connection between 'rosy' and pastoral language is made additionally in James's initial sketch for the novel where, after Felix's 'picturesque imbroglio' succeeds in pairing off the 'maidens' with the 'swains', James light-heartedly imagines that 'the beneficient cousin departs for Bohemia (*with his bride, oh yes!*) in a vaporous rosy cloud, to scatter new benefactions over man – and especially, woman-kind!' (*Letters*, Vol.II, p.106).
51. Poirier, 'Afterword', pp.183–5.
52. Nathaniel Hawthorne, *The Scarlet Letter and Selected Tales* (Harmondsworth: Penguin Books, 1970), pp.64, 66. Oddly, in *The Europeans*, it is Felix who invokes, albeit rather vaguely, some of Hawthorne's terminology in responding to the 'surface' designed by Eugenia: 'His sister, to his spiritual vision, was always like the lunar disk when only a part of it is lighted. The shadow on this bright surface seemed to him to expand and to contract; but whatever its proportions, he always appreciated the moonlight' (p.155).
53. Nathaniel Hawthorne, 'Preface' to *The Marble Faun* (New York: The New American Library, 1961), p.vi.
54. Jean-Christophe Agnew, 'The Consuming Vision of Henry James', *The Culture of Consumption*, ed. R.W. Fox and T.J. Jackson Lears (New York: Pantheon Books, 1983), p.84.
55. Idem.
56. Ibid., p.85.
57. The narrative provides a nicely understated commentary on his insensitivity: 'this young man's brilliantly healthy nature spent itself in objective good intentions which were ignorant of any test save exactness in hitting their mark' (p.94). Such 'ignorance' is clearly displayed in his conversation with Mr Brand about Charlotte's love (pp.160ff.), and in his request for Gertrude's hand (pp.180ff.). And in that notable scene with Mr Wentworth where Felix proposes to sketch him, we witness not so much an opposition between New England distrust of art and European promise of transformation as, again, a display of Felix's benevolent insensitivity – we leave the scene with a sense not of Wentworth's naïveté but of Felix's lack of tact and understanding.

58.   Agnew, 'The Consuming Vision of Henry James', p.97.
59.   Notions of 'natural' feelings, desires, behaviour are tested con-
      tinually throughout the novel, principally by Eugenia's contempo-
      rary artifice which deploys the 'natural' in the service of an idea of
      naturalness, the 'air' of the natural. Against this deployment, the
      Wentworths and Felix rely on the 'sincerity' of the 1840s to
      maintain the 'natural' in its conventional sense. When, for exam-
      ple, Eugenia instructs Felix early on to 'Tell my story in the way
      that seems to you most – natural' (p.45), her pause is that of
      calculation; the calculation of the effect of that story upon the
      Wentworths: the design of Felix's narration. The complex of
      'natural' and 'naturalness' extends beyond Gertrude's sense,
      exhibited in her conversation with Mr Brand (p.128), that the New
      England 'natural' serves repression: Eugenia's punning on 'relat-
      ives' and 'relations' in the two most important conversations that
      invoke the 'natural', with Mr Wentworth and with Robert Acton
      (see pp.65, 102–3), renders the opposition of 'natural' to 'artificial'
      as precisely a register of the changes wrought by the history of
      consumption. Eugenia's principal 'lie' in the novel is to claim to
      Acton that she has sent off the document of renunciation. The
      occasion is a conversation where Acton, within the terms of what
      he later calls his 'legitimate experimentation' (p.191), is able to set
      'invent' against 'natural' in the unquestioning opposition that was
      meaningful in the 1840s (p.170). The project of 'experimentation',
      legitimate or otherwise, is to test; here to test his feeling where 'She
      is not honest, she is not honest' becomes 'She is a woman who will
      lie'. It is Acton's manipulation that produces the 'lie', and before
      the simple 'Yes' which replies to his question about the document,
      Eugenia 'hesitated for a single moment – very naturally' (p.171).
      Her hesitation, underlined by the typographical pause, is 'natural'
      on behalf of her lie, is appropriate to her calculation of duplicity:
      and, in effect, given the situation, it is precisely 'natural' for her to
      'lie'. The movement in this conversation from the schism between
      'invent' and 'natural' to the naturalness of lying renders the
      'natural' as, above all, a social tactic in both hands. Acton's
      'experimentation' and Eugenia's performance both render that
      manufactured quality whereby the 'natural' reveals its element of
      design.
60.   Halttunen, *Confidence Men*, p.188.
61.   Quoted, ibid, p.167. The shift from the sentimental demand for
      'transparent sincerity' to the more worldly demand for a 'skillful
      social performance' (p.189) incorporates a shift in the nature of
      goods themselves in the marketplace (and this is a connection that
      Halttunen fails to document), where objects become saleable not so
      much for their supposedly intrinsic virtues or functions, but for
      their display of properties and their social resonances, in short,
      their effects.
62.   Ibid, p.189.
63.   This particular piece of information is curious in that it is wholly
      unnecessary to the narrative: its redundancy from the point of view
      of the story is graphed by its parenthetical insertion, suggestive of

an afterthought. The marginality of the item (enhanced by its reference to the 'later years' of Wentworth's career), in narrative and typographical terms, paradoxically (and James is fond of such playfulness with details relating to matters of business) draws our attention by its very curiousness and redundancy; there is, too, a local oddity in that we might wonder why, if he has a 'large' amount of business to transact, Wentworth visits Devonshire Street 'but three times a week'. What our attention is drawn towards is the compacted 'confidential trust-business'. For Wentworth, literally at the end of a dying order where 'confidence' and 'trust' mean what they say, the compaction is wholly unproblematical, but for the post-Melvillean nexus of the 1840s/1870s negotiated by *The Europeans*, it is, at the least, strikingly unstable and readable only as a nostalgic feature of New England's 'silvery prime', as open (sincere) as the door of the Wentworth house itself (p.51).

64. Halttunen, *Confidence Men*, p.190.

65. Poirier is absolutely right in noting that the full name's 'suggestion of a complicated and even contradictory variety of personal roles is thoroughly appropriate to Eugenia's character and to her place in the novel' (*The Comic Sense of Henry James*, p.100). It is instructive that no other character in the James canon enjoys such a cornucopia of denominative flourish.

66. Halttunen, *Confidence Men*, pp.198, 204.

8 The Self's Representations

1. Rachel Bowlby, *Just Looking: Consumer Culture in Dreiser, Gissing, and Zola* (London: Methuen, 1985), pp.31–2.

2. Ibid, pp.29, 34.

3. Jean-Christophe Agnew, 'The Consuming Vision of Henry James', *The Culture of Consumption*, ed. R.W. Fox and T.J. Jackson Lears (New York: Pantheon Books, 1983), p.85.

4. Ibid, p.97. Peggy McCormack puts it more generally: 'despite their frequent lack of real jobs, James's characters *do* work, but the products of their labor are their social personae' ('The Semiotics of Economic Language in James's Fiction', *American Literature*, 58, 1986, p.541).

5. One response to Madame Merle (William T. Stafford's 'The Enigma of Serena Merle', *The Henry James Review*, 7, 1986, pp.117–23) is a good testimony to the sheer difficulty of deciphering her, finding 'a deep irony in this deeply ironic book that its most troubled villain is simultaneously its most persistent enigma' (p.117).

6. *The Europeans* (Harmondsworth: Penguin, 1984), p.78. All subsequent references to this edition will appear parenthetically in the text.

7. Leo Bersani, *A Future for Astyanax: Character and Desire in Literature* (New York: Columbia University Press, 1984), pp.136–7.

8. 'Appreciation', encoded by desire, lies at the centre of Jamesian epistemology and provides a vital means of liberation. Bersani notes:

What we know we know through appreciation and not perception; knowledge is a kind of seeing which can dispense with the objects of vision. . . . The problematical quality of the correspondence between our mental possessions of reality and reality itself makes the obsession with the latter an unnecessary restriction of freedom. The reality of a thing depends on the quality of the treatment it gets.

It is the desire of treatment which forces the mind from 'the constraints of either internal (psychologically "deep") or external truths' (*A Future for Astyanax*, p.138). Composition, and our apprehension of composition (writer and reader are allied in the lesson James drew from Hawthorne), are liberated thereby from both 'the superstition of truth' and 'the conventions of realistic fiction', and so in a text like *The Turn of the Screw* we have a story where 'the very question of what is "true" is made irrelevant by the consequences of an agitated imagination'. What the story does is to illustrate the power of questions (such as that of the ghosts' 'reality') 'to produce events by the very intensity and consistency with which they are asked', and so:

There is nothing to know about in *The Turn of the Screw*, there are only conjectures to be imposed, conjectures which the governess makes catastrophically credible. We have no analysis of her psychology; we never 'go behind' the children's behaviour: no one authenticates the ghosts' appearance for us. We simply see . . . a conviction about the ghosts strong enough to destroy the children. (Ibid, p.140; compare Millicent Bell, 'The Turn of the Screw and the Recherche de L'Absolu', *Henry James: Fiction as History*, ed. I.F.A. Bell, London and Totowa, NJ: Vision Press and Barnes & Noble, 1984, pp.65–81).

9.   Here also, we may dissociate Henry's understanding of the self from that of William. If, following Frank Lentricchia, William's notion of the self's individuality is a philosophical positive ('a given of liberalism – a holdout in freedom and the site of the personal and of "full ideality"'), then Henry might usefully be situated in Lentricchia's account of Foucault's response to the policing (a permanent anxiety in Henry's fiction) of a disciplinary society:

Foucault's antidote is writing: not as a space for the preservation of identity and the assertion of voice, but as a labyrinth into which he can escape, to 'lose myself,' and, there, in the labyrinth, never have to be a self (a self is a dangerous thing to be) – write yourself off, as it were, 'write in order to have no face.' Give no target to discipline.
(Frank Lentricchia, *Ariel and the Police: Michel Foucault, William James, Wallace Stevens*, Brighton: Harvester, 1988, p.26; compare Michel Foucault, *The Archaeology of Knowledge*, trans. A.M. Sheridan Smith, London: Tavistock, 1972, p.17)

In the labyrinth of signs and surfaces that constitutes the consumptive world, a self is indeed dangerous because it runs the risk of, simultaneously, an overly dense solidity as a means of resisting its dispersal through the play of performance and dispersal itself. Style, in both writing and social intercourse, emerges as both control and antidote to control, and acknowledges again the double function of liberation and prison within the performances occasioned by consumption. The instability produced by this acknowledgement is registered, for example, in Eugenia being 'restless', which is one of the defining adjectives used of her throughout the novel. Felix, by comparison, and a figure from an earlier historical period, the 1840s, is very much at home wherever he finds himself (for example, pp.37–8, 82).

10. *The Portrait of a Lady*, New York: The New American Library, 1963 (from the first edition of 1881), p.176. All subsequent references to this edition will appear parenthetically in the text.

11. We are told early on that 'Isabel was in a situation which gave a value to any change. She had a desire to leave the past behind her, and, as she said to herself, to begin afresh' (p.30). Her 'beginning afresh a great many times' is in part the consumptive urge for origination through novelty and in part an Emersonian predilection for the present self free from the bindings of past and future. The two come together in her ambition for a life which 'should always be in harmony with the most pleasing impression she should produce; she would be what she appeared, and she would appear what she was' (p.48). Caught here is the disabling contradiction of her ambition for uncalculated flexibility, a flexibility which is not only naïve (an unwillingness for 'giving up other chances', p.122) but illusory in that it fails to understand true freedom of the self as a recognition of the limits within which the self may move (compare Arnold Kettle, *An Introduction to the English Novel*, London: Hutchinson, 1969, Vol.II, p.30).

12. I would not want to go as far as Richard Poirier's second adjective in describing Madame Merle as 'a later and corrupt version of the Baroness' (*The Comic Sense of Henry James*, London: Chatto & Windus, 1960, p.234). The unjustly hostile response she attracts, almost universally, from the commentators seems impelled by a critical stance which sentimentalises Isabel's temperament even while remaining alert to its limitations.

13. In a rather exaggerated comment upon the business of being an American expatriate in Europe, just prior to her case for the 'expressive' self, Madame Merle adopts more conventional senses of 'surface' and the 'natural' (a 'conventional language' being part of her performative equipment, as Isabel has recently recognised: see p.178) to locate the particular position of the female:

> You should live in your own country; whatever it may be you have your natural place there. If we are not good Americans we are certainly poor Europeans; we have no natural place here. We are mere parasites, crawling over the surface; we haven't our feet in the soil. At least one can know it, and not have illusions. A woman, perhaps, can get on; a woman, it seems to me, has

> no natural place anywhere; wherever she finds herself she has
> to remain on the surface and, more or less, to crawl.   (p.181)

This is followed by her dismissal of 'an American who lives in
Europe' as an epithet which signifies 'absolutely nothing' (p.182).
The point is that against her 'conventional' meaning Madame
Merle effectively disperses standard recognitions of place, status,
role and so on. Such dispersal is an important aspect of her
variousness; while seemingly criticising their absence of 'position',
she simultaneously disposes of the sureties which sanction notions
of 'position' in the first place. And, as I shall argue later, it is crucial
that such dispersal is envisaged as a female issue.

14.   Thomas Carlyle, *Sartor Resartus* (London: Chapman & Hall, 1890),
      pp.36, 165, 21.
15.   Ibid, p.21.
16.   Ibid, p.33.
17.   Isabel has learned much since the occasion of her first meeting with
      Osmond where she is largely silent through a fear of spoiling his
      'delicacy' and we are told: 'Isabel had little skill in producing an
      impression which she knew to be expected . . . she had a perverse
      unwillingness to perform by arrangement' (p.229). At this stage,
      she can understand performance only as a prescription from others
      rather than as a function of appreciation. Again, the distance
      between the two is the distance of the changing sociability of
      manners.
18.   R.W. Emerson, 'Wealth', *The Conduct of Life* (Boston: Houghton
      Mifflin, 1896), p.100.
19.   Ibid, pp.100–1.
20.   Ibid, pp.101–2. Earlier in the essay, Emerson offered one of his
      most direct statements on money's relation to ethics:

> The subject of economy mixes itself with morals, inasmuch as
> it is a peremptory point of virtue that a man's independence be
> secured. Poverty demoralizes. A man in debt is so far a slave
> . . . when a man or a woman is driven to the wall, the chances
> of integrity are frightfully diminished; as if virtue were coming
> to be a luxury which few could afford.   (p.90)

21.   The essay on 'Wealth' continues by claiming that 'the current
      dollar, silver or paper, is itself the detector of the right and wrong
      where it circulates', and that 'The value of a dollar is social, as it is
      created by society' (ibid, pp.102, 103).
22.   See my 'The Hard Currency of Words: Emerson's Fiscal Metaphor
      in *Nature*', *English Literary History*, 52 (1985), pp.733–53.
23.   Emerson, 'Wealth', p.101.
24.   Ibid, p.85.
25.   Andrew Carnegie, 'Wealth', reprinted in *Builders of American
      Institutions: Readings in United States History*, ed. Frank Freidel and
      Norman Pollack (Chicago: Rand McNally, 1963), p.309.
26.   Idem.
27.   Emerson, 'Wealth', p.96.

28. We may see this moment in the different discourses Carnegie and Emerson employ for their shared insistence on the necessity for competition. In 1889, the argument is sanctioned by an unquestioning social Darwinism, 'while the law may be sometimes hard for the individual, it is best for the race, because it insures the survival of the fittest in every department' (Carnegie, 'Wealth', p.307), where the tactic of 'insures' against the customary 'ensures' provides a nicely understated reminder of commerce's more intimate invasions. In 1860, the sanction is provided by organic images of checks and balances:

> Each of these idealists, working after his thought, would make it tyrannical, if he could. He is met and antagonized by other speculators as hot as he. The equilibrium is preserved by these counteractions, as one tree keeps down another in the forest, that it may not absorb all the sap in the ground. And the supply in nature of railroad-presidents, copper-miners, grand-junctioners, smoke-burners, fire-annihilators, etc., is limited by the same law which keeps the proportion in the supply of carbon, of alum, and of hydrogen. (Emerson, 'Wealth', pp.93–4)

29. *Henry James Letters*, ed. Leon Edel (Cambridge, MA: Harvard University Press, 1975), Vol.II, pp.105–6. James's use of 'picturesque' throughout his work is both extensive and various in implication. One of the best accounts of his use is given by Viola Hopkins Winner, who claims his most frequent deployment of the term is that exemplified by the art historian Heinrich Wolflin whom she quotes to good effect:

> over the solid, static body of things there will always play the stimulus of a movement which does not reside in the object and that also means that the whole only exists as a *picture* for the eye, and that it can never, even in the imaginary sense, be grasped with the hands.
> (*Henry James and the Visual Arts*, Charlottesville: University Press of Virginia, 1970, p.34)

The implication here that the 'picturesque' has a capacity for construction rather than reflection, for the flexibility of the relational rather than the stasis of things understood in essentialist terms, matches closely James's general project for the liberation of writing and of the self.

30. *Literary Criticism. French Writers, Other European Writers, The Prefaces to the New York Edition*, ed. Leon Edel (New York: The Library of America, 1984), pp.229–31.

31. Isabel repeats the image shortly afterwards in noting that 'Pansy was really a blank page, a pure white surface; she was not clever enough for precocious coquetries' (p.291). The technical literariness of the image reminds us of the extent to which James's thematic interrogation of representation intimately involves a concern with his own practice.

32. *The Tragic Muse* (New York: Dell, 1961; from the first edition of 1890), p.71. All subsequent references to this edition will appear parenthetically in the text.

33. Fredric Jameson, *Marxism and Form: Twentieth-Century Dialectical Theories of Literature* (Princeton, NJ: Princeton University Press, 1971), p.132.

34. The argument of James's Preface to the New York edition of *The Tragic Muse* works productively against itself in its professing of 'a certain vagueness of remembrance' about the 'origin and growth' of the novel:

> If it be ever of interest and profit to put one's finger on the productive germ of a work of art, and if in fact a lucid account of any such work involves that prime identification, I can but look on the present fiction as a poor fatherless and motherless, a sort of unregistered and unacknowledged birth.

Simultaneously, he proposes the value of both origin (without which there is 'no clear vision of what one may have intended' and thus 'no straight measure of what one may have succeeded in doing') and the dispersal of origin (where the world becomes 'a conception that clearly required, and that would for ever continue to take, any amount of filling-in'). James concludes that, given his general theme of the conflict between 'art' and the 'world', the opposition 'would beget an infinity of situations' (*Literary Criticism. French Writers*, pp.1103–4). It is James's commitment to 'any amount of filling-in', to 'an infinity of situations' engendered by the absence of origin, that ensures his faith in the liberation of the open text, in the 'not-yet-existent' which frees writing and character from the closure of formulae.

35. *The Bostonians* (Harmondsworth: Penguin, 1966), pp.160–1.

36. Oscar Wilde, 'The Relation of Dress to Art. A Note in Black and White on Mr. Whistler's Lecture'; reprinted in *The Artist as Critic. Critical Writings of Oscar Wilde*, ed. Richard Ellman (London: W.H. Allen, 1970), p.17.

37. Wilde, 'The Decay of Lying'; reprinted in *The Artist as Critic*, p.301.

38. Wilde, 'The Critic as Artist'; reprinted in *The Artist as Critic*, p.386.

39. Lionel Trilling, *Sincerity and Authenticity* (Oxford: Oxford University Press, 1972), p.120.

40. Wilde, 'The Truth of Masks'; reprinted in *The Artist as Critic*, pp.427, 430.

41. Ibid, p.432.

42. Trilling, *Sincerity*, p.121.

43. Wilde, 'The Truth of Masks', p.432.

44. Wilde, 'Pen Pencil and Poison'; reprinted in *The Artist as Critic*, p.323.

45. Wilde, 'The Critic as Artist', p.389.

46. Ibid, pp.391, 393.

47. Ibid, pp.382–4.

48. Walter Pater, *The Renaissance*, 1873 (London: Macmillan, 1920), pp.125–6.

49. Wilde, 'The Critic as Artist', p.398.
50. Poirier, *The Comic Sense of Henry James*, p.224.
51. Ibid, p.235.
52. John Carlos Rowe has seen how Isabel is 'caught in the fiction of a self complete in its own right, remote from the destructive elements of time, change, and social relation'; while, in contrast, Madame Merle 'defines the self in its flow' and so prefigures William James's formulation of consciousness as 'a function and relation rather than a substance' (*Henry Adams and Henry James: The Emergence of a Modern Consciousness*, Ithaca, NY, and London: Cornell University Press, 1976, pp.32–4). Rowe argues, rightly, that the distinction is central to the morality of James's fiction in general:

   > Any closed world is fatal for the Jamesian character . . . Meaning depends upon the openness of the structures of thought . . . The closure of social worlds and the tendency of language to degenerate into convention restrict individual freedom and thus the vitality of social relations . . . constant interchange of fictions, lies, actual experiences invest society with its changing meaning. Ethical judgements in James's fiction are curiously dependent upon the affirmation or denial of this essentially intersubjective mode. (pp.40–1)

   It is a concern with the 'play' rather than the 'accretion' of meaning which characterises Jamesian epistemology (p.239), and this is inevitably a relational activity.
53. Robert Clark, 'The Transatlantic Romance of Henry James', *American Fiction: New Readings*, ed. Richard Gray (London and Totowa, NJ: Vision Press and Barnes & Noble, 1983), pp.111–12.
54. Elizabeth Allen, *A Woman's Place in the Novels of Henry James* (London: Macmillan, 1984), p.8. Isabel Archer provides the apposite example:

   > Isabel fails to understand what the world is doing *to* her . . . how it defines her as lady and uses her. Only by understanding her existence as sign, as carrier of potential meaning, could Isabel begin to make any real 'choice' at all. As it is, she accepts others' image of her and can therefore experiment only within the limitations of that image. (p.83)

55. Ibid, pp.9–10.
56. Judith Fryer, *The Faces of Eve: Women in the Nineteenth-Century American Novel* (New York: Oxford University Press, 1976), pp.126, 127. For a brilliant discussion of James and sexual identity, see Alfred Habegger, *Gender, Fantasy, and Realism in American Literature* (New York: Columbia University Press, 1982); in particular the chapter on 'Henry James and W.D. Howells as Sissies' and the section on 'The Gentleman of Shalott: Henry James and American Masculinity'.
57. Theodor Adorno, *In Search of Wagner*, trans. Rodney Livingstone (London: New Left Books, 1981), pp.83–4.

58. Jean Baudrillard, *For a Critique of the Political Economy of the Sign*, trans. Charles Levin (St Louis, MO: Telos Press, 1981), p.91.
59. Ibid, p.94.
60. Helene Keyssar, *Feminist Theatre* (London: Macmillan, 1984), p.xiv.
61. Idem.
62. Hans Vaihinger, *The Philosophy of 'As If': A System of the Theoretical, Practical and Religious Fictions of Mankind*, trans. C.K. Ogden (London: Routledge & Kegan Paul, 1924), pp.258–9.
63. *The American* (New York: The New American Library, 1963), p.7. The novel's debate about copies and originals lacks the complex sense of the representational that we find in *The Tragic Muse*: M. Nioche's French lessons for Newman include the advice that 'if he wanted the real thing, [he] should go to the Théâtre Français' (p.47), but it is in the domestic context of refining his pronunciation. Nevertheless, the roles of money and how it is earned in the novel remind us of the extent to which James conceives the debate in economic terms. It is important, for example, to resist an assumption that Newman's financial response to art is simply philistine, and, equally, his interest in copies at the expense of originals cannot be sanitised merely as the judgement of 'aesthetic verdancy' (p.55). The relation between copy and original anticipates the concern with coined and paper money which structures *Washington Square* the following year and, literally, in the question of Noemie's dowry, the fake (her copies) are converted into the real, 'converted into specie' (p.44) by Newman's purchase. And the deadness of the Rue d'Enfer at the end of the novel registers the consequence of Newman's commercial enterprise: the place where the frozen qualities of objects in the marketplace (which Newman, early in the novel, romanticises as a 'bazaar' – p.58 – which promises no 'obligatory purchase') become mortified. It is here, too, that Newman himself is brought to his own form of stasis, that 'rest' (p.321) which bespeaks not tranquility so much as the weariness from the final surrender of the novel's battles.

Index

abstraction, 22–3, 27, 28, 30, 31, 33, 49, 59, 66, 127, 191
Adams, Henry, 213
Adorno, Theodor, 71, 108, 201–2, 219, 225
advertisements, 9, 11, 13, 64, 66, 127, 131, 133, 144
Agnew, Jean-Christophe, 5, 63–4, 65, 167–8, 174, 231, 233
Allen, Elizabeth, 199–200
alterability, 12–13, 36, 152, 157, 161, 168–9, 203, 204, 213, 253
Anesko, Michael, 208
Arnold, Matthew, 31
Austen, Jane, 26–7
authenticity (and sincerity), 28, 31, 71, 85, 87, 108, 124, 144, 147–205, 258

Bakhtin, Mikhail, 10–11
balance, 19–21, 22, 23, 26, 33, 55
Balzac, Honoré de, 4, 33–4, 35, 40, 43, 49, 51, 89, 90–1, 192, 228
Barthes, Roland, 20, 22, 59–60, 160, 225
Baudrillard, Jean, 13, 132, 160, 167, 202
Beard, George M., 49, 68–9
Bell, Ian F. A., 239
Bell, Millicent, 27–8, 31, 33–4, 222, 229
Benjamin, Walter, 66, 108
Berger, John, 199
Bersani, Leo, 7–8, 35–6, 174–5, 210–11, 223, 260
Besant, Walter, 2
Bewley, Marius, 235

Bland, Richard, 47–8
Bloch, Ernst, 191
Bowlby, Rachel, 69–70, 94–5, 127, 133, 173, 231, 245
Brewster, Henry B., 228
Brodhead, Richard H., 244–5

Carlyle, Thomas, 31, 101, 103–5, 109, 111, 112–13, 115, 116–17, 119, 136, 178, 190, 238–9, 241, 242–3
Carnegie, Andrew, 182, 263
Carton, Evan, 210–11
Clark, Robert, 199, 212
Coleridge, S. T., 166
commerce, 17–8, 22–3, 30–2, 34, 42, 49, 57, 59, 69–70, 88–9, 107–10, 111, 122, 153, 266
commodification, 22–3, 26–7, 28, 30, 49, 55, 57, 66, 76ff, 108, 121, 125–6, 151, 169, 191, 192, 199, 201, 203, 204, 205, 229, 230, 243–4
Conrad, Peter, 215–6
consumer culture, 3–4, 5–6, 7, 8, 9, 11, 12, 26, 63–4, 66, 70, 72, 75, 76ff, 81, 84, 89, 94–5, 107, 125, 127, 130, 131, 135, 144, 148, 150–1, 153ff, 210–11, 213, 214, 234, 245, 246, 248, 252, 258, 261
Crane, Stephen, 2
Culver, Stuart, 208
currency, 42–52, 209–10, 225–9, 262, 263, 266

Debord, Guy, 9, 66, 125–6, 232
design, 35, 160, 167–9

desire, 7–8, 9, 11, 12, 13, 71, 111, 131, 132, 133, 144, 202, 211, 260
Dickens, Charles, 73, 97, 164, 165
Dietrichson, Jan W., 227
Dreiser, Theodore, 58, 128
Dunne, Gerald T., 50
Dupee, F. W., 229

Eagleton, Terry, 31, 32
Eakin, Paul John, 243
Edel, Leon, 38, 239, 249–50
Emerson, Ralph Waldo, 30, 31, 51–3, 101–6, 107–12, 116–17, 118–19, 131–2, 136, 141, 149, 150–3, 160, 161, 176, 177, 180–3, 237, 239–41, 242–3, 252–3, 262–3

Featherstone, Mike, 214
female, presentations of, 1, 3, 95, 118–19, 121ff, 137, 142–3, 147–205, 234, 244, 245–6, 249
Fincham, Gail, 257
Flaubert, Gustave, 40
Forster, E. M., 58
Foucault, Michel, 260
freedom, 35–6, 41, 72, 175, 196, 198, 234, 264
Fryer, Judith, 201
Fuller, Margaret, 105, 112, 199, 243

Gilmore, Michael T., 207
Gissing, George, 147–8
Godden, Richard, 64, 214, 231, 234
Goode, John, 231
Gordon, D. J., 241
Greenslade, William, 211
Grimsted David, 221

Habegger, Alfred, 70–1, 120, 128–9, 130, 245–6, 249, 250
Halttunen, Karen, 149, 170, 172, 214, 258
Harriman, E. H., 220

Hawthorne, Nathaniel, 2, 3, 4, 5, 34, 35, 36–42, 43, 49, 51, 54, 80, 112, 149, 156, 166–7, 175, 198, 201, 204, 213, 222, 223, 228, 230–1, 235, 238, 244, 255, 257
Hegel, Georg, 196
Henderson, Harry B., 156, 255
historical sense, 3, 9, 13, 32, 92 *et passim*
Hoffman, Frederick J., 212–13
Hofstadter, Richard, 227
Horkheimer, Max, 219, 225
Horowitz, Daniel, 210, 252
hotels, 92–4, 95
Howard, David, 90, 128, 141, 143, 232, 244, 249–50, 251
Howe, Irving, 246
Howells, William Dean, 39, 40, 53, 128, 160, 245–6
Hutchinson, Stuart, 2, 208–9, 229

Jackson, Andrew, 31, 42, 43, 44–7, 48, 171, 225–7
James, Henry, *passim*
books by: *The Ambassadors,,* 3, 9, 154, 165; *The American,* 67, 149, 204–5, 266; *The American Scene,* 65, 94; *The Bostonians,* 1, 11, 17, 63–144, 151, 175, 176, 183, 187, 189–91, 192, 194, 201, 203, 208, 228; *The Europeans,* 1, 8, 71, 107, 111, 130, 147–205, 209; *Hawthorne,* 32, 37–41, 47, 54, 58, 149, 161, 237–8; *The Portrait of a Lady,* 1, 5, 6, 71, 111, 130, 176–87, 193, 195, 196, 197, 198–9, 201, 203, 204, 232; *The Princess Casamassima,* 17, 228; *The Tragic Muse,* 1, 187–95, 204; *The Turn of the Screw,* 260; *Washington Square,* 1, 17–60, 91, 107, 130, 149,

151, 154, 161, 180, 181, 209

prefaces by: *The American*, 3–4; *The Aspern Papers*, 3; *The Awkward Age*, 222–3; *The Tragic Muse*, 264; *The Wings of the Dove*, 153

essays by: 'Anthony Trollope' 239; 'The Art of Fiction', 2, 129, 130, 134; 'Frances Anne Kemble', 242; 'Honoré de Balzac', 90–1

reviews by: Cabot, *A Memoir of Ralph Waldo Emerson*, 101–3; Dickens, *Our Mutual Friend*, 97, 164; Eliot, *Middlemarch*, 222; Nordhoff, *The Communistic Societies of the United States*, 232–3; Sainte-Beuve, *Premiers Lundis*, 248, 249; Swinburne, *Note of an English Republican on the Muscovite Crusade*, 239; Whitman, *Drum-Taps*, 99–101, 112, 248; *The Correspondence of Thomas Carlyle and Ralph Waldo Emerson*, 103–5, 111, 116–17, 136, 237; *The Correspondence of William Ellery Channing, D.D., and Lucy Aikin*, 67–8; *Lettres d'Eugenie de Guerin*, 149–50; *Correspondance de C.A. Sainte-Beuve*, 135–6

James Sr, Henry, 30, 221
James, William, 237, 260–1
Jameson, Frederic, 191–2
Johannsen, Robert R., 229

Kemble, Frances Anne, 242
Kenney, William, 229
Kettle, Arnold, 261
Keyssar, Helene, 203–4

Knights, L. C., 25
Kronick, Joseph G., 213

Lawrence, D. H., 58
Lears, T. J. Jackson, 74, 127–8, 144, 251
Lee, Brian, 220
Le Fanu, Mark, 218
Leggett, William, 45
Leiss, William, 6, 7
Lentricchia, Frank, 260–1
Lewis, Wyndham, 253
Lincoln, Abraham, 52
Locke, John, 42
Lucas, John, 27, 28, 56–7, 229

Macherey, Pierre, 157–8
Marx, Karl, 76, 233
Melville, Herman, 2, 28
McCloskey, Robert Green, 220
McCormack, Peggy, 214, 259
Michaels, Walter Benn, 133, 148, 247
Miller, Douglas T., 215
Miller, Theodore C., 244
Mizruchi, Susan L., 233, 243
Morgan, J. P., 220

newspapers, 64–6, 73–4, 92, 143, 144
Nugent, Walter T. K., 227

Pater, Walter, 138, 190, 197
Peabody, Elizabeth, 237
perception, 4–5, 11, 66, 70, 81, 84, 119, 120, 129, 130, 133, 156, 159–60, 165ff
performativeness, 1–2, 3, 5, 6–7, 11–13, 127, 142, 143–4, 147–205, 210, 258, 262
Pessen, Edward, 17
Poe, Edgar Allan, 43
Poirier, Richard, 56, 149, 157, 158–9, 166, 174, 198, 229, 255, 259, 261
Posnock, Ross, 11, 213–14
Poulet, Georges, 212
Pound, Ezra, 235–6

power, 8–9
publicity, 63–80, 81, 92–6, 104, 106, 107, 108, 114–15, 122, 123, 125, 127–8, 131, 132–3, 134, 141, 142, 143, 144, 190, 192, 194, 201, 242, 246, 247, 250, 251

Quebe, Ruth Evelyn, 233, 250

reconstruction, 42, 43, 47
reform, 68, 102, 104–5, 107–11, 122, 127, 141
relation, 10, 35, 84, 85, 86, 121, 129, 144, 177, 191, 192, 198, 252–3, 263, 265
representation, 3–5, 7, 8–10, 36–42, 42–52, 71, 84, 130, 147–205, 209–10, 214, 264, 266
Rich, Adrienne, 204
Riesman, David, 172
Ripley, George, 31
romance form, 2–13, 35, 36–42, 213, 223
Rowe, John Carlos, 265
Ruskin, John, 31

Sainte-Beuve, C. A., 131–2, 135–6, 139, 248, 249
Schlesinger, Arthur M., 221
Schmitz, Neil, 210
scientific temperament, 21–3, 25, 28, 35, 43, 52, 55, 60, 230
self, presentations of, 2, 6–8, 9–10, 11–13, 63, 69–72, 74ff, 81, 84, 96ff, 105, 107, 108, 109, 111–12, 131ff, 147–205, 210–11, 212–13, 246, 247, 250, 260–1, 263, 265
Seltzer, Mark, 8–9, 208
setting, 18–19, 26, 29, 89–95
Sharp, James Roger, 44, 225–6
Shell, Marc, 43–4, 50–1, 229
Sohn-Rethel, Alfred, 22–3, 34, 48–9, 220
Springer, Mary Doyle, 229, 230

Stafford, William T., 259–60
Stevenson, Robert Louis, 2, 207, 213
Stoehr, Taylor, 224, 228
Stoval, Floyd, 236
Stowe, William W., 222
Sundquist, Eric, 12
surface, 1–3, 5, 7, 8–9, 13, 21–2, 35, 148–205, 210–11, 212–13, 253, 254, 257, 261, 264
Swann, Charles, 251
Swedenborg, Emanuel, 52
Swinburne, A. C., 239

Tanner, Tony, 149, 158, 159, 160
telegrams, 65–9
Thomas, Brook, 41, 50, 223
time, 17, 28–30, 33, 34–5, 213
Todorov, Tzvetan, 36, 223–4
Trachtenberg, Alan, 66, 74, 94
Trilling, Lionel, 195, 196
Trollope, Anthony, 239
Tuttleton, J. W., 257
Twain, Mark, 241

Unger, Irwin, 227, 228–9

Vaihinger, Hans, 204
Veblen, Thorstein, 20, 127
Vernon, John, 209
Volosinov, V. N., 28, 218–19, 219–20

Ward, Mrs Humphrey, 141–2
Ward, J. A., 229
Wells, H. G., 1–2
Westbrook, Wayne W., 208
Whistler, James McNeill, 4–5
Whitman, Walt, 97, 98–101, 112, 135, 235–6, 248
Wilde, Oscar, 138, 190, 195–8
Williams, B. J., 228
Winner, Viola Hopkins, 263
Winter, J. L., 220
Wolflin, Heinrich, 263

Zola, Emile, 40, 134